The Social Epistemology of Experimental Economics

Any experimental field consists of preparing special conditions for examining interesting objects for research. So naturally the particular ways in which scientists prepare their objects determine the kind and the content of knowledge produced. This book provides a framework for the analysis of experimental practices – the social epistemology of experiment – that offers a comprehensive account of scientists practical engagements with their objects of study and the knowledge they acquire as a result. The social epistemology of experiment is applied to experimental economics and in so doing it introduces the epistemic role of the participation of human subjects in experiments and the causal efficacy of institutions in constraining and enabling human behaviour. It also develops the role of the social and socially established practices in overcoming the methodological difficulties associated with experimenting with human subjects in the social sciences as well as the effect of scientists' interventions in the laboratory worlds.

This book offers an historical and contextualized account of the emergence of experimental economics, the methodological discussions that have informed and constituted it, its main research programmes and stylized facts. The analysis of its three main research programmes – market experiments, game theory experiments and individual decision-making experiments – shows how economics experiments are particularly tailored to produce knowledge about market institutions and human behaviour.

This book will be of interest to researchers in the fields of philosophy of science, science, technology and society studies, sociology of science, economic methodology, history of economics and experimental economics.

Ana Cordeiro dos Santos is Researcher at the Centre for Social Studies (CES), University of Coimbra, Portugal. She obtained her Ph.D in Philosophy and Economics from Erasmus University of Rotterdam, The Netherlands.

Routledge Advances in Experimental and Computable Economics
Edited by K. Vela Velupillai
National University of Ireland, Galway and Francesco Luna, International Monetary Fund (IMF), Washington, USA

The Economics of Search
Brian and John McCall

Classical Econophysics
Paul Cockshott et al.

The Social Epistemology of Experimental Economics
Ana Cordeiro dos Santos

Economics Lab
An intensive course in experimental economics
Alessandra Cassar and Dan Friedman

The Social Epistemology of Experimental Economics

Ana Cordeiro dos Santos

Routledge
Taylor & Francis Group
LONDON AND NEW YORK

First published 2010
by Routledge
2 Park Square, Milton Park, Abingdon, Oxfordshire OX14 4RN

Simultaneously published in the USA and Canada
by Routledge
711 Third Avenue, New York, NY 10017

First issued in paperback 2014

Routledge is an imprint of the Taylor and Francis Group, an informa business

Typeset in Times New Roman
by Taylor & Francis Books

British Library Cataloguing in Publication Data
A catalogue record for this book is available from the British Library

Library of Congress Cataloging in Publication Data
Santos, Ana Cordeiro dos.
The social epistemology of experimental economics / Ana Cordeiro dos Santos.
p. cm.
Includes bibliographical references and index.
1. Economics–Research. 2. Experimental economics. I. Title.
HB74.5.S325 2009
330.072'4–dc22

2009002010

ISBN 978-0-415-48050-5 (hbk)
ISBN 978-1-138-80509-5 (pbk)
ISBN 978-0-203-87433-2 (ebk)

To Conceição e António

Contents

Illustrations

Figures

Table

Acknowledgments

The Social Epistemology of Experimental Economics is about the inescapably collective nature of knowledge production, in time and space. This project is no exception. Even though it is singly authored, it certainly would not have been possible without the support and collaboration of a great many. This collaborative work started in 2001 at the Erasmus Institute for Philosophy and Economics (EIPE), Erasmus University of Rotterdam, when, as a PhD student, I first started the epistemological study of economics experiments; and it was concluded at the Centre for Social Studies (CES), University of Coimbra.

I first want to thank to José Castro Caldas and Helena Lopes, my senior research colleagues at DINÂMIA – Research Centre on Socioeconomic Change, who introduced and encouraged me to study the philosophy of economics and supported this project throughout the years.

I am particularly indebted to Uskali Mäki, my PhD supervisor at EIPE, with whom I learned to appreciate the merits of intellectual rigour as well as the importance of sheer and shared enthusiasm in doing research whose outcomes are not always certain and predictable. Part of this package was the amazing freedom Uskali gave me to take the paths of my own choosing and the confidence he demonstrated in having done so. This encouragement and support lasted until the very end of this project, culminating in the publication of this book, which is a substantially revised version of my PhD thesis. My thanks for all that.

Special thanks are also due to John B. Davis and Päivi Oinas whose encouragement and support was critical in reaching this final stage of publicly reporting the work carried out over the last seven years. I also want to express my grateful recognition to Caterina Marchionni for her generous, attentive and valuable suggestions on the final version of this book.

There are many other contributors who have commented on previous versions of parts of the present work presented in seminars and conferences. I especially thank Francesco Guala, who not only commented on a substantial part of a previous version of this book, but also provided hospitality during my research visit in 2005 at the University of Exeter, UK. I acknowledge helpful comments from Emrah Aydinonat, José Castro Caldas, Luís Francisco

Carvalho, Ana Costa, John B. Davis, Igor Douven, Fredrik Hansen, George Hendrikse, Frank Hindriks, Marteen Janssen, Arjo Klamer, Aki Lehtinen, Deirdre McCloskey, Mary Morgan, Roberta Muramatsu,João Rodrigues, Arthur Schram, Joep Sonnemans, Gülbahar Tezel and Jack J. Vromen. Needless to say, all remaining mistakes are of my own making.

I must also gratefully acknowledge the financial support of Fundação para a Ciência e a Tecnologia (FCT, Grant SFRH/BD/2822/2000), Portugal, and Vereniging Trustfonds Erasmus Universiteit Rotterdam, The Netherlands. FCT funded my visiting periods in Rotterdam. Vereniging Trustfonds funded my visit to the University of Exeter, UK, in 2005. I also thank the Executive Board of CES for providing me with the conditions for completing this project, the support of the research group Studies on Governance and Economic Institutions, at CES, and to Monica Varese Andrade for her promptness and careful revising of the manuscript. Finally, I thank Taylor & Francis Ltd for permission to publish a substantial part of my 'The "Materials" of Experimental Economics: Technological versus Behavioural Experiments' (*Journal of Economic Methodology* 14:3, 311–37, September 2007) in Chapter 10 of this book, and my 'Behavioural Experiments: How and What can we Learn About Human Behaviour' (*Journal of Economic Methodology* 16:1:71–88, March 2009) in chapter 11 of this book.

1 Introduction

epistemology, experiments and economics

> I. Man, being the server and interpreter of nature, can only do and understand so much and so much only as he has observed in fact or in thought the course of nature: beyond this he neither knows anything nor can he do anything.
>
> II. Neither the naked hand nor the understanding left to itself can effect much. It is by instruments and helps that the work is done, which are as much wanted for the understanding as for the hand. And as the instruments of the hand give motion or guide it, so the instruments of the mind supply either suggestions for the understanding or cautions.
>
> XCV. Those who have handled sciences have been either men of experiment or men of dogmas. The men of experiment are like the ant, they only collect and use; the reasoners resemble spiders, who make cobwebs out of their own substance. But the bee takes a middle course: it gathers its material from the flowers of the garden and of the field, but transforms and digests it by a power of its own … Therefore from a closer and purer league between these two faculties, the experimental and the rational (such as has never yet been made), much may be hoped.
>
> (Bacon 1620, Book I)

Practical and rational faculties at work in the laboratory

This book is about the things scientists do in the world with the help of instruments and the understanding they acquire of it as a result. Already in 1620, Francis Bacon could foresee that much could be hoped for from the collaborative work of the hand and of the mind, and alerted to the sterility of the 'naked hand' and of the 'understanding left to itself'. The naked hands of practical scientists ('men of experiment'), who were like ants, could only collect and use their gatherings. The minds of the theoretical scientists ('reasoners'), who were like spiders, could only produce material out of their own substance. Scientists should instead combine both practical and rational faculties. They should be like the bee that transforms its gatherings by a power of its own. The course of science indeed has followed Bacon's prescriptions and it did so at an ever-increasing pace. The interactive work performed by the hand and the mind has also been extended to the human world, of which experimental economics is a case in point.

Yet experiment did not attract the attention of philosophers of science. Scientists' practical engagements with the material world were not considered a philosophically interesting subject matter. This is not to say that the role of experiment in science was denied. Quite the contrary. Experiment and the empirical base it provided were simply taken-for-granted. Theory was philosophy's subject matter *par excellence.*

Only in the latter quarter of the twentieth century did experiment start to attract philosophers' interest. But experiment still remains an under-studied subject matter. This book is therefore intended as a contribution to the understanding of the work performed by the hand and the mind in the laboratory. It offers a comprehensive account of scientists' practical engagements with their objects of study and the knowledge they acquire as a result – the social epistemology of experiment. And it applies this account of experimental practice to the recently established experimental field of economics.

This chapter sets the stage for the present work. It briefly reviews the studies of experiment undertaken thus far and presents the field of experimental economics. The overview of the book is given in the last section.

The neglect of experiment

The causes of the neglect of experiment can perhaps be traced back to the classical divide that opposed 'reason' to 'experience', and the long lasting idea that experience is what is acquired through the immediate, passive and unmediated senses. As experiment became a more pervasive practice, it was simply assumed that it was capable of delivering an unproblematic empirical base for science. By the mid twentieth century the view that scientific practice consists of the proposal of theories and of its submission to empirical testing was widespread. Experiment was subservient to theory and its role was to test and adjudicate among competing theories. It was the theoretician who showed the experimenter the way: 'The theoretician puts certain definite questions to the experimenter, and the latter by his experiments tries to elicit a decisive answer to these questions, and to no others'. This was the case, because '[t]heory dominates the experimental work from its initial planning up to the finishing touches in the laboratory' (Popper 1959 [1934]: 107).

The status of the empirical basis of science started to be questioned and along with it the idea that experiment could play the adjudicator role in science. It became increasingly recognized that observational reports are not neutral claims about the world. They are 'interpretations in the light of theories' and 'fallible' because their acceptance relies on agreement by 'convention', given the set of 'background knowledge' established at a given time. To use the jargon of the philosophy of science, observational reports were deemed 'theory-laden'. The recognition that there is no univocal relation between a theoretical hypothesis and an empirical proposition, i.e. that theory is 'under-determined' by data, introduced the consideration of the overall context of knowledge production.

Thomas Kuhn's *The Structure of Scientific Revolutions* (1970 [1962]) was most influential in challenging the view that science follows the pattern described by the proposal, testing and rejection of falsified theories. Scientists are instead engaged in minor theoretical tinkering within the limits defined by a 'paradigm' that is not easily questioned. Paradigmatic change is based on contingent social conditions, given that there is no objective basis, empirical or otherwise, on which to base the replacement of one paradigm by another. Paradigms are 'incommensurable'.

Even though these critiques targeted the empirical base of science, they were informed by a theory-oriented view of science. They all pointed to the absence of a neutral empirical basis for theory testing and choice. The actual processes of knowledge production, and in particular those concerned with the construction of the empirical basis of science, remained largely ignored.

Sociologists were the first students of experiment interested in determining how the empirical basis of science is actually arrived at. The so-called strong programme, or the Edinburgh School, associated with the work of Barry Barnes (1974) and David Bloor (1976), set out to study how social milieu influences the formation of belief in science. The new focus of sociological analysis put experiment, the hallmark of science, in the foreground. Detailed case studies have been since carried out from the historiography of science and from sites of scientific practice (based on field work, ethnographic inquiry and participant observation) to account for how experimental knowledge is actually generated. The long sequential phases of trial-and-error, dead-alleys, failed attempts at constructing and calibrating material apparatuses, experimenters' personal and social skills, and the historical and social milieu embedding scientific production, all became part of the studies of experiment. The view that experimental practice follows a linear and logical sequence of actions leading to firm observational reports was no longer tenable.

Two accounts of experimental practice were critical to assail the privileged status of experiment: Bruno Latour's and Steve Woolgar's *Laboratory Life* (1986 [1979]) and Harry Collins's *Changing Order* (1985). Adopting the anthropological approach to the study of scientific communities, *Laboratory Life* focuses on the material, technical, literary and social practices that transform initial 'literary inscriptions' generated by 'inscription devices' into scientific papers, allegedly the ultimate goal of scientific activity. Experimental practice is, in this view, the outcome of a long process of social negotiation that produces and transforms experimental results into 'scientific facts'.

Changing Order focuses on the presumed lack of standards for experimental practice, which is deemed to create an 'experimenter's regress' problem. The problem arises from the difficulty in determining whether a clash between a result and an expectation is resolved by accepting the result, and hence that the apparatus has worked properly, or by rejecting the result, and thus attributing the result to a failure of the apparatus. Lacking a criterion to judge the functioning of the apparatus, there is no secure way to ascertain what the proper outcome is. And lacking an account of the phenomenon, nor are there means to ascertain whether the apparatus operated adequately. Scientists are, then, trapped in a regress, because determining the correct functioning of the apparatus depends on having knowledge of the phenomenon of interest, which is what scientists are trying to learn about. The absence of objective criteria leaves room for a high degree of arbitrariness, which renders experimental results vulnerable to scientists' predispositions and to the interference of non-epistemic factors. As Collins states: '[i]t is not the regularity of the world that imposes itself on our senses but the regularity of our institutionalized beliefs that imposes on the world' (Collins 1985: 148).

The private nature of the bulk of experimental practice, moreover, renders the experimental process relatively inaccessible to those who did not take part in it; it is not easily transferred to others because it is part of 'tacit' knowing (Polanyi 1958). This means that not only are there no *a priori* criteria to assess experimental results, but there are also no intersubjective criteria. The implication of this is that the replication of experimental results, i.e. the reproduction of somebody else's processes and results, is also contextual and open to negotiation.

The problems posed by the theory-ladenness of observation, the underdetermination of theory by data, paradigms' incommensurability, experimenter's regress and the tacit nature of experimental practice, opened experimentation's flank to the interference of 'social factors'. From an unproblematic activity that generated knowledge about the natural world, scientific experimentation became an activity prone to the influence of factors extraneous to science. Given that experimentation had long been a taken-for-granted scientific activity, it is not surprising that interest in experiment arose when its privileged status was called into question. Philosophers became the next students of experiments.[1]

New experimentalism

The view that scientific practice must be understood within its social milieu is a position that most philosophers were willing to accept. But the view that the content of science is prone to the influence of extraneous factors (e.g. social prejudices, ideologies, etc.) was too radical to go unchallenged. By questioning experiment, sociological studies were attacking the 'rational' or 'objective' basis of science. Confronted with this situation, philosophers, as well as other students of experiment, attempted to overcome the problems of the traditional view of science (i.e. its unrealistic depiction and unattainable prescriptions for good scientific practice), while avoiding the radical implications of the sociological approach (i.e. the irrationality of science).

A new philosophical approach – New Experimentalism – set out to restore the credibility of experimentation and hence of science. This endeavour turned to actual experimental practice to find out how experimenters actually ground observational facts, which still offer important objective constraints in knowledge production. This is how Richard Ackermann, one of its proponents, introduced the new research programme:

> [t]he newer concentration on experimentation is that an experiment is a complex activity undertaken over time (involving the design and manufacture of equipment, the calibration of equipment, checks on proper functioning of the equipment, etc.) that may issue in observations that can be reported as data. What's needed in this context is a discussion of whether specific experimental practices can in some sense legitimate or validate observational reports, and how the strength of such legitimation might be taken into account in a philosophy of science.
>
> (Ackermann 1989: 186)

New studies of laboratory science have since been carried out to identify the constitutive aspects of experimental practice and how experimenters reason and justify the assembly of persuasive evidence with a view to restoring the traditional function of experiment as an objective adjudicator in science.

The first 'new experimentalist' contribution is credited to Ian Hacking's *Representing and Intervening*. The main message of Hacking's book is that scientific experimentation is 'a long hard task', the goal of which is 'to create, produce, refine and stabilise phenomena', which calls for a wide range of activities not encompassed in the notion of passive observation. For '[o]nly when one has got the equipment right is one in a position to make and record observations' (1983: 230). Rather than being trapped in an infinite regress, experimenters determine whether the experimental equipment is working correctly in actual practice. How they do that was the subject matter of the new experimentalist approach.

Since the 1980s, historians, sociologists and philosophers of science have been prolific in the production of detailed accounts of scientific experimentation aimed at identifying the practices used and the arguments put forward in experimental practice (e.g. Ackermann 1989; Franklin 1989; Galison 1987; Hacking 1983).[2] The most articulated account of experiment to date sees experimentation as an activity that consists of the progressive elimination, measurement and calculation of 'background effects', 'noise', or 'error', until experimenters are confident that the phenomenon created in the laboratory was successfully isolated from disturbing factors (Galison 1987; Hon 1989, 2003; Mayo 1996; Guala 2005a). In this view, as errors are eliminated, corrected and accounted for, belief is reinforced in the 'reality' of the 'signal' looked for. The process ends when experimenters are convinced that they have accounted for all sources of error.

Interest in experiment has recently waned and especially so in the philosophy of science. This state of affairs has led Hans Radder to declare that 'the philosophy of experimentation is still underdeveloped, especially as compared to historical and social scientific approaches' (Radder 2003b: 1–2).

The social epistemology of experiment

This book proposes a comprehensive framework – the social epistemology of experiment (SEE) – that aims to account for and appraise the processes and practices by which knowledge is produced by experimental means.

The social epistemology of experiment shares with new experimentalism the principle that the methodological and epistemological study of experiment must take into account the actual processes by which knowledge is produced and validated. Based on various studies of experiment, SEE puts forward a comprehensive account of experimental knowledge production that is mobilized to formulate and answer key methodological and epistemic questions pertaining to experiment. It aims in particular to provide a framework that helps answer the two key questions of experiment: (1) How do experimenters come to believe that they have created the phenomenon of interest rather than an artefact of the experimental apparatus? (2) What are the grounds for belief in knowledge generated by a process in which both the means and the outcomes of that process are at stake?

The social epistemology of experiment is built upon various studies of experiment – philosophical, historical and sociological – that provide rich accounts of actual experimental practice and that uncover human action relevant to the production and establishment of experimental results, which is, however, often hidden in the final reports of experiments. These studies comprise various episodes of experimental practice that differ in genre and size, and vary in time and place. The various studies taken together therefore contribute to form a general view of experimental practice that is able to identify the inner processes and epistemic attributes of experiment. This does not mean that the studies of experiments share the same view. In fact, these studies use experiments to make different, and at times conflicting, arguments. Whereas some aim more explicitly to restore the traditional role of experiment or to make more salient the social dimension of knowledge production, others may be placed in the continuum delimited by the more sociologically oriented and the more traditional approach to science.

I will argue that they all support a reconstructed account of experimental practice based on a general principle of coherence. Experimental practice is here reconstructed as an activity that consists of forging relations of coherence among heterogeneous items of scientific culture, which gives experimenters confidence in their practice and in the outcome of practice. The conceptualization of experimental practice as an endeavour in which scientists strive for the attainment of coherent resolutions pays special attention to scientists' predispositions to produce results that fit their conceptual frameworks while overlooking conflicting results, as well as the enforcement of group commitments by scientific communities. The social epistemology of experiment therefore presents an account symmetrical to that supplied by the error-elimination approach.

Whereas the error-elimination account of experiment presupposes that scientists and scientific communities strive for the identification and correction of error, the social epistemology of experiment conceives of scientific practice as an endeavour that strives for a coherent resolution between scientists' prior expectations and the outcome of their actions in the material world. When scientists confirm their expectations, they tend, often too hastily, to believe that their apparatuses have worked properly and thus they tend to overlook potential sources of error. When their prior expectations clash with their results they first attempt to protect their conceptual models and blame the experimental equipment for the failure.

By acknowledging the confirmation biases of scientists, which may have many causes (e.g. resistance to acknowledging error, preferences for given theories and instruments, political interests and so forth), SEE brings to the fore the factors that get in the way of finding support for one's prior beliefs – the direct participation of the material world and the social dimension of knowledge production – which are the main epistemic factors of scientific experimentation but are only presupposed in the error-elimination accounts of experiment.

The direct participation of the object under scrutiny and the social dimension of knowledge production force scientists to identify and correct error and thereby explore relevant courses of action in their attempts at finding persuasive arguments for their results. These two factors are what ultimately convey epistemic value to scientists' confirmations, or coherent results, if and when arrived at. These two factors are thus two critical variables in SEE that aim to provide a framework for the analysis and appraisal of experimental practices and results. The examination of experiments is, then, devoted to assessing the actual participation of the material and the social worlds in knowledge production and thus the extent to which knowledge production strived for the identification and elimination of error.

The social epistemology of experiment calls attention to two pairs of factors that have not been sufficiently integrated in previous studies of experiment. First, it integrates the analysis of the *processes* of knowledge production with the analysis of the *products* of experiments. Second, it appraises the participation of both the *material* and the *social* worlds. The social epistemology of experiment emphasizes that the epistemic value of experimental results depends on the processes of knowledge production and on the role of the material and the social worlds in those processes. The inclusion of the two pairs, processes/products and nature/society, in the same framework allows for building an account of scientific experimentation that can be applied to any stage of experimental practice, rather than to the finished products of science, and attributes epistemic value to both 'material world' and 'social world'.

The 'materiality' and the 'sociality' of scientific experimentation have been recognized as relevant elements of scientific experimentation. However, they have often been presented as epistemically conflicting and contrasting factors.

Indeed, the participation of the material world in knowledge production is often presented as a countervailing factor to the detrimental effects of social factors, while the positive effects of the latter are overlooked. The social dimension of knowledge production is, in turn, evoked as a counterargument to the view that takes the results of experiment as objective and neutral outcomes. Given that the balance tips in favour of the material aspects of experiments and the role of the material world in them, the epistemology of experimentation I put forward here is called a 'social' epistemology to emphasize the epistemic value of the social dimension in scientific experimentation.

To conclude, the social epistemological framework provides a descriptive and a normative device for understanding and appraising the practices and products of experiments. It is built upon accounts of actual scientific practice to capture the fundamental features of the processes through which practising scientists, embedded in scientific communities, produce and establish new claims to knowledge. In this view, coherence is the underlying principle that guides experimental practice and grounds experimenters' belief in their claims to knowledge. The epistemic value of experimental results is an empirical question, the answer to which requires assessing the levels of materiality and sociality of the coherent relations supporting them. The higher the participation of both the material and the social worlds in knowledge production, the higher the epistemic value of practices and results. How coherent resolutions are obtained in actual practice depends on the problem-situation at hand, which varies both within single disciplines and across disciplines. In this book I show how economists do this in various episodes of experimental practice, research programmes and experiments.

Experimental economics

The experimental field of economics is an achievement of the second half of the twentieth century, which has only recently gained the discipline's recognition. Economics was considered a non-experimental discipline at least until 1985. In this year, Paul Samuelson and William Nordhaus still presented economics as a non-laboratory science in their best-selling textbook *Economics*, and comforted economists to 'be content largely to observe' (p. 8).

The evolution of the discipline was, by and large, affected by this consensual shortcoming and by attempts to overcome or attenuate it. Economists, in their efforts to make economics a scientific discipline, tried to make do with other methods and techniques. But their acquaintance with experimental practices in other human sciences eventually brought the experimental method into the discipline, and economics ultimately became an experimental science.

Experimental work in economics took off in the 1980s. A large and increasing community of economists now conduct experiments in laboratories, whose numbers keep growing everywhere around the globe. The community of experimenters present and discuss their work under the auspices of their official association, the *Economic Science Association*, founded in 1986. Reports of experiments are published in top journals such as *Econometrica*, *The American*

Economic Review and the *Economic Journal,* and since 1998 also in the specialized journal *Experimental Economics.* Experimental Economics is now part of the curricula of undergraduate and graduate courses and it is a field with one recipient of the Bank of Sweden Nobel Memorial Prize, awarded in 2002 to Vernon Smith 'for having established laboratory experiments as a tool in empirical economic analysis, especially in the study of alternative market mechanisms'. This prize was jointly awarded to the psychologist Daniel Kahneman 'for having integrated insights from psychological research into economic science, especially concerning human judgment and decision-making under uncertainty'.[3] The success of the field has been such that it has also given rise to a new industry in the business of consultancy services, particularly in the design of market mechanisms. In short, economics has become an experimental science.

The methodological and epistemic discussion of the experimental method of economics has, however, lagged behind the rapid growth of the field. Three main phases can be identified. The first phase, in the 1980s, consisted of experimenters' first attempts at justifying the role of experiments in economics and of their responses to sceptical charges that attacked the relevance of experiments to provide knowledge of real world economies. The second phase, since the late 1990s till the present, has seen a more reasoned debate about the role and function of experiments in economics, which has greatly benefited from the contribution of philosophers of science. At the present time, interest in methodological and epistemic discussion seems to be fading.

In the 1980s, pioneers in the field were more concerned with persuading the profession about the legitimacy of the experimental method in economics rather than with developing thorough analyses of its methodological and epistemic functions. Early methodological discussion, as we will see, was ill-informed by an inadequate conception of science and of experiment which failed to provide full-blown methodological and epistemic answers. *The Methodology of Experimental Economics* by Francesco Guala (2005a) offers the single philosophically informed and comprehensive analysis of experimental economics to date. The overarching theme is inference; inference 'from data to phenomena, and from phenomena to their causes within a given experimental setting' and inference 'from laboratory circumstances to some real-world situation' (p. 6).

The Social Epistemology of Experimental Economics is meant as a contribution to the methodological and epistemological analysis of the experimental field of economics. It offers a broad portrayal of experimental economics along with a more fine-grained analysis of particular episodes of experimental practice and results. These include the scrutiny of arguments intended to justify the relevance of the experimental method in economics, the analysis of research programmes, experiments, experimental procedures and social practices. And it does so by focusing on two epistemic factors of experiments – the participation of experimental subjects and the social dimensions of knowledge production – and their relevance to the type and content of knowledge that economics experiments produce about human behaviour and the economy.

The social epistemology of experiment focuses in particular on Vernon Smith's trajectory in his attempt to win the profession's recognition of the relevance of the experimental method. Smith is the field's prominent practitioner who has most contributed to the establishment of the field of experimental economics. He did in fact win the *Bank of Sweden Nobel Memorial Prize* for having done so. Notwithstanding the prominence given to Smith's contributions, and to the market experiments to which Smith most contributed, I also discuss exemplars from other contributors and critics of the experimental method.

Now that the field has been established within the discipline, we are witnessing decreased interest in methodological and epistemic reflection. The growing use of experimental results in the development of new theories of human behaviour and the use of experiments in market design, however, raise new questions which require a good understanding of economics experiments. The present book aims also to assist in answering the new questions raised by these recent developments.

Overview

This book is organized in two parts. Part 1 constructs the social epistemology of experiment and Part 2 applies its analytical framework to experimental economics. Part 1 comprises five chapters. Chapter 2 presents the questions that are the focus of SEE: (1) How do experimenters come to believe that they have created the phenomenon of interest rather than an artefact of the experimental apparatus? (2) What are the grounds for belief in knowledge generated by a process in which both the means and the outcomes of that process are at stake? And it provides a first sketch of an answer based on the general guiding principle of coherence. Chapter 3 introduces experimental economics. It presents the practices whereby economists create and study microeconomic phenomena in their labs. Chapter 4 analyses the role of the material world in scientific experimentation and Chapter 5 focuses on the epistemic contribution of the social dimension of knowledge production. Chapter 6 presents four tests for the appraisal of the processes and products of scientific experimentation: the materiality test, the stringency test, the social robustness test and the technological test. Part 2 is composed of the subsequent six chapters. Chapter 7 presents the historical context of the emergence and establishment of the experimental method of economics. Chapter 8 presents early methodological discussion that aimed to justify the use of experiments in economics, in particular the relation between experiment and theory. Chapter 9 presents recent methodological discussion around the relation between experiment and the real world. Chapter 10 analyses the roles of the 'materials' of economic experiments – the participation of experimental subjects and the institutions that regulate their actions. Chapter 11 puts forward criteria to assess the participation of human subjects in economics experiments. Chapter 12 illustrates the relevance of the social dimension of experimental practice in economics. Chapter 13 concludes by applying the social epistemological framework to the work carried out.

Part I

The social epistemology of experiment

2 Creating phenomena in the lab

This chapter presents a brief account of scientific experimentation and identifies the key methodological and epistemic questions that concern the production of knowledge by experimental means. It also sketches a first response to these questions, which are tackled in more detail and elaborated in subsequent chapters of the first part of the book.

Learning to move around in the laboratory world

Experiments are used in science because naturally occurring phenomena are either too complex to understand or do not occur in conditions that allow for close scrutiny. Experimenters have to engage in the production of the phenomenon of interest in order to study it under the favourable conditions of the laboratory. And they have to control the interference of factors – known as 'backgrounds' – that may have an effect on it. Only then can experimenters be sure that the data obtained pertain to the object of study and to this object only. The control exercised over experimental conditions ensures, in turn, the stability of the phenomenon produced.

The production of a stable phenomenon is not a trivial accomplishment. It involves a long sequence of operations before the recording of evidence for the phenomenon can take place. Experimenters need to design, build and implement a special apparatus to produce and explore as yet unknown aspects of the phenomenon of interest. In the process, unexpected events inevitably arise that call for adjustments to the experimental apparatus, the refinement of experimental procedures, the revision of working assumptions, and so forth. The process ends only when the phenomenon of interest is believed to have been successfully produced. In Ian Hacking's words:

> There is designing an experiment that might work. There is learning how to make the experiment work. But perhaps the real knack is getting to know when the experiment is working. That is one reason why observation, in the philosophy-of-science usage of the term, plays a relatively small role in experimental science. Noting and reporting readings of dials … is nothing. Another kind of observation is what counts: the uncanny ability

> to pick out what is odd, wrong, instructive or distorted in the antics of one's equipment. The experimenter is not the 'observer' of traditional philosophy, but rather the alert and observant person. Only when one has got the equipment right is one in a position to make and record observations.
> (Hacking 1983: 230)

To experiment is thus to gain expertise in experimental apparatuses so as to build confidence that the phenomenon of interest has been produced and the recording of evidence for it can take place. From this brief account of experimental practice, the central methodological and epistemic questions of scientific experimentation already emerge:

1 How do experimenters come to believe that they have got the equipment right or that they have created the phenomenon of interest rather than an artefact of the experimental apparatus?
2 What are the grounds for belief in knowledge generated by a process in which both the means and the outcomes of that process are at stake?

Whereas the first question calls for the identification of the standards that guide experimenters' actions and decisions in the construction of novel resources for scientific practice, the second question invites inquiry into how those standards provide warrant for belief. Answers to these questions are not straightforward. Even a simple experimental task like observing through the microscope calls for a wide range of activities that extend beyond the notion of passive observation. Here is Hacking's stance when referring to the observation of a cell through a microscope:

> Our conviction arises partly from our success at systematically removing aberrations and artifacts … We are convinced about the structures [of the cell] we seem to see because we can interfere with them in quite physical ways, say by microinjecting. We are convinced because instruments using entirely different physical principles lead us to observe pretty much the same structures in the same specimen. We are convinced by our clear understanding of most of the physics used to build the instruments that enable us to see … We are more convinced by the admirable intersections with biochemistry, which confirm that the structures that we discern with the microscope are individuated by distinct chemical properties too. We are convinced not by a high powered deductive theory about the cell – there is none – but because of a large number of interlocking low level generalisations that enable us to control and create phenomena in the microscope. In short, we learn to move around in the microscopic world.
> (Hacking 1983: 208–9)

Hacking suggests that confidence in experimental results is given by a variety of resources and practices, which together provide reasons for believing that the phenomenon created in the laboratory is real rather than the product of a malfunctioning apparatus. Hacking stresses in particular that the possibility of interfering with the object of scrutiny and the confirmation of the expected outcomes of these interventions strengthen belief in both the proper operation of the apparatus and in the results obtained with it. This is the case, for example, when observing a change in the colour of a cell after injecting colorant fluid, which reinforces the belief that the microscope is functioning well and that the observations made with it are valid.

Producing the same results with different apparatuses is also an important means of building confidence in scientific experimentation. The independent confirmation of the results simply renders implausible (this is also known as the 'no miracle' argument) that they are caused by the same systematic 'backgrounds' that the various apparatuses generate. This is so because different apparatuses are associated with different backgrounds, which make the coincidence of errors extremely unlikely. The attribution of the same results to the correct operation of the various instruments is reasonable and understandable. As Hacking puts it, again referring to observing through a microscope, 'it would be a preposterous coincidence if, time and again, two completely different physical processes produced identical visual configurations which were, however, artifacts of the physical processes rather than real structures in the cell' (1983: 201). Finally, the production of experimental knowledge relies also on well-established theories of instruments and phenomena as well as on low level generalizations that support both the use of the instruments and the observations.

Hacking's list of resources and practices, however, does not provide a comprehensive view of experiment that enables us to answer the key questions of experiment. It is not clear what it is that the interventions of scientists, the use of various instruments while doing so, and the mobilization of theories of instruments and phenomena accomplish. Hacking does not say what, in the end, gives scientists confidence that they have produced the phenomenon of interest. Nor does he spell out what scientists do when they do not have a well-furnished toolbox for building new apparatuses for the exploration of unknown phenomena. In sum, in Hacking's account the identification of a general principle that guides experimenters' actions and warrants belief in their results is missing.

The three-way coherence

Drawing closely on the reconstruction of scientific experimentation by the sociologist Andrew Pickering (1987, 1989, 1995), I take coherence as the general principle that guides experimenters' actions and warrants belief in experimental results.

Coherence is an epistemically esteemed value in science. Scientists adopt coherence as a criterion for the appraisal of single theories, the relation between theories and evidence and, ultimately, all established knowledge. Philosophers of science have, in turn, built theories of science on the basis of various coherence criteria, such as Whewell's notion of *consilience* (1967 [1840]), Popper's falsificationist methodology (1959 [1934], 1965 [1963]), or Solomon's (2001) social empiricist epistemology. These theories, however, focus on theory choice, taking the empirical propositions of science as given. The coherence account of scientific experimentation put forward here concerns instead the production of empirical propositions, which are to be supported by relations of coherence. These are relations of mutual support of various and heterogeneous items of science that extend beyond the establishment of inferential relations between theoretical and ready-made empirical propositions. And they are part of the process of knowledge production, along with the empirical propositions that they sustain.

Pickering construes experimental practice as an endeavour that consists of the manipulation of the three components that make up an experimental system – the *material procedure*, the *instrumental model* and the *phenomenal model* – until a *three-way coherence* obtains. The material procedure comprises 'experimental action in the material world: setting up the apparatus, running and monitoring it in the laboratory'. The instrumental model refers to 'the experimenter's conceptual understanding of how the apparatus functions'. And the phenomenal model refers to 'the conceptual understanding of whatever aspect of the phenomenal world is under investigation' (Pickering 1989: 276–77).

Figure 2.1 presents a schematic representation of the practice leading to the three-way coherence and to the experimental result it supports. Experimental practice starts with the identification of a research problem. This may, for example, arise from a clash between a piece of established knowledge and recent results of scientific practice that conflict with it. Experimental inquiry then continues with the exploration of feasible ways of investigating the natural world. This requires searching through the available items of scientific culture for the material and conceptual resources that may be mobilized to solve the problem at hand. When experimenters believe they have identified a potentially workable material apparatus, the operation of which can provide the information sought about the phenomenon of interest, a 'two-way coherence' is achieved between the instrumental and the phenomenal model (Figure 2.1a).

Experimental practice then continues with the material implementation of the instrumental model. Because experimenters cannot fully anticipate the outcome of their actions, experimental practice will most probably give rise to unexpected results that call for further intervention in the natural world so that experimenters can make sense of those results. Material and conceptual manoeuvrings upon the experimental system then feedback upon the various components that comprise it (Figure 2.1b). In the process, new material apparatuses and techniques may be tried out, and the understanding of how the phenomenon under scrutiny is to be investigated may be substantially revised.

When the implementation of the instrumental model finally produces results that can be explained by the phenomenal model, a 'three-way coherence' obtains (Figure 2.1c). Experimenters then believe that they have understood their practice and the outcome of that practice and hence that they

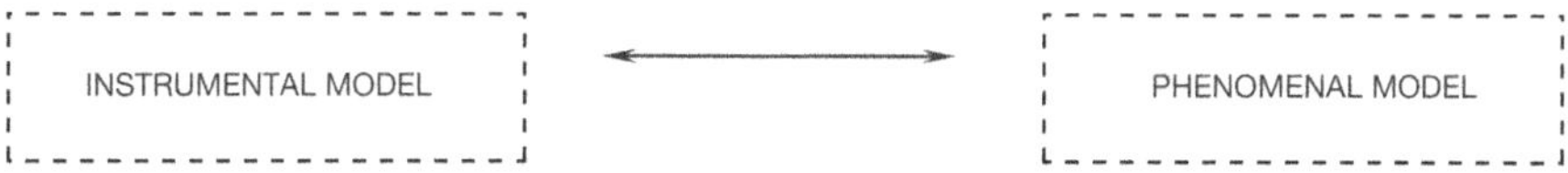

a) The two-way conceptual coherence between the instrumental and the phenomenal model: establishing how a given phenomenon is to be investigated by experimental means.

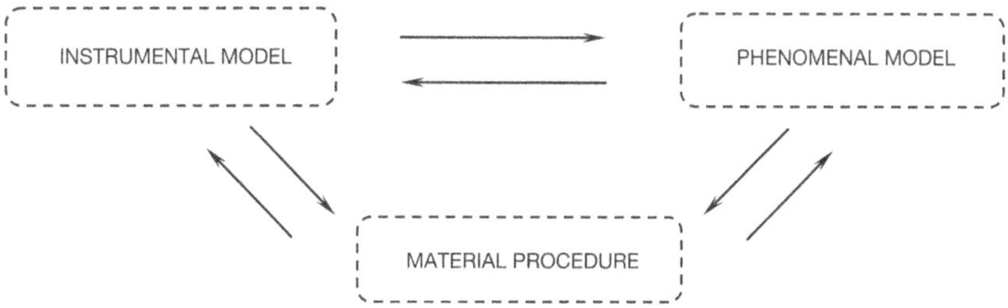

b) The forging of the three-way coherence by material and conceptual maneuvering.

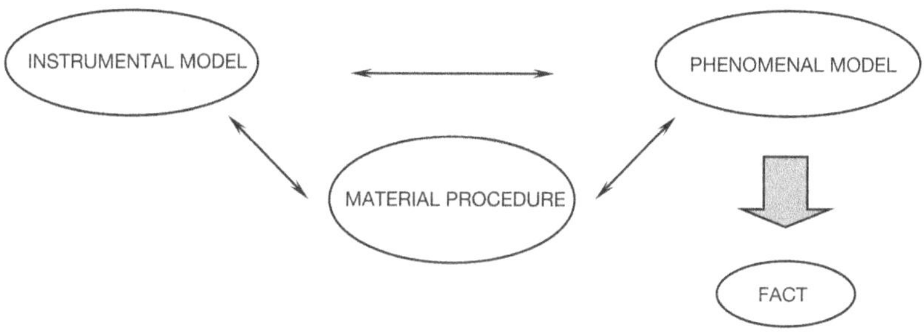

c) The end of the experimental process of knowledge production: the attainment of the three-way experimental coherence.

Figure 2.1 The experimental process of knowledge production

have produced valid results. The experimental process of knowledge production ends. As Pickering notes, '[a]chieving such relations of mutual support is … the defining characteristic of the successful experiment' (Pickering 1987: 199). This is so because

> [t]he output phenomenal model, and the fact it carries, must be right, it seems, because it is implied by the material procedure and the

> instrumental model which lie behind it. Of course, as a plastic resource, there is no guarantee that this particular instrumental model is right, but it fits so nicely between the fact and the material procedure that it is hard to doubt. On the other hand, there is no guarantee that the material procedure is the correct one, material procedures are plastic, too, but … and so on.
>
> (Pickering 1989: 280)

Achieving the three-way alignment is critical when experimenting with new apparatuses to explore unknown phenomena. This is so because the experimental systems have not yet been established as adequate resources for practice and therefore they are still amenable to a wider range of material and conceptual manipulations, which make it difficult to determine when to end the experiment. That is, new experimental systems are plastic systems. The plasticity of the experimental systems and of their components is, of course, a matter of degree. Conceptual models are, for instance, constrained by boundary conditions, and instruments work only under a set of what are taken to be proper operations (the plasticity of experimental systems is addressed in detail in Chapter 4).

The three-way coherence is nonetheless an epistemically relevant outcome and this is why the experiment ends. When the experiment ends, the components of the experimental system crystallise in their final versions. The instrumental model then provides the description of how the material apparatus is to be implemented and operated to generate information about the phenomenon under investigation. By conveying the conceptual understanding of the material procedure, the instrumental model gives scientists confidence that the phenomenon was generated by valid means. The phenomenal model interprets the results produced by the material procedure and thereby gives scientists confidence that the outcome of the experiment carries knowledge about the natural world. The material procedure, in turn, acquires significance as an adequate means of investigating that particular aspect of the natural world. The three-way coherence, however, has only achieved a temporary stabilization. It may be destabilized in subsequent practice as the experimental results are subjected to the scrutiny of the scientific community. In Figure 2.1b the material and conceptual manipulations of the components of the experimental system are depicted by the arrows connecting them, which represent how each component feedbacks upon each other and by the change in their shapes during the various stages of knowledge production. The replacement of the dashed lines by the straight lines in the final stage depicts the stabilization of the coherent components when the process ends.

It should be pointed out that the phenomenal model contains a characteristic that is absent in the other two experimental components. The phenomenal model is both the input and the output of experimental practice. The experiment is ultimately designed and implemented to produce a phenomenon that experimenters want to know more about. This is the fundamental objective behind the experiment. If experimenters had full knowledge of the phenomenon there would be no purpose in conducting the experiment in the first place. The original input phenomenal model therefore conveys an expectation about the phenomenon to be investigated, which is to be corrected and adjusted in the course of experimental practice. The output phenomenal model in turn conveys what has been determined in the course of practice. Once established, the output phenomenal model gains autonomy from the material and conceptual work that generated it and becomes a fact (Figure 2.1c).

The view that coherence is the underlying principle that gives scientists confidence that they have produced and understood the phenomenon of interest is well supported by other studies of experiment. David Gooding (1990) thinks of experimentation as a learning process that 'may show convergence of successive material arrangements (the apparatus) and successive construals (or models) of manipulation of and with apparatus, and its outcomes … to a stable state in which all three are mutually compatible' (p. 166). The significance of this stable state is that it 'indicates that the process is locally convergent, that is, producing sense or order that can be reproduced'. Otherwise, 'it fails to make experience intelligible and reproducible' (p. 167). Ian Hacking (1992) has also conceived of experimentation as a practice that achieves the 'mutual adjustment' of the 'matériel', 'ideas' and 'marks' until they are brought into a relation of consilience, which accounts for the self-vindication of experimental results. In his view, in laboratory sciences theories and laboratory equipment evolve until they match each other and become mutually self-vindicating. Finally, Hans Radder (1995) conceives of the experimental process as involving 'the material realization and the theoretical description or interpretation of a number of manipulations of, and their consequences for, the object and the apparatus, which have been brought into mutual interaction' (p. 58, emphasis omitted).

I am now in a position to sketch the answers to the key methodological and epistemic questions of experiment that I develop in the first part of the book. Taking as a starting point Pickering's reconstruction of experimental practice as an activity that consists of the establishment of a three-way alignment between the components of the experimental system, the social epistemology of experiment takes coherence as the central principle guiding experimental practice and grounding belief in the results of experiment. In this view, experimenters strive to attain a three-way coherence between the components of the experimental system, which then forms a unified, organized and structured whole. When coherence obtains, the material procedure interpreted through the instrumental model produces a phenomenon that is interpreted by the phenomenal model. Experimenters then believe they have made sense of their practices and respective outcomes.

Experimental coherence is worked out during knowledge production via conceptual and material manoeuvring of the experimental system until scientists succeed in making sense of the phenomenon produced. Experimental practice is thus part of a cognitive process whereby scientists attempt to make sense of their interactions with their objects and try their tentative interpretations against the natural world as well as against other scientists. When coherence is attained, the inquirers no longer have the inclination to revise the elements of the system any further. The experiment ends.

Scientists are then confident that they have produced the phenomenon of interest or that they have controlled the influence of extraneous factors so that there is no need to introduce further amendments to the experimental system. And they believe that the scientific community will also believe them. This means that the making of relations of experimental coherence is also part of an epistemically relevant social process that produces results that have to win the consent of the larger scientific community, or even of the general public. Experimental practice is intrinsically a social endeavour undertaken by collectives of scientists in well-organized and structured scientific institutions that validate the work of their members. The social epistemology of experiment (SEE) hence stresses that the three-way coherence is pivotal to persuade the wider community of scientists that the experiment is valid and, therefore, that there are objective grounds for belief in its results. But the social validation of experimental results can only be determined in subsequent practice (the subject matter of Chapter 5).

Establishing relations of coherence

The conception of experimental practice as an endeavour that consists of the design, implementation and manipulation of a material apparatus and of the ongoing revision of related conceptual models until a three-way coherence obtains is still a crude simplification of experiment. Pickering emphasized that an experimental apparatus is rarely capable of producing a valid experimental result in its first trial, and thus further adjustments have to be made before scientists trust their results. But Pickering did not elaborate on how the relations of mutual support are actually obtained and what their epistemic import is.

The overall fit between the material procedure, the instrumental model and the phenomenal model involves a variety of resources and practices to produce a web of relations of coherence in support of the experimental results. The complexity of this web depends on the reliability of the resources used. This means that the construction of new equipment requires the establishment of a more intricate network of coherent results in its support than the use of well-established apparatuses. The latter do not require such work because their reliability has already been determined in prior practice.

I now use Allan Franklin's list of 'epistemological strategies' of experiment (1986, 1989, 1990, 2007) to illustrate how a three-way coherence is built up in practice and how this constructive work depends on the reliability of the resources of practice. Franklin presents the strategies as 'arguments designed to establish, or to help establish, the validity of an experimental result or observation' (1989: 437). But he is careful to note that the list provided is not exhaustive and that no single argument, or subset of arguments for that matter, is meant as 'necessary or sufficient condition for rational belief' (1989: 459). Nor does it guarantee that the results are correct. Experiments are fallible. They are nonetheless capable of providing scientists with good reasons for belief in experimental results.

I take Franklin's list as a set of *coherence strategies*, that is, means of establishing coherent relations between resources of practice and hence of establishing the alignment between the material procedure, the instrumental model and the phenomenal model. These strategies assist in generating partial and local relations of coherence which help the construction of the three-way coherence. The strategies of experiment are:

1 Independent confirmation using different experiments.
2 Experimental checks and calibration, in which the experimental apparatus reproduces known phenomena.
3 Confirming the predicted effects of intervention.
4 Reproducing artefacts that are known in advance to be present.
5 Using an apparatus based on a well-corroborated theory.
6 Using an independently well-corroborated theory of the phenomenon to explain the results.
7 Using the results themselves to argue for their validity.
8 Elimination of plausible sources of background and alternative explanations of the result.
9 Using statistical arguments.

Experimenters obtain the highest degree of confidence when the same results are produced by alternative and well-established apparatuses (strategy 1, cf. Hacking 1983). This means that distinct material apparatuses, each with a well-defined instrumental model describing its appropriate operation, produce exactly the same results; or, to put it in another way, various three-way coherences support the same fact. The reproduced result is then accepted with the force of certainty because it is a highly replicated and robust result.[1] When scientists do not have alternative apparatuses at their disposal, they have to build their confidence on the available apparatus by other means. They can test the reliability of the equipment for the purpose at hand by reproducing well-known phenomena. The confirmation of what is already known will then reinforce belief in it (strategy 2).

The use of an experimental apparatus that has not yet achieved the status of a reliable instrument requires a tighter relation between material procedure, instrumental model and phenomenal model. Observing the predicted effect of an intervention strengthens belief in both the proper operation of the apparatus and in the observations made with it (strategy 3, cf. Hacking 1983). Observing known background effects associated with particular apparatuses will also give confidence that the apparatus is working properly (strategy 4). The weak epistemic value of such three-way coherences may be further enhanced by coherent relations between the apparatus and the theory of the apparatus (strategy 5) or between the observations and the theory of the phenomenon (strategy 6). The observations obtained with the apparatus may be further supported if they cannot be attributed to a plausible malfunction of the apparatus (strategy 7) or if no other plausible and alternative interpretation, given the state of current knowledge, can account for the results (strategy 8). Finally, statistical analysis can be carried out and further assurance provided on the significance of the data collected (strategy 9).[2]

It is now easy to see how the web of partially coherent relations to be worked out in practice depends on the availability of well-established resources. Well-established resources are the outcome of previous three-way coherences that produced and established them as reliable means of knowledge production. Experimental resources become reliable means of knowledge production in practice as they themselves become tools for the making of new three way coherences in the resolution of new problems. When using a well-established apparatus, scientists only need to be assured that it has worked properly. This assurance is given by the shared understanding of what an appropriate operation amounts to, which a two-way coherence between the material procedure and the respective instrumental model has previously defined. The material apparatus is thus a 'black box' autonomous from the processes that produced it and that have established an invariant relationship between its operations and the world (Ackermann 1985; Schaffer 1989); it is perceived as a reliable transmitter of 'nature's messages' (Schaffer 1989) that allows 'direct observations' from nature (Franklin 1986).

New resources have yet to be socially validated. Their use in practice requires the making of a tighter set of partially coherent relations between the material apparatus and the theory of the apparatus, between experimental evidence and the theory of the phenomenon, and so forth. A complex array of coherences must sustain experimental results. If these coherences were not established in the past they have to be worked out in current practice.

Conclusion

In this brief introductory chapter two methodological and epistemic questions were identified: how do experimenters come to believe the phenomena they create? What are the grounds for belief in knowledge generated by a process in which both the means and the outcomes of that process are at stake? Coherence was presented as the general principle guiding experimental practice that helps answer both questions. Experimenters are dedicated to making relations of coherence among various heterogeneous items until a three-way coherence is achieved among the material procedure, the instrumental model and the phenomenal model.

Coherence grounds experimenters' beliefs in experimental results because the mutual support the components of the experimental system provide each other gives experimenters confidence in their practice and in the outcome of that practice. But the answers are not yet completed. I must still justify the epistemic value of the three-way coherences. The account of experiment presented is vulnerable to the objection that the epistemic value of the three-way coherence is affected by scientists' confirmation biases. The conceptualization of experimental practice as an endeavour in which scientists' strive for the attainment of coherent resolutions must accommodate the possibility that scientists may produce results that are significantly influenced by attempts to obtain their anticipated phenomenal models while overlooking important backgrounds or errors. As a result, scientists may prematurely end the experiment.

In Chapters 4 and 5 I show that the epistemic value of the three-way coherence stems from the direct participation of the natural world and the social validation of knowledge claims. These two factors prevent experimental outcomes being solely determined by scientists' material and conceptual actions. Before that, in the next chapter I introduce experimental economics.

3 Creating microeconomic phenomena

This chapter presents the experimental method of economics as conceptualized by one of its founding fathers, Vernon Smith. It presents the procedures whereby economists create and study microeconomic phenomena in their labs, and provides an illustration of how economists do this – Smith's first market experiments. It shows that, similarly to experimentation in the natural sciences, the practice of experimental economists can also be depicted as the forging of three-coherences until they are confident that the phenomenon created is no artefact of the experimental procedures.

The microeconomic experimental system

As Vernon Smith put it in his 'Microeconomic Systems as an Experimental Science' (1982), in economics the fundamental objective behind a laboratory experiment is to create a microeconomy in the lab for the purpose of observing and measuring variables relevant to the study of microeconomic institutions and human behaviour.

Closely following the work of welfare economists, in particular their work on the design and evaluation of resource allocation mechanisms, Smith defines an experimental microeconomy as a system made up of two component parts: the environment and the institution. The *environment* (e) defines the initial circumstances of the microeconomy and consists of the collection of the characteristics of N economic agents: $e = (e^1 \ldots e^N)$. Each agent i is characterized by a utility function u^i, a technology endowment T^i, and a commodity endowment w^i: $e^i = (u^i, T^i, w^i)$. The *institution* (I) consists of the collection of the rules of individual property rights, $I = (I^1 \ldots I^N)$, under which each economic agent communicates, exchanges or transforms commodities for the purpose of modifying the initial endowments in accordance with their preferences and knowledge. More specifically, the institution comprises the *language* (M^i) that defines the set of admissible messages that each individual may use in communication; the *adjustment process rules* (g^i) that govern the sequence and exchange of these messages; the *cost imputation rules* (c^i) that assign the costs to be applied to these messages; and, finally, the *allocation rules* (h^i) that compute the outcome of the exchange process for each agent and that are a function of the messages sent by all. For each agent these rules define the messages that i has the right to send, the rules that govern these communication rights and the right to claim commodities or payments as a result of that process: $I^i = (M^i, h^i, c^i, g^i)$. For example, the first-price sealed-bid auction is an allocation mechanism for the sale of a single item that enforces the same rules on every trader. It begins with a request for bids after which each buyer submits one bid price. When all bids have been received, the allocation rule determines that the item should be awarded to the highest bidder who buys the item at her or his bid price.

To sum up, a microeconomic system is composed of an environment and an institution, $S = (e, I)$, the performance of which depends on both the behaviour of individual agents and the institution. Economic agents do not choose commodity allocations (X). Agents choose messages, $m^i = \beta\ (e^i \setminus I)$, which depend on their individual characteristics (e^i) and the institution (I) that organizes their actions. Nor does the institution (I) determine the final outcomes (X). The institution simply determines how individual messages are to be exchanged and translated into final outcomes $X = H\ (m^i \ldots m^N)$ (see Figure 3.1).

After creating the microeconomy in the lab (to be developed in the next section), the microeconomic system is examined experimentally by manipulating the elements of the environment and of the institution (depicted with the large arrows in Figure 3.1) and by observing the impact of these manipulations on the messages sent and the resulting individual and aggregate outcomes (the shaded area in Figure 3.1). Given that the performance of the microeconomy is determined by the joint effect of the institutional rules and of the decisions of the agents operating under these rules, the microeconomic system is examined by investigating the effect of varying one of the system's variables at a time while keeping the rest constant. The performance of the microeconomic system and the examination of individual behaviour can then be evaluated by reference to relevant criteria such as incentive compatibility and utility maximization.

The experimental method of economics offers the possibility of studying the relationship 'environment (e) – institution (I) – behaviour (m) – outcomes (X)', which has for long been central to economic analysis but which was largely unobservable and undetectable by non-experimental means. The major difficulty concerned the measurement of microeconomic environmental variables. In Smith's own wording:

> Among the observable elements of an economy are (i) the list of agents, (ii) the list of physical commodities and resources, (iii) the physical commodity and resource endowments of individual agents, (iv) the language and property right characteristics of institutions, and (v) outcomes. What is not observable are (vi) preference orderings, (vii) technological (knowledge, human capital) endowments, and (viii) agent message behavior … These last items are not observable because they are not only private but

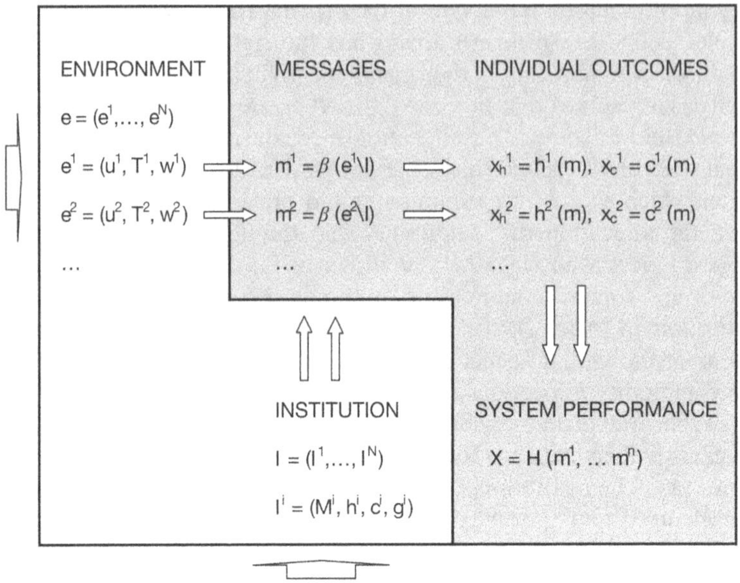

Figure 3.1 The experimental microeconomic system

> to a degree *unrecorded*. Willingness to buy (preferences) and willingness to produce (technology and preferences) can at best only be inferred from agent point actions in the message space. Often we cannot even observe point messages, for example, we may know allocations and prices, but not all bids. In any case, we cannot observe the message behavior *functions* because we cannot observe (and vary) preferences.
>
> (Smith 1982: 928, emphasis in original)

Field data (i.e. data obtained from uncontrolled and naturally occurring economic processes) provide information about economic agents, institutions and market outcomes. But this information constitutes only indirect evidence for issues relevant to economics such as incentive-compatibility, a key evaluative criterion in mechanism design.

Economists have been particularly interested in determining whether the rules that are specified in the institution, together with the behaviour of the agents, generate a choice of messages that are incentive-compatible, that is, rational from the individual viewpoint as well as for the system as a whole. Economists want to know if a given institution leads each agent to choose a strategy that is the best utility-maximizing response to the other agents' strategies and if the situation arrived at is a social optimum in the sense that no one can increase her utility without decreasing that of others (in other words, if the institution is capable of generating a Nash equilibrium the outcomes of which are Pareto optima). And this assessment requires information about individual preferences as well as about production possibility sets that are only obtainable by experimental means. Field data may provide proxies for these variables, but they cannot aspire to be more than very unreliable estimates for the relevant measures. A substantial amount of conceptual and statistical work must be done to convert field data into those estimated values.[1]

The 'material apparatus' of economics

In contrast to experimentation in the natural sciences, where it is common to find the coexistence of various experimental traditions even within the same field of research, in economics experimenters follow a fairly stable set of standard procedures that are shared among the various fields that make up the discipline of experimental economics. That is, economists share the same experimental apparatus. Whereas biologists may resort to different microscopes (e.g. ordinary, polarizing, phase-contrast, fluorescence, etc.) to observe the cells of the same specimen, and high-energy physicists may use different apparatuses (e.g. the visual bubble chamber and the electronic scintillation counters) to detect the existence of a particular particle, experimental economists use a fairly stable 'material procedure' that helps them to create their microeconomic systems in the lab. In other words, in economics experimenters do not have the possibility of obtaining independent confirmation by the use of experimental apparatuses based on radically different principles. The results of experimental economics can only be confirmed by experimental microeconomies that are built on the same experimental principles.

The 'material procedure' of experimental economics is specifically tailored to create and control microeconomic systems in the lab, as defined above. Economists create and control microeconomic systems by designing and enforcing the microeconomic institution that regulates the actions of the participants in the course of the experiment. The microeconomic institution is easily created and controlled by design. It consists of the rules of communication and exchange that define the experimental task and how it is to be carried out. The major methodological difficulty in experimenting in economics concerns the control of the microeconomic environment, namely, the control of the preferences of the experimental subjects. This problem was addressed in 'Induced Value Theory', where Smith (1976a) presented a method for controlling subjects' preferences, which has since become a standard tool in experimental economics to that end. Control over preferences is exercised in economics 'by using a reward structure to induce prescribed monetary value on action' (1976a: 275). This means that the pay-off function must take the variables of the experiment as arguments, and subjects must be given the property rights over the monetary outcomes of the actions taken during the experiment. Even though it was not originally mandatory, the use of money to induce value onto abstract experimental outcomes became the exclusive reward medium of participants in economics experiments. The reward structure therefore applies to the experimental context the same principles that are prevalent in real economic systems. As Smith remarks, in an economic system agents also have property rights over 'intangible property on which value is induced by specifying the rights of the holder to claim money or goods' (1982: 931, n. 11). In addition, the reward structure must satisfy what Smith later dubbed the 'precepts' of experimental economics, which are 'the set of sufficient conditions for a valid controlled microeconomic experiment'. These include non-satiation, saliency, dominance and privacy (1982: 931–35).

Non-satiation dictates that the amount of the reward earned by participating in the experiment must be important to experimental subjects, who must prefer more to less of it. *Saliency* imposes that this amount must be positively correlated with the outcomes of the individual actions, i.e. the rewards must increase with the good outcomes and decrease with the bad outcomes of the experiment. In the double auction experiment, for instance, value is induced on the commodities transacted by (i) a reward structure that pays the redemption values of the goods to buyers and pays the market price of the units sold to sellers, and (ii) by property rights rules that confer on subjects the right to claim the amounts earned in these transactions (obtained after deducting the prices buyers paid and sellers' costs of producing the goods sold).

The reward structure must be sufficient to guarantee effective control because there might be non-monetary subjective costs and values associated with subjects' participation in the experiment. For instance, the 'subjective cost of transacting, that is, the cost of thinking, calculating, and acting' may offset the value induced by the reward structure. Moreover, 'individuals may not be autonomous own-reward maximizers' as 'interpersonal utility considerations may upset the achievement of well-defined induced valuations' (1982: 933–35). In order to exercise control over these factors, the conditions of dominance and privacy must also be implemented. *Dominance* thus requires a reward structure capable of offsetting the subjective costs or values associated with the process of making and executing individual decisions during the experiment. *Privacy* restricts the information on pay-offs to own rewards to impede interpersonal considerations to get in the way.

These conditions were initially meant to apply to market experiments. They were specifically conceived to induce supply and demand valuations, which were critical to the creation of the experimental markets. But they have gradually become part of the standard procedures of experimental economics. It is now widespread practice in economics to pay subjects for their participation in the experiments on the basis of their performance. The goal is to ensure that the experimental situation is relevant to subjects as intended by the experimenters so that they can interpret the behaviour and functioning of the experimental microeconomies. Only then can experimenters understand how the environment and the institution translate into individual behaviour and how this, in turn, affects the performance of the microeconomy. As Smith justifies it:

> When great care is used in an experiment to make induced value be the primary source of motivation, it is *not* for the purpose of making sure that subjects have self-interested motivations; it is for the purpose that we *know* what were the preference patterns of the subjects in the experiment.
> (Smith: 1982: 933, n. 13, emphasis in original)

A controlled experiment in economics is, then, a microeconomic system that elicits behaviour that can be interpreted in the light of preferences induced by the reward structure and the institution that organizes subjects' interactions.

The design of a reward structure that fulfils the 'the set of sufficient conditions for a valid controlled microeconomic experiment' does not exhaust the 'material procedure' of experimental economics. Experimenters follow a larger set of principles and practices to create transparent experimental microeconomic systems.

Simplicity is a key principle. The design of simple tasks is crucial to guarantee that subjects understand the experimental problem in the intended way and can solve it within the time available and with a reasonable amount of effort. The reason is that subjects' misunderstandings, or excessive mental effort, may jeopardise the whole enterprise. The now widespread use of computers in experimental economics contributes significantly to the simplification of experimental tasks. It allows presenting experimental problems in a more comprehensible way and facilitates problem-solving by ruling out expected sources of mistake by design. To facilitate the understanding of experimental tasks, subjects are also given time to read the instructions carefully, to clarify doubts that may arise and to practice trials.

The principles of *abstraction* and *neutrality* are meant to control the interference of individuals' subjective perceptions of the context of interaction. The conception of abstract tasks (i.e. avoiding as much as possible depicting real-world situations) that are described in fairly neutral terms (i.e. avoiding as much as possible loaded terms such as 'maximization') aims to control the effect of subjects' perceptions of the problem at hand and the 'right' answer to it (so-called demand effects). The concern is to prevent subjects acting so as to conform with, or defy, what they might perceive is expected from them. The goal is then to ensure that they act in accordance with the experimental situation as it is presented to them. The *prohibition of deceiving subjects* is another important rule that aims to assure subjects that they can trust the stated purposes of the experiment and act accordingly. It does so, so experimental economists argue, by developing the experimental economists' reputation for honesty among the subject population.

Anonymity aims to control the effect of intersubjective considerations, i.e. subjects caring about the impact of their actions on other subjects. In addition to the implementation of the precept of privacy (i.e. restricting subjects' pay-offs information to their own rewards), anonymity is promoted by avoiding as much as possible contact between subjects prior to, during and after the experiment. The use of computers in experimental economics is critical here, too, because it can limit face-to-face interaction between the experimenters and the subjects and among subjects.

These standardized procedures highlight a key methodological issue of scientific experimentation in the human sciences – the fact that experimentation involves conscious human beings whose behaviour depends on how they perceive the situation they are in. Economists deal with this issue by erasing the social load of the experimental context as much as possible in order to make experimental subjects focus on the structure of the decision problem at hand.

The way in which control is achieved in experimental economics is now well ingrained in the field. The conceptualization of a microeconomic experiment, the set of sufficient validity conditions, and the principles and procedures of experimental economics are all part of the field's established culture. Taken together they help to describe what may be labelled as the 'instrumental model' of experimental economics. This can be easily ascertained by the textbook depiction of the field of research (Davis and Holt 1993; Friedman and Sunder 1994; Hey 1991) or by the field's methodological discussions (e.g. Loomes 1991; Starmer 1999a; Guala 2005) and, most expressively, by experimenters' disputes that often revolve around conformity to these standards (see Chapter 12).

The stability of experimental lore has favoured the replicability and robustness of experimental results. In fact, the adoption and adaptation of previous designs in the making of new experiments is another pervasive practice of experimental economics. This practice is promoted by the report of fairly complete accounts of experimental procedures in the published reports of experiments and by the norm of making them available upon request. In this way experimenters have easy access to recruitment methods, procedures used for matching subjects to roles, composition of the subject pool, instructions given to subjects, experimental data, and so forth.

To summarize, the creation of laboratory microeconomic systems is conceptualized by a well-established 'instrumental model' that justifies the effectiveness of the 'material procedure' in producing meaningful knowledge for economics. This includes:

1 The definition of a salient reward structure capable of inducing the desired set of motives onto the experimental subjects.
2 The creation of fairly neutral and abstract experimental contexts to avoid the interference of background factors.
3 Guaranteeing anonymity among subjects to avoid the effect of interpersonal considerations.
4 The banning of deceiving experimental subjects to enhance the efficacy of the experimental instructions (in present and future practice).
5 The convention of providing fairly complete reports of the procedures underlying the production of experimental results so that they can be replicated and checked for robustness by other experimenters.

Every experiment in economics follows these procedures.[2] In each experiment, however, a particular 'material procedure' creates a particular microeconomic system, and the respective 'instrumental model' justifies how this system will contribute to the acquisition of knowledge of a particular aspect of human behaviour or the institution. The interpretation of the behaviour observed in this context or the performance of the institution consists, in turn, in the experiment's 'phenomenal model'. Similarly to experimentation in the natural sciences, when a three-way coherence obtains experimental economists acquire confidence that they have understood the behaviour of the subjects or made sense of the microeconomic system. How this is achieved in practice is now illustrated with Smith's first market experiment.

The market experiment

Smith's first contact with market experiments dates back to 1952 when he was a graduate student at Harvard. It all started when Smith participated as a subject in one of Edward Chamberlin's pedagogical experiments that allegedly demonstrated the predictive failure of the standard neoclassical model of a market under perfect competition. At that time Smith thought that 'the whole exercise was sort of silly'. It was impressive enough, however, to catch his attention during a night of insomnia when it occurred to him that 'the idea of doing an experiment was right'. What was wrong was Chamberlin's experimental design. A more powerful design would have to give the theory of competitive markets a better chance so that its failure would be a more powerful result. These thoughts kept him dwelling on what could possibly be an appropriate design for 'the more credible job of rejecting competitive price theory' (1991: 370). In 1956, now as an assistant professor at Purdue, he decided to give it a shot. In so doing, he initiated the process that would significantly contribute to the foundation of the discipline of experimental economics.

Smith's impulse to conduct the first market experiments was triggered by his discomfort with Chamberlin's design and the expectation that he could improve it. To that end, Smith resorted to Chamberlin's experiment and competitive market theory. The theory predicts that a competitive market reaches a state of equilibrium (defined by an equilibrium price and an equilibrium quantity) in a market characterized by atomistic buyers and sellers (no one has significant power to affect the terms of trade of a homogeneous good), perfect information (regarding the terms of trade and the good) and perfect mobility of factors (factors can be put to alternative uses at no cost). At equilibrium buyers and sellers can do no better. At the equilibrium price, no buyer wants to buy an extra unit of the good nor does any seller want to sell an extra unit of it. In other words, at equilibrium supplied quantity equals demanded quantity. Moreover, this is a point where efficiency is maximized because total surplus is at its maximum level.

In Chamberlin's (1948) market experiments, students would circulate in the classroom and engage in bilateral bargaining, acting as either buyers or sellers of one unit of a fictitious good, until a contract was made or the trading period ended. In Smith's view a more appropriate setting would have to be more favourable to the theory so that a negative result would be more compelling. This would require a different microeconomic institution. Smith then introduced two important modifications. First, the bilateral bargaining institution was replaced by a multilateral mechanism to better capture the informational structure of competitive markets. The problem, as Smith saw it, was that bilateral bargaining did not provide opportunity for the dissemination of information, but 'perfect' competition is characterized by 'perfect' information about market conditions, namely about the offers to buy and sell and the transactions made. Smith chose the auction mechanism of the stock exchange markets as the microeconomic institution to allow the simultaneous eliciting of quotations for the whole trading group, rather than to a single trader at a time. All traders could thus observe the tendered offers and bids and whether they were accepted or not. Second, he substituted the single period design with a multi-trading period set-up to test the hypothesis that markets tend to approach equilibrium over time (rather than the implausible alternative hypothesis of instantaneous equilibrium). The multi-trading period set-up would also provide students the opportunity to acquire experience, as it was typical of 'real' market traders (Smith 1962, n. 5).

Smith's intervention over environmental variables followed Chamberlin's experimental procedure closely. Subjects were randomly assigned the roles of a seller or a buyer. Each seller was given a card containing a number that represented the minimum price for which she/he should be willing to sell one unit of a fictitious indivisible commodity (i.e. her/his reservation price). It was also explained that sellers could not sell the commodity at a lower price but could sell it at a higher price and thereby earn the difference between the actual contract price and the minimum reservation price marked on the card (i.e. the seller's surplus). A seller's reservation price was private information. Similarly, each buyer was assigned a private reservation price representing the highest price at which the unit of the commodity should be acquired. Purchases at a price lower than the reservation price would result in earnings of the difference between the maximum reservation price and the actual contract price (i.e. the buyer's surplus). Moreover, subjects were told that they should be willing to make contracts at their reservation prices rather than leaving their needs unsatisfied (1962: 112). By assigning reservation prices for each trader, Smith defined the market's supply and demand curves, i.e. the set of possible supply and demand quantities at each price, and the equilibrium values for quantity and price (obtained at the intersection of the supply and the demand curves, which assume that buyers and sellers are willing to trade at their reservation prices). Because reservation prices were private information, experimental subjects could not possibly compute the equilibrium price. In this way the material procedures implemented the supply and demand of a market of the kind depicted in Figure 3.2.

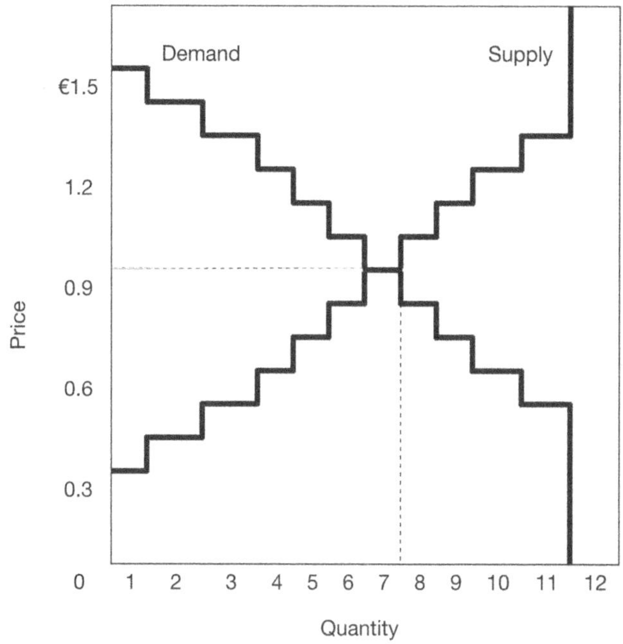

Figure 3.2 An experimental market: supply and demand curves and equilibrium price and quantity

Students would then engage in multilateral bargaining by orally stating intentions to buy or sell one unit of a fictional commodity to the whole group of traders. Whenever a match was reached, a binding contract would be closed for the agreed contract price. If there were no more offers or the trading period finished, a new trading period would resume and the same conditions would be restored for each subject. The data of the experiment would consist of the reservation prices (induced by Smith) and the contract prices for each commodity traded during market exchange. These were determined by the joint action of both the environmental and institutional variables. The institution of the microeconomic system (later to be known as the double auction) determined how students were to exchange one unit of a fictional commodity. The environment of the microeconomic system was characterized by the number of traders and their reservation prices, which defined agents' willingness to buy or to sell one unit of the commodity and hence the overall supply and demand for each price.

Even though the 'instrumental model' of experimental economics had not yet been fully spelled out at the time, this set of experiments closely follows the rules described in the previous section. This is so despite the fact that in the first experiments subjects did not earn monetary rewards. But Smith insisted that '[t]he present experiments have not seemed to provide motivation problems' since 'subjects have shown high motivation to do their best even without monetary payoffs' (1962: 121). The set of sufficient conditions for a valid experiment might have been guaranteed by the hypothetical pay-offs that were deemed important to experimental subjects who might have wanted to make the highest hypothetical earnings anyway. Figure 3.3 depicts Smith's practice leading to the publication of the report of his first market experiments.

Smith implemented a substantially different market from Chamberlin's. Exchanges in this market were regulated by a new institution regarded as a better test of competitive market theory because it had 'key features of the organized markets and of competitive markets generally' (1962: 111). The failure of competitive price theory under these more favourable conditions would be a far more compelling result. This was the particular *instrumental model* that would lead to the refutation of the theory if the experimental market failed to achieve the equilibrium price and quantity – the *phenomenal model* Smith was willing to accept and that would render the experiment meaningful and intelligible (see Figure 3.3a).

Even though the new experimental microeconomic system was favourable to competitive price theory, Smith noted that there would be room for market failure:

> The mere fact that, by any definition, supply and demand schedules exist in the background of a market does not guarantee that any meaningful relationship exists between those schedules and what is observed in the market they are presumed to represent. All the supply and demand schedules can do is set broad limits on the behavior of the market.
>
> (Smith 1962: 114–15)

In other words, Smith is here claiming that even though the experimental procedure could make subjects' behave as buyers and sellers, it did not mandate that they would trade at equilibrium, which was not known to them. The contracts could be closed for a wide range of prices different from the equilibrium price. But, in fact, they did not. Rather than obtaining a categorical rejection of competitive price theory, the experiment produced confirming evidence (see Figure 3.3b_1).

As Smith recounts, because the results of the first experiment yielded the opposite phenomenal model – the success of the competitive market in reaching equilibrium – Smith doubted them. The three-way coherence achieved was not convincing enough. Full confidence could only be achieved by way of conducting more experiments. And so he did. Smith carried out new experiments to check whether or not the original result could be attributed to a faulty experimental procedure. But subsequent experiments replicated the original result: the competitive experimental market converges to equilibrium (see Figure 3.3b_2).

Smith needed to build a strong coherent system in support of both the experimental results as well as the experimental method, which was not yet part of the established culture of economics. Smith reported eleven experiments, not only to demonstrate that he had collected sufficient evidence that supported his main result, but also to argue for the legitimacy of the experimental method. He did so by supplying further evidence that the result is robust to altering conditions of the experimental design. Indeed, the results were reproduced under different supply and demand conditions (i.e. changes in the position and shape of supply and demand schedules), different subject pools (e.g. sophomore and junior engineering, economics and business majors, and a graduate class in economic theory), different market mechanisms (auction and retail market), and so forth. Hence, Smith's support for his results and for the experimental method is grounded on a complex web of three-way coherences that sustain various microeconomic systems, each of which yielded the same result: convergence of the experimental market to equilibrium (see Figure 3.3c). The results should then be accepted as valid rather than as artefacts of the material procedure. But these results were not yet robust because the experimental method of economics had not yet been established.

The results were nonetheless sustained by a coherent resolution between theory and evidence. Not only was the theoretical prediction towards equilibrium supported by the results, but the effects of altering conditions were also correctly predicted by theory (e.g. decreases in demand reduce market prices). Moreover, the statistical tests carried out after the data had been collected rejected the null hypothesis of instability, thus providing further assurance that the data constituted significant evidence for the equilibrating tendencies of the experimental markets.

Smith also used the data collected to test various hypotheses concerning the mechanism of market adjustment, which failed to confirm the Walrasian hypothesis according to which the rate of increase in exchange price is an increasing function of excess demand at that price. He found instead support for the conjecture which takes the speed of adjustment to depend on the relative magnitude of buyers' and sellers' rents (determined by the difference between traders' reservation prices and the theoretical equilibrium).

Coherence was not complete, however. One out of the eleven experiments did not support the equilibrating tendency of the market. But this did not pose a special problem because it was a result that Smith could understand and explain. The result occurred under very special conditions that intended 'to simulate an ordinary retail market', i.e. a market characterized by an asymmetry between buyers and sellers where only sellers were allowed to make price quotations. Buyers could only accept or reject the offers of the sellers. Under such circumstances the disequilibrating tendency operated in favour of the buyers as they could conceal their eagerness to buy. By explaining the disequilibrium, Smith undermined the significance of the conflicting result. In fact, it contributed to reinforce the general conclusion, as this market deviated from the theoretical competitive market. That is, the apparent destabilization also supported the main experimental result.

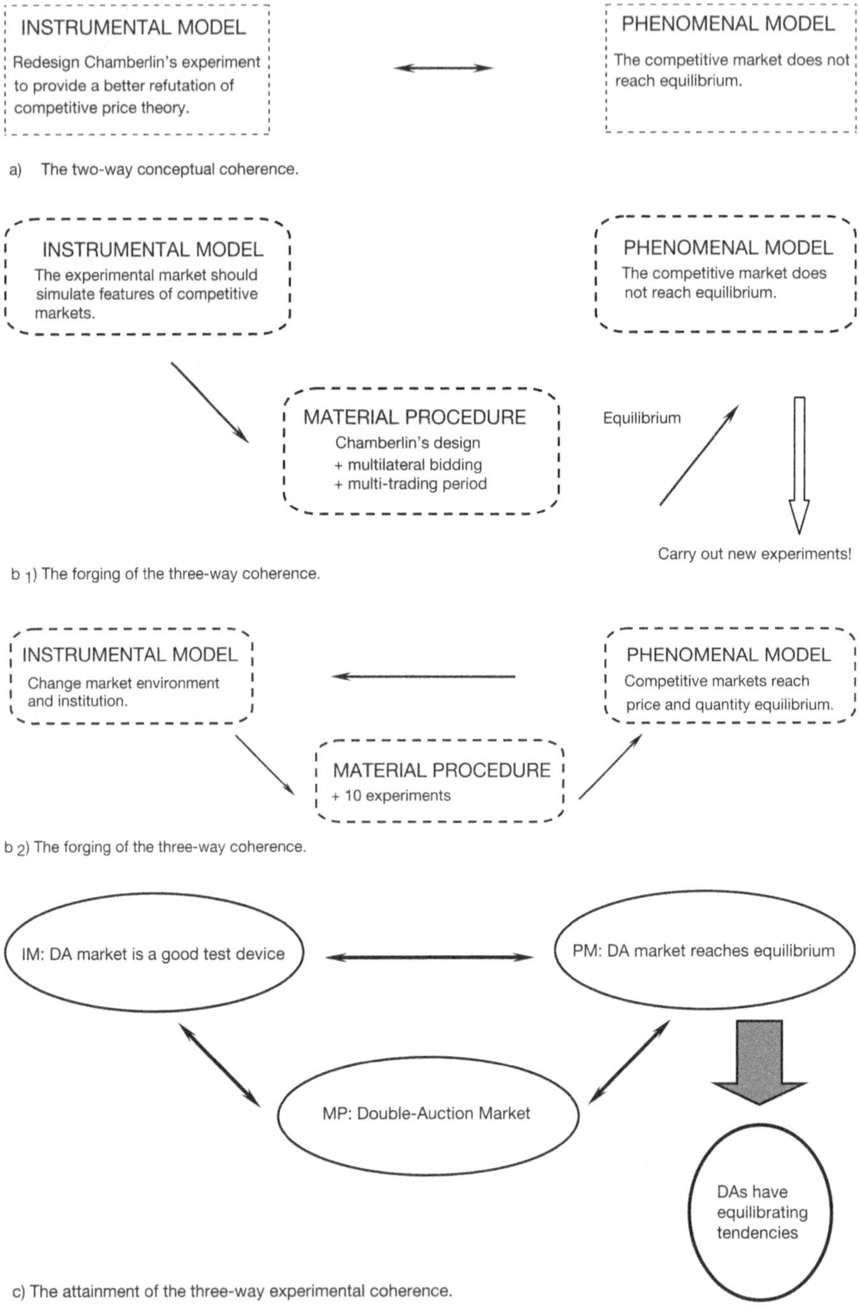

Figure 3.3 The market experiment

The analysis of Smith's experimental practice illustrates well the difficulties inherent in scientific practice in new fields of research. In unexplored fields a more complete set of coherence arguments must be provided in support of the results and of the means by which the results were generated. Similarly to experimental physics, these arguments rely on coherence strategies that help construct a strong net of relations of coherence. The results of the market experiments were thus supported by: various experiments that showed convergence to equilibrium under different environmental and institutional conditions; confirmation of the predicted effects of changes introduced to the experimental microeconomies; data concentrated on equilibrium prices and quantities; use of statistical significance tests; explanations of deviations from equilibrium by reference to known theory; and last but not least, consistency with a major item of economics culture – competitive price theory.

It should be noted again that Hacking's argument that confidence in experimental results may be obtained by independent confirmation does not apply to experimental economics. As argued, economics experiments share 'the same physical principles', which makes independent confirmation by the use of radically different physical processes simply unavailable in economics. In economics there are no 'preposterous coincidences' to evoke. Economists can, however, confirm their results by using different microeconomic systems. That is, rather than observing or measuring the same phenomena by different means, economists can reproduce the same phenomena by different microeconomic systems, which are created by fairly similar means.

Smith was very cautious in deriving implications from his first set of experiments because experiments were alien to most economists at the time. The market experiments were modestly presented as 'experimental games designed to study some hypothesis of neoclassical competitive market theory' (1962: 111), and the results were simply evidence for the success of theory in predicting equilibrium in those markets. No further implications were derived. The theory simply predicted well there.

Smith was more concerned with explaining the concept of an economic experiment. To that end, the experimental design and procedure were carefully described with the help of the conventional supply and demand charts depicting the crucial aspects of the experiments. The experimental data (i.e. the experimental contract prices for each trading period) were presented with the use of diagrams and were subjected to statistical and econometric tests. This is rhetorically ingenious. After all, Smith's experiments are all about markets, supply and demand curves, and equilibria – the key concepts of economics – and their analysis uses techniques familiar to economists. That is, besides the coherence strategies that helped forge the three-way coherence that sustained his results, Smith also appealed to the values of the economics community.

In 1960 Smith finally decided that he had accumulated sufficient data to demonstrate the validity of his results. In 1961 Smith submitted his findings to the *Journal of Political Economy*, which were published in 1962, after two revisions, four negative referee reports and an initial rejection (Smith 2003). Five years of supporting results were necessary to give Smith confidence in his own results or, perhaps more importantly, assurance that the community of economists could also trust them. Smith's willingness to report these experiments was ultimately encouraged by his co-practitioners who persuaded him to publish what he knew was a controversial proposal: the experimental method for economics. This is how Smith recalls it:

> Whatever the exact genesis, I got up the courage to write a paper reporting on all the experiments I had done from 1956 to 1960. It wasn't easy. People had been sceptical that there was a trick, some people reason why the experiments worked that had *nothing* to do with economics or theory or that overused, undefined thing that economists call the 'real world'. But there were also those who consistently encouraged me – John Hughes and Em Weiler, in particular.
>
> (Smith 1991: 372, emphasis in original)

Conclusion

This chapter introduced experimental economics. It presented Vernon Smith's definition of an economics experiments and the standard procedures used to conduct experiments in economics. It illustrated how economists create microeconomic phenomena in their labs with Smith's first market experiments. No critical examination of the experimental method of economics or of the market experiments has been carried out. This will be postponed until Chapter 6 and the second part of this book. Before that I need to spell out the criteria for assessing experiments. This is the purpose of the next three chapters.

4 Intervening in the 'material world'

Chapter 2 presented scientific experimentation as an endeavour that produces phenomena in the laboratory for scientific scrutiny. Coherence was selected as the fundamental principle that guides experimental practice and grounds belief in experimental results. In this chapter I argue that the epistemic value of coherence stems from the direct participation of the natural world. This participation renders the coherent results no trivial achievements because the actual properties of the aspect of the world under scrutiny play an active role in the production of knowledge about them. This participation may, however, vary, and thus the potential to generate knowledge.

The participation of the 'material world' in experiments

In order to examine how experimenters engage the material world in knowledge production, I draw again on Pickering's account of experiment, namely on his description of scientists' intervention in the 'material world' as a *dialectic of resistance and accommodation*. In his view, the engagement of the material world in knowledge production

> takes the form of a *dialectic of resistance and accommodation*, where resistance denotes the failure to achieve an intended capture of agency in practice, and accommodation an active human strategy of response to resistance, which can include revisions to goals and intentions as well as to the material form of the machine in question and to the human frame of gestures and social relations that surround it.
>
> (Pickering 1995a: 22, emphasis in original)

In Pickering's view, experimental practice proceeds in a 'dialectic' way whereby scientists act on the material world and the material world reacts to these actions. These reactions then trigger a succession of subsequent actions and reactions until the three-way coherence is finally obtained. The reactions of the material world are 'resistances' to scientists' intentions that are frustrated in the course of practice. These resistances may manifest themselves in many different ways. The material world resists when scientists fail to produce the phenomenon of interest or they produce results that do not fit within the framework of their phenomenal models. In other words, material resistances pose obstacles on the way to the three-way coherence between the material procedure, the instrumental model and the phenomenal model. Scientists then attempt to 'accommodate' these resistances by introducing amendments to the material and the conceptual components of the experimental system. They may try out new techniques or revise working assumptions in their efforts to solve the mismatch between the interventions in the material world and the conceptual understanding of these interventions and of their respective outcomes. When the three-way coherence obtains, experimenters finally succeed in making sense of both interventions and resulting outcomes.

The dialectic of resistance and accommodation stresses the unpredictability of experimental activity. Even though experimenters may start with well-defined conceptual models and material procedures and be confident about them, the participation of the material world carries a potential to generate unexpected results that trigger unforeseen sequences of actions, the final outcomes of which are not known in advance. This is so because there are always unknown or insufficiently understood aspects of the material world and of how to interfere with it. This is what, in the end, explains the purpose of conducting experiments: to learn about the material world.

But the potential to produce new knowledge does not derive only from the ignorance of the scientists. It derives also, and more fundamentally, from scientists' incapacity to manipulate the material world, in particular, from scientists' incapacity to have it conform to their anticipated phenomenal models. This means that despite scientists' expectations and consonant interventions in the material world, the outcomes arrived at also depend on how the world is. In Pickering's words, 'how the material world is leaks into and infects our representations of it in a nontrivial and consequential fashion'. The dialectic of resistance and accommodation hence 'displays an intimate and responsive engagement between scientific knowledge and the material world that is integral to scientific practice' (1995a: 183). Were scientists able to control the material world at will, the results of science would convey scientists' actions rather than how the material world is, and scientific results would no longer carry new knowledge about it.

Mary Morgan (2003, 2005) expresses the epistemic superiority of scientific experimentation relative to mathematical modelling in terms of 'confoundment' and 'surprise'. Although scientists can be confounded by experimental results, she argues, they can only be surprised by the results of models. And this cognitive difference depends on scientists' capacity to control the objects of inquiry. In 'mathematical model experiments', scientists know the resources for their results because they built those resources into the model that constitutes the experimental set-up. Only their computational limitations prevent them from knowing beforehand the models' solutions. In contrast, in laboratory experiments 'the resources for the result we expect to find are not necessarily present in the experimental setup: we might have the wrong account or theory about what will happen or our knowledge of the world might be seriously incomplete' (2003: 120 emphasis omitted). 'Confoundment' in scientific experimentation then expresses scientists' incapacity to exercise full control over the material world. As Morgan puts it, 'however ingenious the scientist, the material world can only be controlled and manipulated to an extent' (2003: 119). Scientists' control is, however, the most effective in 'mathematical model experiments' in which the material world is absent.

One implication of this is that the potential for generating new knowledge depends on the extent to which the experimental set-up constrains the participation of the material world. But control is necessary to produce valid results, i.e. results that scientists believe are not artefacts of the experimental procedures. In experimental practice there is, thus, a trade-off between the exercise of control and the potential to generate new knowledge. The more control is exercised, the more the results are the outcome of scientists' actions rather than the agency of the material world. This trade-off between control and material agency is thus the central epistemic issue of scientific experimentation. And it calls for the analysis of the extent to which the results of experiments are determined by the agency of the material world or that of the experimenters.

The participation of the material world in knowledge production is particularly evident when experimenters obtain unexpected results, or when they are at pains to obtain the three-way alignment between the components of the experimental system. By the same token, the production of new knowledge about the material world is particularly salient when scientists revise their goals, theories, underlying assumptions, conceptual models, instruments, techniques and so forth. This means, as Pickering stresses, that scientists' purposes, goals and plans are not immune to the 'dialectic'. They, too, can be revised as a result of encounters with the material world.[1] The engagement of the material world in the experimental process of knowledge production is, therefore, what confers objectivity to experimental results; and it does this by controlling the interference of the subjectivity of individual scientists (1995a: 195).

To conclude, the participation of the material world in scientific experimentation conveys epistemic value to the three-way coherences, and thus to the experimental results they support, because it prevents knowledge from being the sole realization of scientists' prior beliefs. The three-way coherences are objective because the 'interactive stabilizations that characterize the objective contents and products of science are hard to come by; their achievement is difficult and uncertain' (1995a: 195–96).

In Figure 4.1 the added epistemic value of the three-way coherence conveyed by the participation of the material world in knowledge production is depicted by the reduced dimension of the elliptic representing the phenomenal model. The smaller shape of the phenomenal model represents the more limited range of admissible options, which is the direct consequence of the participation of the material world in knowledge production.

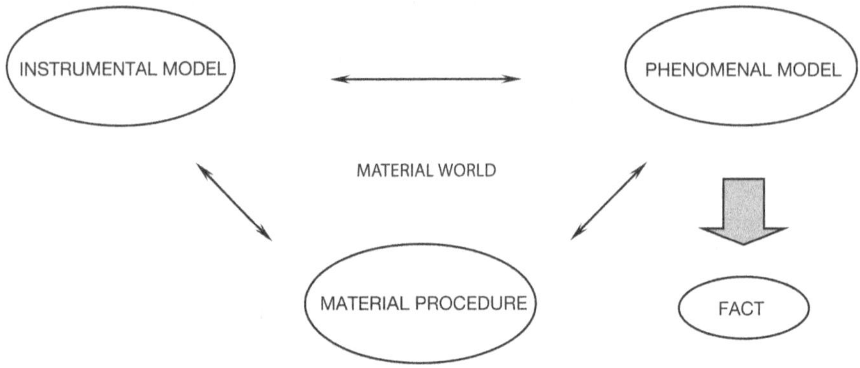

Figure 4.1 The material world and the three-way experimental coherence

The 'materiality' of economics experiments

In economics, as we have seen in the previous chapter, experimenters interfere with experimental microeconomic systems – the 'material world' of economics experiments. They interfere in particular with the 'microeconomic environment' and the 'microeconomic institution', or more generally, the experimental participants and the institutional rules that define the experimental problem and structure participants' actions. The goal is to study the relationship 'environment (*e*) – institution (*I*) – behaviour (*m*) – market outcomes (*X*)' (cf. Figure 3.1).

We have also seen how the 'material world' of experimental economics is controlled by the design of the institution and by the inducement of self-interested and income-maximizing motives. But from this it does not follow that the actions of the participants cannot 'resist' economists' expectations. Like any other experimental discipline, control can only be exercised to some extent. The 'material world' of economics also resists experimenters' intentions and thus, as in any other experimental science, the epistemic value of economics experiments derives from the capability of its objects of inquiry to frustrate experimenters' expectations.

Experimental participants have a crucial role in economics experiments. This is obviously so given that this is the distinguishing feature of economics experiments as compared to other modes of inquiry. In experimental economics the study of human behaviour and of the performance of the microeconomic institution is always carried out by observing the actions of the experimental participants and the resulting outcomes. The epistemic value of economics experiments hence derives from the participation of experimental subjects who may behave differently from the behaviour experimenters induce on to them.

The epistemic value of the participation of human subjects in experiments was acknowledged by Smith in his seminal article, 'Microeconomic Systems as an Experimental Science', in the following terms:

> The experimental laboratory, precisely because it uses reward-motivated individuals drawn from the population of economic agents in the socioeconomic system, consists of a far richer and more complex set of circumstances than is parameterized in our theories. Since the abstractions of the laboratory are orders of magnitude smaller than those of economic theory, there can be no question that the laboratory provides ample possibilities for falsifying any theory we might wish to test [i.e. for frustrating economists' expectations].
> (Smith 1982: 936)

Experimental participants therefore 'resist' when they take actions that depart from the behaviour postulated by economic theory and induced in the laboratory. Insofar as experimenters induce self-interested and income-maximizing actions, the resistances of the participants in economic experiments manifest themselves when subjects behave in a non-self-interested manner or fail to maximize the experimental pay-off.

From this it follows that the central methodological and epistemic issues of experimental economics concerns the trade-off between the actions of the experimenters and those of the participants. This trade-off has already been noted by Mary Morgan (2005: 325) who stresses the importance, for experimental design, of questioning: 'Where is the potential for independent action in the experiment?' From this it follows that in any experiment economists must ensure that the actions of the participants are not constrained in such a way that their behaviour is entirely determined by the experimental set-up and procedures. Even though the relevance of Morgan's question varies with the purpose of the experiment, as we shall see in Chapter 10, this question should be posed in any experiment. The epistemic added value of economics experiments is given by the participation of human subjects.

This concern was clearly present in Smith's (1962: 114–15) first market experiments reviewed in the previous chapter. Even though the experimental set-up was favourable to competitive price theory, Smith was careful, noting that there would be room for market failure. He explicitly says that the induced supply and demand schedules only 'set broad limits on the behavior of the market'. Subjects could have resisted Smith's interventions in the experimental microeconomy by closing contracts at other prices than the equilibrium price. In Chapter 6, however, I will argue that this was not in fact the case. But for now it suffices to note that the main epistemic source of economics experiments is the participation of human subjects, and this is recognized by experimenters even when they fail to provide participants with the conditions for independent action. Whether or not the experimental set-up provides these conditions is an empirical matter that should be addressed in every case.

Scientists' agency versus material agency

We have seen that scientific experimentation is informed by a difficult trade-off between the exercise of control and the participation of the material world.

Control is necessary to produce the phenomenon of interest under suitable conditions for scientific inquiry. But the more control is exercised, the more the results are the outcome of scientists' actions rather than the agency of the material world (or that of experimental subjects in economics). This trade-off constitutes the central epistemic issue of scientific experimentation, which calls for the close scrutiny of the participation of the material world or that of the experimenters.

Two polar situations may be distinguished: experimenting with *plastic* and with *rigid* experimental systems. Plastic experimental systems are amenable to a high degree of material and conceptual manipulation, which reduces the participation, or the relevance of the participation, of the material world. Plastic systems are often used when scientists lack well-established resources and standards for dealing with new problem-situations. Knowledge production is then guided by tentative trials at implementing an operational material apparatus and by speculative ideas about the phenomenon of interest. A clash between an expectation and a result is more likely to be resolved by attempting to obtain support for prior beliefs rather than by revising them. And this may be done by further manipulating the material apparatus so as to eliminate the conflict materially, or by explaining the effect away by conceptual manoeuvring. Experimental practice is in this way more vulnerable to the influence of preconceptions regarding the problem at hand and how a solution to that problem can be obtained. The results of plastic systems are hence more critically the realization of scientists' preferred solutions to the selected problem-situations. The problem-solutions obtained are, as a result, highly disputable. In the absence of shared standards of appraisal scientists also disagree on what a legitimate test for the solutions might be.

Rigid experimental systems, in contrast, delimit the range of admissible material and conceptual manoeuvrings. They employ material apparatuses for which the proper operation and purposes have already been stabilized in prior scientific practice. Therefore, consensus is relatively unanimous when working with them. Even though rigid experimental systems exercise a high level of control over the actions of scientists, they may also limit the participation of the material world in experimentation. Rigid experimental systems may limit the participation of the material world by delimiting its scope of action to fairly circumscribed and familiar problem-situations. Thus, whereas the participation of the material world may be materially or conceptually constrained by scientists' actions when they experiment with plastic systems, rigid experimental systems may constrain the agency of the material world to fairly confined and recognizable problem-situations. To put it in yet another way, whereas rigid experimental systems may constrain the choice of problem-situations, plastic systems produce yet to establish problem-solutions.

Various studies of experiment reflect the centrality of the trade-off between scientist's agency and material agency and thus the concern with the predominant role of scientists' actions in determining the results of experiments.

Even though Pickering recognizes the epistemic value of the participation of the material world in experimentation, as we have seen, he attributes to scientists an almost unlimited scope for action. That is to say, Pickering depicts experimental activity as a practice that consists of the design, implementation and manipulation of plastic experimental systems. The plasticity of the experimental systems, together with the unpredictable nature of experimental practice, result in the production of a potentially indefinite number of equally valid results none of which can be singled out as superior to the others. These results are the outcome of scientists' engagement with the material world, each of which realizes specific interactive stabilizations. The implication of this is that plastic experimental systems produce incommensurable results (Pickering 1995a: 188).

Nonetheless, Pickering takes plastic systems to realize relevant 'captures and framings' of the material world. That is, the material interactions of scientists with the material world are informed by the way the material world is. The problem for him is that these interactions and their respective representations are incommensurable. The material world is not sufficiently decisive to produce unique 'captures' or to declare some 'captures' superior to others. Pickering illustrates this with the famous study on the search for quarks. The fact that only one team, Fairbank's, declared it had found quarks after two decades of research is not particularly telling. According to Pickering the interactive stabilizations obtained in the field are all equally valid. He says 'It just happened that the contingencies of resistance and accommodation worked out differently', and concludes '[d]ifferences like these are, I think, continually bubbling up in practice, without any special causes behind them' (1995a: 211–12).

Actual experimental practice combines elements of plasticity and rigidity. Scientists never start from scratch and scientists' minds are not *tabula rasa*. The problems scientists select are influenced by current scientific practice and they employ recognizable means to solve them. At the same time they have a reasonable degree of freedom concerning the choice of the sorts of problems to embrace and the kinds of solutions to favour. Briefly, scientists try to check whether their anticipated solutions are right while following shared standards of practice and accommodating the resistances of the material world. In any case, the degree of scientists' freedom increases as problem-situations deviate from conventional research and scientists rely more and more on plastic resources of practice. As scientists move more freely in the laboratory worlds, the participation of the material world in knowledge production decreases.

The idea that the epistemic value of experimental systems varies was somehow implicit in Franklin's strategies of experiment. When experimenters can resort to well-established (rigid) resources of practice, their behaviour is predominantly guided by routine procedures associated with the operation of a reliable material apparatus (cf. strategy 1). When the resources are produced along with the results of practice, scientists' expectations and actions assume a more significant role in knowledge production (e.g. confirmation of predictions, cf. strategy 3). As a result, scientists have to build a more complex web of relations of coherence to obtain support for their results.

Normal science and rigid experimental systems

I now look at experimentation with fairly rigid experimental systems, which can be framed within the framework of what the historian Thomas Kuhn called 'normal science' (1970 [1962]). In contrast to experimenting with plastic systems, rigid experimental systems, by constraining and limiting the actions of individual scientists confer objectivity to the results of experiment.

'Normal science' is the practice exercised within the limits defined by the 'paradigm' that supplies the criteria for selecting problem-situations and the tools to solve them. The paradigm guides scientists to focus on research questions that can be solved with available resources and assessed by accepted standards. And scientists conform to these standards because they want to be acknowledged as competent practitioners. This, then, accounts for the cumulative nature of normal science.

Normal science hence delimits the scope of scientific practice to well-circumscribed problems. The problems that cannot expectedly be solved with the paradigm's resources are not conceived of, ignored or rejected as inadequate scientific inquiries. By the same token, the problem-solutions that conflict with the paradigm are deemed erroneous, set aside and neglected. This means that normal scientific practice consists to some extent of 'an attempt to force nature into the preformed and relatively inflexible box the paradigm supplies' (Kuhn 1970 [1962]: 24). Such a practice not only does not promote novelty, but it also leaves it unnoticed when it does occur. Phenomena that do not fit the paradigmatic box are not seen and new theories are not developed to account for them. Normal-scientific research is instead oriented towards the articulation of those phenomena and theories that the paradigm already supplies.

Kuhn does not perceive this limitation as particularly troublesome. The accumulation of failures in problem-solving eventually generates new problem-situations that ultimately give rise to a new basis for the practice of science, i.e. a new paradigm. Science shifts from paradigm to paradigm. A paradigm's potential is fully explored and a new paradigm emerges to replace the old one. In the meantime, normal science extends the knowledge of those facts that the paradigm displays as interesting.

Experimenting with rigid experimental systems can thus be depicted as part of normal science where scientists know which research projects to take on and how to pursue them. Peter Galison (1987) provides such an account in his *How Experiments End*. Galison is here particularly concerned with the identification of the criteria that guide scientists in deciding the termination point of their experimental process of knowledge production, or in determining the attainment of the three-way coherence. Even though he recognizes that there is no experimental algorithm to determine the conclusion of an experiment, the various items of scientific culture impose 'constraints' on experimental practice that aid scientists in narrowing down the 'alternatives of what the experimentalist takes to be reasonable beliefs and actions' until the decision to end the experiment is reached (p. 246). The 'constraints' of scientific culture jointly define and delimit the field of inquiry and thereby contribute to the closure of the experimental process of knowledge production, thus performing the role of an experimental algorithm. In other words, the rigidity of the various items of scientific practice reduce the admissible range of scientists' material and conceptual actions until the three-way coherence is attained and the experiment ends.

Galison distinguishes three categories of items of scientific culture that differ in their relative capability to work as a 'constraint'.[2] To put it briefly, *long-term constraints* comprise metaphysical commitments, meta-level theoretical and experimental presuppositions that single out particular phenomenal domains and adequate modes of inquiry, instrumentation and techniques. These constraints are widely accepted and assumed by scientists in the design and interpretation of experiments in such a way that 'if a result contradicted it, the experimentalist would look again at his instruments and procedures' (p. 246). These constraints are long lasting because they survive the constitution and conclusion of shorter term projects. The long-term constraints of experimental economics, for example, include the general presupposition that economics experiments are useful tools to study human behaviour and microeconomic institutions, and that the methods, procedures, and benchmarks are adequate means to produce what can be recognized as valid work in the field.

Middle-term constraints consist of theoretical and experimental 'programmatic goals' that are 'attached to specific institutions and people' (1987: 249). They set the experimental work within the framework of a particular theory and the material practice within the realm of a specific device taken as valid for the investigation at hand. According to Galison, middle-term constraints reduce the number of alternatives taken as reasonable grounds for belief by directing scientists towards the most relevant background factors and the most adequate means to tackle them. In economics, middle-term constraints are defined by its research programmes. Experimental economics, as we shall see, contains three grand areas of research – market experiments, game theory experiments, and individual decision-making experiments – each of which is associated with particular theories, benchmarks and procedures. In Smith's market experiments, for example, competitive price theory was critical to the design and implementation of the experimental market, as well as to interpreting the results.

The application of particular theoretical models or phenomenological laws and specific experimental practices introduces *short-term constraints* on experimental practice. These constraints are the less rigid or the most plastic. Because different theories or models may be compatible with the broad constraints of any given programme, they are more easily discarded and replaced by others. But they are just as valuable heuristics as the other constraints are. Whereas long-term constraints help define the problem-situation and middle-term constraints build confidence in the means of problem-solving, short-term constraints help decide when the solution has been obtained. According to Galison, short-term constraints do this by the formulation of precise predictions. The experiment stops when experimenters find empirical support for their predictions. It gives them confidence that they have managed to produce the phenomenon of interest. Otherwise, they go on trying to work out what went wrong in their experiments (p. 252). In the market experiments, to continue with the same example, the observation of the evolution of prices and quantities towards the theoretical predictions gave Smith confidence that equilibrium had been attained. But if it had not, Smith would not have rejected competitive market theory. He would probably have concluded that the theory does not apply to experimental markets; as he did not claim that the theory had been confirmed when he obtained supporting evidence.

The constraints of scientific culture, experimental and non-experimental, provide scientists with standards that help them to identify interesting problem-situations and the resources to solve them. These also guide them in selecting the parts of the experimental system to revise in the face of confounding results. In so doing, scientific culture delimits the range of possibilities that appear reasonable until the three-way coherence is finally attained. When the experiment ends, scientists' expectations are met. Scientists believe they have made sense of their practices and results. The confirmation of expectations may, however, lead to the premature end of the experiment. As Galison puts it: 'This stopping place is, naturally enough, all too dangerously often the predicted result' (1987: 74).

But expectations are not always met. Although restrictive, the resources of practice are not absolutely rigid. That is, they are not rigid to the extent 'that makes it impossible (or unreasonable) for the physicist to start with one set of beliefs and come … to experimental conclusions contradicting the starting assumptions' (p. 258). Implicit in Galison's argument is also the agency of the material world, or the 'stubbornness', as he puts it, of the effect despite all efforts to eliminate it (p. 259). Thus, in Galison's view, the epistemic value of experimental results lies both in scientific culture, which prevents or substantially reduces experimenters' arbitrariness, and the agency of the material world which cannot be completely manipulated. But the participation of the material world is critical. The material world resists scientific culture, too, or, more precisely, the expectations that they produce.

The epistemic value of experimental results may be improved by 'increasing the *directness* of measurement and the growing *stability* of the results' (1987: 259 emphasis in original). That is, belief in experimental results can be improved by making new relations of coherence with a more active participation of the material world (e.g. by directly measuring a previously estimated value) and by reproducing these results in other experimental systems. In sum, the epistemic value of experimental practice lies in making a robust three-way coherence (or more) with well-established items of scientific culture where the material world has a direct participation in it.

Similarly to Pickering, Galison's account suggests that the 'stubbornness' of the material world can attenuate the inevitable dependence of knowledge production on both established knowledge and scientists' beliefs. Galison, however, stresses the role of the 'resistance' of scientific culture that constrains scientists' actions. The 'agency' of scientific culture places limits on scientists' agency. But it may also limit the participation of the material world. Problem-situations deeply embedded in existing scientific culture restrict the participation of the material world by limiting scientific problem-solving to well-defined domains of research whose problem-solutions are by and large anticipated by established knowledge.

Hacking (1992) also distinguishes the resources of practice in terms of their degrees of rigidity. Hacking identifies three categories. 'Ideas' include conceptual items such as questions, background knowledge, systematic theory, topical hypotheses, and models of the apparatus. 'Matériel' includes the material components such as the target, detectors, various tools and data generators. 'Marks' include the results of experiments such as the data and data processing techniques as well as their interpretation. Among the listed resources of laboratory practice, 'topical hypotheses' are among the most revisable elements of the system. They are propositions about the phenomenon of interest that are derived from the more stable 'systematic theory' about the subject matter and what is known about it. Material apparatuses vary, too, in their degree of rigidity, ranging from off-the-shelf apparatuses to devices constructed anew for specific purposes. The procedures of 'data assessment' or 'data reduction' are taken for granted, whereas 'data analysis' depends on the research 'question'. The most rigid resources of practice are the 'styles of scientific reasoning', which are 'the expectations about what the world is like and practices of reasoning about it' that 'govern our theories and our interpretation of data alike'. The laboratory sciences' style is characterized by two main metaphysical presuppositions: '(a) the expectation that we find out about the world by interfering with it', and '(b) the expectation that nature "herself" works that way, with forces and triggering mechanisms and the like, and in general a master-slave mode of interaction among her parts' (p. 50). These elements are so rigid that they do not even feature on the list of resources of practice because scientists do not use them. They can be ignored because 'experimenters do not change ideal conceptions of the universe in the course of, or at any rate because of, experimental work' (p. 44–54). But Hacking accepts the revisability of any of the resources of practice. Even though they are established before the experiment, they are not immutable (p. 50).

According to Hacking, the degree of plasticity of the resources of practice is much more slender than Pickering admits. In contrast to the latter, who considers the possibility of having an indefinite number of solutions to the same problem-situation, Hacking says that 'it is extraordinarily difficult to make one coherent account, and it is perhaps beyond our powers to make several' (p. 55). In his view, regardless of the rigidity or plasticity of scientific culture, the associations established are hard to come by, so that they hardly allow scientists to produce results that fit their prejudices. To put it another way, even though the resources of practice are plastic, the coherences they bring about are not, nor are the results they yield. This then explains the stability of laboratory science and its autonomy from the rise and fall of theory.

The stability of experimental knowledge derives from the mutual reinforcement of the various components of the experimental system. The material apparatus, the phenomenon and the theory that account for it evolve in a mutually self-enforcing way that is not destabilized by work done in other fields. Once a coherence relation is established, theory and instruments remain valid in their data domain. According to Hacking, the stability of experimental knowledge is, in fact, the characteristic trait of 'laboratory science' that underlies the 'self-vindication' of its results.

It should be noted, however, that Hacking's analysis is not applicable to all experimental sciences; it applies only to sciences 'whose claims to truth answer primarily to work done in the laboratory' (1992: 33). In any case, Hacking takes scientific experimentation as a far less contingent endeavour than Pickering. What is contingent is scientific culture (which he dubs the '*form* of a branch of scientific knowledge') that arises out of a historical process. Scientific results (which he dubs the '*content* of science') are determinate (1999). Scientific culture evolves in time and determines the classes of problem-situations considered as relevant, but once a problem-situation is defined, the problem-solution is determined. Scientific culture, therefore, takes a more central role in Hacking's account. It constrains the production of knowledge and it generates unique and stable solutions. In the course of practice of laboratory sciences, new theories arise and new problems emerge, but old solutions remain valid in their domains of application.

The various accounts presented here do not necessarily provide conflicting views on the plasticity or rigidity of experimental systems. They can instead be taken as depictions of various stages of the experimental process of knowledge production. Mature fields of experimental research can rely on rigid experimental systems and they may have already given rise to theories that account for those phenomena that have already been stabilized in their domains. These rigid experimental systems, however, substantially determine the solutions reached while producing reliable results. New fields of research are still at the stage of 'extraordinary science'. They have to make do with plastic experimental systems. The relevance of the problem-situations, the adequacy of the means and the reliability of the solutions are highly contestable and vulnerable to scientists' prior beliefs.

Normal experimental practice contains elements of rigidity and plasticity. Scientific culture influences the kinds of problem that are selected and scientists are irremediably dependent on the available resources of practice to solve them. In any case, in the course of practice there is some degree of freedom concerning the choice of the types of problem to embrace and the kinds of solution to pursue.

Conclusion

Experimental practice is an endeavour that aims at establishing a three-way coherence among the material procedure, the instrumental model and the phenomenal model. The three-way coherence provides scientists with reasons to believe in their results because the alignment of the components of the experimental system is hard to come by. It 'accommodates' the 'resistances' of both scientific culture and the material world. The participation of the material world in knowledge production is critical. But insofar as the participation of the material world depends on the plasticity of the experimental systems, the present analysis stresses the importance of assessing the participation of the material world in knowledge production.

The analysis developed in this chapter, therefore, brought to the fore the experimental version of the underdetermination problem, which is particularly acute when experimenting with plastic experimental systems. Under these circumstances, the conflict between an expectation and an observation may be resolved in an undetermined number of ways, both material and conceptual. It will most likely be solved by attempting to obtain data that fit the framework of the preferred phenomenal model. When experimenting with rigid experimental systems, conceptual and material manoeuvring with the experimental system is more difficult and therefore the severity of the underdetermination problem is significantly reduced. In the next chapter I argue that the underdetermination problem is also tackled by the critical interaction of scientists, which narrows down the range of admissible interpretations of practice and results even when working with plastic experimental systems. This means that a resolution for the underdetermination problem may be worked out collectively and at community level.

5 Intervening in the 'social world'

To experiment is to produce phenomena in the laboratory for scientific scrutiny. Scientists ground their belief in the phenomena they produce by establishing three-way coherences among the material procedures, the instrumental models and the phenomenal models of their experimental systems. In the previous chapter we have seen that these three-way coherences 'accommodate' the 'resistances' of the material world and thereby convey knowledge about the aspects of the material world under scrutiny. In this chapter I argue that the 'social world' also creates resistances that need to be accommodated. This means that the collective way through which knowledge is produced also conveys epistemic value to the experimental coherences and the experimental results they support.

Socially established culture and social resolutions

The social dimension of knowledge production was implicit in the accounts of experiment reviewed in the previous chapters. We have seen that scientists' material and conceptual interventions in the course of practice are guided by the socially established items of scientific culture. This is so because scientific communities organize their practice in such a way as to ensure that scientists select relevant problems, solve them with recognizable methods and tools, and assess the solutions to these problems by shared standards. Well-defined research programmes, well-established methods, procedures, instruments, theories, and standards reduce the range of possibilities that appear reasonable in the course of experimental practice until the three-way coherence is attained. When the experiment ends, scientists believe they have made sense of their practices and results. The material procedure interpreted through the instrumental model produces intelligible results within the framework of the phenomenal model. By constraining the actions of the scientists, socially established practices and resources confer objectivity on the results of scientific practice.

But scientists do not always have at their disposal the necessary means that help them to solve the problems that emerge in the course of practice. Or they may produce conflicting results for which there is not as yet a socially established way to adjudicate among them. In these circumstances, experimental closure has to be worked out in actual practice by collectives of scientists.

The social dimension of scientific experimentation, as expressed by the enforcement of socially established practices and the attainment of social resolutions when these practices do not suffice to achieve experimental closure, has been treated differently by students of experiment.

Pickering acknowledges that experimental practice is a social activity in which collectives of scientists employ socially established items of scientific culture and resolve points of contention. But Pickering does not grant epistemic value to these social resolutions. In his view, as we have seen, experimental systems are as incommensurable as the results they produce and hence none of them can be considered superior to the others. No objective adjudication among alternative results is forthcoming. Collective resolutions are instead based on factors external to the alternatives in dispute. In Pickering's view, they are most likely driven by conformity to dominant and established scientific culture. The process of collective appraisal will thus be biased towards the 'socially sustained matrix of commitments' as 'scientific communities tend to reject data that conflict with group commitments and, obversely, to adjust their experimental techniques and methods to "tune in" on phenomena consistent with those commitments' (1981: 236). The enforcement of the established items of scientific culture by scientific communities does not have a particularly relevant epistemic value. Any resolution would be equally valid.

Hacking and Franklin completely dismiss the social dimension of experimental practice. Hacking states that, while science as a process is undoubtedly a social activity, it is trivially so. Science as a product, that is, as a set of accumulated knowledge, does not need to invoke its context of production (1999: 67). Nor does Franklin attribute an important role to the social validation of scientific beliefs. In fact, the 'epistemological strategies' of experiment (cf. Chapter 2) are taken as socially neutral arguments that provide reasons for rational belief. They are 'independent' and 'reasonable' arguments that suffice to justify the rationality of science (1989: 459). Franklin's underlying presupposition is, however, that scientists pursue all relevant strategies and that social resolutions are based on them. But that scientists do not fully explore their problem-situations, due to both individual and collective biases, and especially so when working with plastic experimental systems, is a central issue of scientific experimentation that the social epistemology I am advocating places in the foreground.

The social epistemology of experiment does not take for granted that scientists pursue and stretch to their limits all reasonable courses of action. Nor does it presuppose that social resolutions achieve the best epistemic state given what is known at the time. Scientists and communities of scientists may resist abandoning favoured commitments, methods, theories and instruments despite the evidence available suggesting otherwise. The social epistemology, however, advocates that the critical interactions of scientists with partially overlapping and partially distinct scientific beliefs can resolve some of the ongoing disagreements, and that these resolutions are epistemically relevant. I draw now on Galison's reconstruction of experimental practice in physics to show that dialogue is possible and that conflicting results can be collectively worked out.

We have seen in the previous chapters that Galison's (1987) *How Experiments End* concerns experimental closure. Based on the history of experimental physics in the late nineteenth century and in the twentieth century, Galison reconstructs experimentation as an error-elimination endeavour that lacks a logical termination point, or an algorithm, which could help scientists to decide when to end the experiment. He then argues that the established items of scientific culture together constrain experimental practice in such a way that they reduce the range of available alternatives until closure is reached. But this is not Galison's whole story. He also argues that the joint effort of various groups of scientists can overcome the absence of shared criteria to adjudicate among alternative solutions.

In Galison's historical accounts, it is clear that the absence of such criteria forces scientists to gather a significant amount of persuasive arguments that can stand up in the court of the scientific community. This is especially the case when scientists produce controversial results.

Galison's reconstruction of experimental physics focuses on disputes between rival research groups that bring to the fore 'the characteristic ways each constructed a persuasive demonstration' (1987: 14). In these reconstructions, a very clear view emerges of how scientists' interventions in the material world are affected by the need to collect a substantive amount of persuasive arguments, which scientists then exchange with other scientists in their attempts to win collective assent for their results. In the process, material procedures, instrumental and phenomenal models are revised and corrected until the community agrees on the final resolution and the three-way coherence is achieved at the community level.

Contra Pickering, who stresses the incommensurability of experimental research, Galison thinks that dialogue among groups trained in different experimental and theoretical traditions is possible. But he notes that scientists may disagree on the degree of persuasiveness of the various arguments put forward. This was the case, for instance, in the dispute concerning the existence of neutral currents, at the level predicted by the Glashow–Weinberg–Salam theory, which opposed the group of scientists working at CERN (European Organization for Nuclear Research), Geneva, and the group located at FNAL (Fermi National Accelerator Laboratory), Illinois. This disagreement forced each team to go back over their procedures to work out the points of contention until they agreed that they had grounds to believe in the existence of neutral currents. But this resolution did not require scientists to agree on everything. The bubble-chamber experimentalists, for instance, are deemed to have trusted the 'golden events' more than the statistical demonstrations produced by computer simulations. Experimentalists more familiar with electronic detectors felt otherwise (Galison 1987: 18–19).

Consensus does not require that the members involved in a dispute agree on all the arguments put forward. It suffices that enough arguments are produced so that each group of scientists finds a subset of them sufficient to argue for the validity of the result. Insofar as objections are met, the community as a whole can consent on the final result. Consensus is, thus, a collective achievement that is grounded on the arguments that the parties in the dispute produce and accept as sufficient to establish the validity of experimental results. In Galison's view, this joint endeavour produces a composite argument that rules out alternative interpretations of the phenomenon under scrutiny. He says:

> An argument develops within the community as a whole that is of this form: We think there is an object *a*, because in our historical period there are only a finite set of imitative effects that are plausible: *b*, *c*, *d*, *e*. Furthermore, we have shown that our phenomenon is not one of these.
>
> (Galison 1987: 132)

Galison's account shows how the engagement of different groups of researchers in the appraisal of competing solutions promotes the exploration of unforeseen possibilities, which eventually resolves the dispute. When it is reached, consensus is not only more persuasive, but it also carries new knowledge about the phenomenon of interest. But Galison warns that which alternatives are conceived of and taken seriously at a given period depend on the prior instrumental and theoretical commitments of the experimenters.[1]

Nonetheless, the process of critical interaction among researchers educated in different traditions brings about new problems that would not otherwise be raised and solved. The epistemic value of social resolutions thus derives from the fact that these are the outcome of a process that raised relevant questions and strived to answer them. The consensual results that emerge from these collective resolutions are supported by various three-way coherences that the various groups of researchers produced. To repeat, this does not mean that all inconsistencies have been met and addressed. The results that find collective assent are supported by various coherent arguments which together constitute sufficient justification for belief in them (see Figure 5.1).

The social validation of experimental results

The social dimension of scientific experimentation does not terminate in the enforcement of socially established practices and the attainment of social resolutions when these practices do not suffice to achieve experimental closure. Experimental practice is intrinsically a collective endeavour and its collective nature has epistemic value. In order to spell this out, I now draw on David Gooding's account of experiment, which is based on the practice of Michael Faraday, the nineteenth century British chemist and physicist. Gooding's main point is that experiment implicates both the natural and the

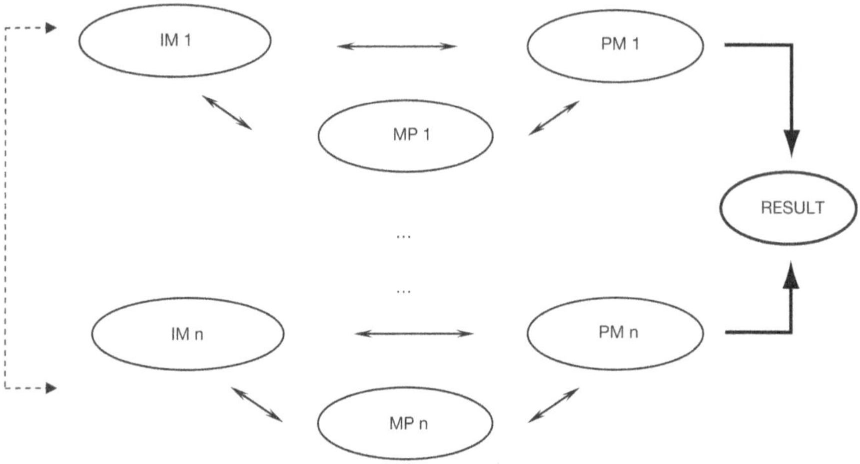

Figure 5.1 The social resolution of conflicting results

social worlds. This is so because 'the natural world does not constrain any one observer sufficiently, *independently* of any other, to explain observational consensus' (1990: 76, emphasis in original).

Individuals need to interact with each other to make sense of their causal interactions with the natural world. This is particularly the case when scientists observe new phenomena. Different perceptions must then be tried against each other until observers reach agreement on what is being experienced. Gooding stresses that consensus is not a matter of certifying that each individual has the same experience when independently observing the same object. It arises instead from a social process of consultation whereby each individual brings her/his contribution to the process of collectively making sense of the new observations.

The collective dimension of experimental practice already occurs at the private stage of knowledge production, that is, prior to the public report of experimental results. At this stage, knowledge production is first and foremost a cognitive process whereby scientists jointly make sense of their practices and outcomes. This collective process involves the formulation, exchange and revision of tentative interpretations of the phenomena of interest. As Gooding puts it, this is a process in which 'observers exchange tentative constructs or construals of their personal experience … [and] construe and reconstrue their own experience in the light of what other observers take theirs to be' (1990: 23, emphasis omitted). Thus, already at the private stage of knowledge production, scientists are confronted with what can now be called 'social resistances' that result from the clash between alternative interpretations of practices and outcomes.

But scientists are particularly concerned with the 'resistances' posed by those who are to evaluate and pass judgement on their results. So, already at the private stage of knowledge production, scientists build arguments that aim at persuading the intended audience of the adequacy of the processes and the validity of the results obtained. Besides conforming to the basic requirements of the profession, which are tacitly or explicitly accepted and used to select the proposals that are worthy of consideration, scientists also try to anticipate potential objections and to answer them.

But it is in the public stage of knowledge production that experimental results are actually put to the test. In order to be accepted as scientific, experimental results must win the consent of those who were not directly involved in the knowledge production process. Only when the relevant community accepts the results of experiments as valid can they be acknowledged as scientific results. As Gooding has it:

> The factual status of the result of an experiment – and therefore its epistemic force – lies in evaluative judgements made by groups of experts about the quality of experiment and its theoretical plausibility (both as to method and to outcomes). On these judgements in turn depend the 'externality' of phenomena or data, that is, their agreed status as real, self-evident, possible, or as artifacts … the 'correct outcome' is [thereby] socially validated.
>
> (Gooding 1990: 211)

The collective acceptance of the results of experiments ensures that these are generated by properly functioning material apparatus(es) that can yield reliable information about the material world. The private results then turn into self-evident natural facts detached from the contexts and practices that generated them. As Gooding puts it, '[t]o be seen as a natural fact it must be seen to exist independently of any particular person, laboratory or experimental technique' (1985: 105).

The public stage of knowledge production depends crucially on experimenters' ability to communicate their findings to 'lay observers', i.e. 'anyone not yet familiar with the observational practices generally necessary to produce and see a phenomenon' (Gooding 1985: 133, n. 8). It depends on experimenters' representational skills that allow other observers to witness phenomena without having to 'tread every turn of the path travelled to produce them'. Successful representations enable lay observers to 'witness' the phenomena and thereby persuade them that 'they could in practice reproduce the same process and would get the same correspondence between concepts and precepts' (Gooding 1990: 167). This is, in fact, what allows the public evaluation of both the processes and products of experiments by those who did not participate in them.

The social validation of experimental results does not require the reproduction of the experiment by third parties to verify whether the same results obtain. It suffices that scientists are persuaded that they would obtain the same results if they had implemented the same material apparatus and followed the same procedures. The process of social validation of experimental results therefore follows a kind of virtual experiment whereby the scientists who did not take part in the experiment evaluate whether the sequence of events described in the experimental reports conceivably yield the reported results.

It should be noted, however, that the published reports of experiment present simplified and idealized versions of practices and phenomena. They erase as much as possible scientists' participation in the process of knowledge production, detaching the phenomena from the actions and the procedures necessary to generate them. The experimental process is thus reconstructed as following a single and linear sequence of operations in which every step leads directly to the outcome conveyed by the output phenomenal model. Only the steps required to produce the phenomenal output are presented. In these accounts, there is thus a more even matching of scientists' interventions in the material world, the material resistances encountered and respective accommodations. Scientists' material and conceptual interventions are more directly aligned with resulting outcomes by an articulated explanation of the purpose of such interventions and the significance of their results. Dead-ends, drawbacks, failed trials and errors are all discarded. The detachment of the phenomena from the actions and the procedures necessary to produce them thereby 'naturalizes' the status of the phenomena depicted in representations (Gooding 1990: 169).

According to Gooding, public reports deliberately attempt to render experiments 'transparent' in the sense that 'the apparatus and procedures appear to contribute nothing to what the experiment shows' (1985: 107). The published reports of experiments therefore constitute an important post-experimental part of practice intended to persuade the community of scientists that the experimental results are not artefacts of the experimental procedure. They aim at persuading that the phenomena that were made accessible only through scientists' agency are accepted as independent of it. As Gooding puts it, in the public accounts scientists' agency becomes invisible and the phenomenon appear as a 'residue' of the experiment and independent of human intervention (1989: 217).[2]

The fact that knowledge production is the joint endeavour of a collective of scientists, who may have been educated in various cultures and may be prone to different commitments, renders the results of science less vulnerable to the biasing effects of particular sets of items of scientific culture and scientists' beliefs. This may already occur at the private stage of knowledge production, given that scientists already bring other viewpoints into the production process. But this is especially the case in the subsequent process of collective appraisal by the wider community. Anticipated and actual critical interactions with other scientists cause 'social resistances' to human intentions that have to be 'accommodated'. These resistances stem from the 'agency' of subsets of scientific culture and beliefs that give rise to alternative interpretations of the instrumental and the phenomenal models and thereby extend scientists' intervention in the material world. In the process, the range of admissible interpretations of practices and results narrows down until a consensual resolution is eventually reached. When consensus is achieved, the community of scientists gives its assent to the interpretation of practice as conveyed by the consensual versions of the instrumental and the phenomenal models. In this view, then, consensus is a social outcome that obtains after confronting different sets of items of culture and beliefs that enhance the autonomy of the results of science from any particular subset of them (cf. Figure 5.1). This critical process may also give rise to new problem-situations, which could not have been conceived otherwise.

To summarize, the epistemic value of the collective nature of experimental practice derives from its potential to promote the confrontation of subsets of scientific culture and beliefs. Socially validated results are as a result more autonomous from particular sets of scientific commitments. The realization of this potential, however, depends on the critical attitude of scientific communities. This attitude is facilitated in heterogeneous communities or in communities that more often communicate with others. The wider the disparity of the views in confrontation, the more interesting and unforeseen questions can be raised and given due attention. The effectiveness of critical evaluation can in turn be assessed by the extent to which prior beliefs were transformed during that process. As Popper puts it:

> I think that we may say of a discussion that it was the more fruitful the more the participants were able to learn from it. And this means: the more interesting questions and difficult questions they were asked, the more new answers they were induced to think of, the more they were shaken in their opinions, and the more they could see things differently after the discussion – in short, the more their intellectual horizons were extended. Fruitfulness in this sense will almost always depend on the original gap between the opinions of the participants in the discussion. The greater the gap, the more fruitful the discussion can be.
>
> (Popper 1994: 35–36)

From this it follows that the potential for critical discussion is pivotal to the social validation of experimental results. We can then conclude that, whereas the epistemic role of the 'material world' is limited by the plasticity of the experimental systems, the epistemic role of the 'social world' is limited in homogeneous scientific communities or by their resistance to acknowledge as relevant criticisms from outsiders. This role may indeed be more difficult nowadays given the growth in specialization of scientific practice.

Scientific communities tend to organize themselves around professional associations that promote research within well-defined and circumscribed research programmes and that disseminate its results in specialized venues and journals. It is in this way that disciplinary professions enforce their standards of practice and ensure that good work is done in their fields. And scientists tend to follow these standards because they want to be recognized as competent researchers. These standards, as we have seen, constitute an important condition for the growth of knowledge. Scientists know where promising research lies and how to carry it out. But it may also narrow the scope of science. Scientists tend to focus on the research that is recognized by the profession as worthy of consideration and perceive the work carried out in other fields of research as irrelevant to their own. This makes communication across different groups of researchers difficult, and this in turn hampers what Popper called the 'friendly-hostile co-operation of many scientists' through which scientists identify and eliminate each others' errors (Popper 1979 [1972]: 217).

Outsiders are indeed in a particularly privileged position to identify and demonstrate the inadequacies of the results produced by others. Scientists need others to correct their prejudices and 'to get rid of that strange blindness concerning the inherent possibilities of … [their] own results (Popper 1979 [1972]: 219, emphasis omitted). Popper alerted to the fact that the effective exercise of this friendly-hostile cooperation requires adequate social institutions to foster critical discussion (p. 218). But he did not examine which social institutions best promote the cooperative interaction of scientists. This topic was only recently taken up by philosophers of science, and I examine it in the next section.

Scientific communities and the organization of science

Philosophers devoted to the study of experiment have not yet paid due attention to the epistemic role of the social dimension of the experimental process of knowledge production. In the book recently edited by Hans Radder (2003b), entitled *The Philosophy of Scientific Experimentation,* none of the thirteen contributions discuss the topic.

The field of social epistemology, however, has focused on the analysis of the epistemic value of the social character of scientific inquiry and, in particular, on the centrality of critical interaction to the validation of knowledge claims. This interest has in turn brought to the fore the relevance of the social organization of scientific inquiry to the fulfilment of the epistemic goals of science, as well as broader social goals. Even though these contributions do not specifically address experiments – they have in fact focused on issues of theory choice – they do offer important insights to the social epistemology of experiment I am advocating here (e.g. Kitcher 2001; Longino 1990, 2002; Solomon 2001). They all highlight that the way scientific work is socially organized has important epistemic consequences and underline, in particular, the role of diversity or of heterogeneous scientific communities.

Of relevance for the present purposes is Longino's (1990, 2002) analysis of the conditions for critical interaction within and between scientific communities. Longino's starting point is the underdetermination problem. The problem is that theoretical choice cannot be solely determined by evidence. It is also determined by background assumptions for which there is no empirical support. Not only is there no empirical grounding for them, but also these background assumptions are protected from critical reflection given that they are often unconsciously held by the members of particular scientific communities. This means that knowledge production is inevitably affected by subjective preference and especially by dominant values within the community. Objectivity in science thus requires the possibility of controlling the influence of subjective preference at the level of unconsciously held background assumptions that determine the extent to which a particular piece of evidence is considered significant to a particular hypothesis. This possibility, in Longino's view, requires the critical examination of these background beliefs.

Longino (2002: 129–31) proposes a set of conditions that an 'idealized epistemic community' should aim at in order to promote 'effective or transformative criticism'. It does not suffice that scientific communities institutionalize critical practices, such as peer review, but these practices must also be effective in promoting critical interaction. Longino identifies four conditions that a well-organized science should satisfy to this effect. First, it must have publicly recognized fora for the exercise of criticism. This means that the scientific community at large must recognize the role of criticism and be supportive of its practice by creating conditions to that end. But a critical community is not simply one that tolerates dissent. Scientists must actively engage in the practice of criticism, by criticizing and responding to counterarguments, and by being open to adjusting their views as a result of it. Therefore, the second condition is that there must be uptake of criticism.

Because the active engagement of scientists in critical discussion requires that those who hold the position being criticized must perceive the critiques as relevant, there must also be shared standards of scientific practice so that the contending parties may agree on the points of convergence and divergence and the means by which the conflict is to be resolved. Thus, the third condition is that there must be publicly recognized standards by reference to which criticism is made relevant to the goals of the inquiring community. Fourthly, there must be 'tempered equality' of intellectual authority to guarantee that all relevant perspectives can be represented, though qualified by the intellectual differences that may exist between them.

Even though this is meant as a characterization of an 'idealized epistemic community', i.e. the state scientific communities should aspire to, the four criteria may be taken as general guiding rules to that end. They can be taken as general rules that promote 'effective or transformative criticism', which allow for transcending the historical, geographical and social contingency of knowledge production. To that effect, the fourth condition is pivotal. The objectivity of science ultimately lies in the promotion of intellectual democracy whereby all participants, and in particular members of under-represented groups of society, are given a fair hearing. The latter are in an especially advantageous position to identify and criticize the dominant value system, which is unconsciously presupposed by the majority.

The possibility of effective criticism hence requires a social organization of science that takes active steps to ensure that relevant members of the community participate in knowledge production and that alternative points of view are developed. This is a pre-condition for the friendly-hostile cooperation that is critical to the growth of knowledge. And this requires deliberate measures, given that critical interaction among members of different groups is difficult. The engagement of groups from different communities is difficult because they do not share criteria for critical appraisal. Members of different groups adhere to different sets of standards, which may be perceived as impeding factors to critical discussion, and thereby reasons for dismissing each others' criticisms as irrelevant. This is even more problematic given that these standards are not often neutral to the positions under confrontation. Proponents of a given position tend to favour a sympathetic set of standards (e.g. theoretical parsimony), whereas opponents tend to favour one that renders that position more vulnerable to challenge (e.g. descriptive accuracy). Failure to reach agreement on common standards may be disruptive of criticism inasmuch as proponents will not perceive critical charges as relevant and, as a result, will not respond to them. Dialogue across cultures will be rare and the identification and scrutiny of unreflectively held beliefs meagre.

That scientific communities and scientists offer opposition to results that conflict with their culture has important implications for the social organization of science. It should encourage the making and the uptake of criticism. This often means that challengers of dominant cultures must be encouraged to make and demonstrate the relevance of their critiques to those educated in and familiar with conventional research. While the 'challengers' of dominant cultures may have the burden of articulating controversial results with established knowledge, the advocators should feel compelled to respond to those challenges. The progress of science depends on having both parties engaged in the resolution of the points of contention. The absence of critical discussion perpetuates the coexistence of dogmatic and conflicting cultures whose work is more fundamentally guided by the survival of its own community.

To conclude, the collective way whereby knowledge is produced has epistemic value because it brings to knowledge production various cognitive resources, which promote the revision of unreflectively held values and commitments. In so doing, it renders the results of science less dependent on particular subsets of items of scientific culture. The collaborative work of scientists is possible and capable of solving conflict even in the absence of shared criteria to discriminate among alternatives. This epistemic value, however, depends on the critical nature of scientific debate and this in turn depends on the organization of science that must actively promote and foster criticism. This requires active measures because to put our most ingrained beliefs to the test is not something that we tend to do naturally. Having completed the analysis of the social dimensions of knowledge production, I now turn to what happens to the products of experiments, once they have been validated by the community.

Knowledge and technology

The success of science is often associated with the technological innovations it brings with it and that have substantially altered human life. Scientific experimentation has a particularly critical role here. Most technological innovations start in the lab. This is not surprising given that scientific experimentation is to some extent a technological achievement in that it attempts to produce reliable equipments tailored to intervene in the material world in predictable and stable ways.[3] Besides producing knowledge about the natural world, scientific experimentation also produces machines and tools of various kinds, which can be used in future scientific practice but not only here.

But a distinction should be drawn among the three final products of experiment: the material procedure, the instrumental model and the phenomenal model. The final versions of material procedures and instrumental models that underlie the production of experimental results yield devices, instruments and machines that generate stable outcomes when operated in a regular manner under similar conditions. The two-way coherence achieved between the material apparatus and the instrumental model defines its appropriate operation for specific purposes. The material apparatuses become 'black boxes' (Pinch 1986; Latour 1987). They become routinely used apparatuses, the full understanding of which is no longer necessary and they thereby become autonomous from their context of production. When a scientific product becomes a black box it becomes a reliable object that can be routinely applied without its users being conscious of the processes (technical and social) that brought it about. Thus, from the viewpoint of the users, and when referring to material apparatuses, a black box is a complex object, of which it is only necessary to know its input and output.

The same holds for phenomenal models. When phenomenal models are adopted for the solution of new problem-situations, either in experimental or in conceptual practice, they become factual statements detached from their production processes, even though they would not exist without the interactively stabilized material procedures and conceptual models that produced them. Nonetheless, they become facts, the status of which is no longer in question.

Socially validated experimental phenomena become part of the field's stylized facts that can be used in subsequent experimental practice, in the exploration of new phenomenal domains or in the development of old or new theories. In theoretical work, the fact becomes empirical evidence for a theoretical argument of a deductive or inductive kind. It becomes a part of an argument with a well-defined structure, an internal 'logic', which may be independent from the context of its production. However, it might take quite some time until scientists can use experimental facts in the construction of new theories. Experimenters and theoreticians have first to become full experts in the phenomenal world. When experimental phenomena become part of the field's stylized facts, they become established items that convey epistemic value to new scientific results.

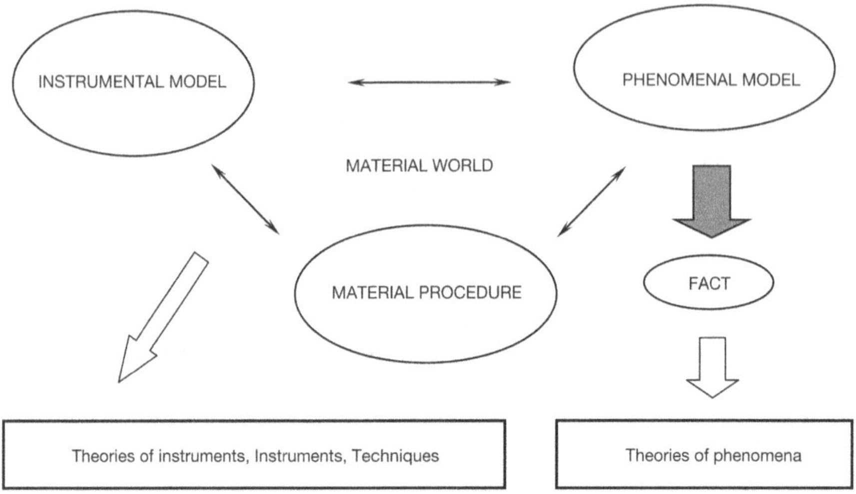

Figure 5.2 The 'technological' products of experiments

To conclude, subsequent practice consolidates previous results by adopting them in knowledge production. Insofar as these results are brought to bear on new problems, their understanding evolves and, consequently, they may be modified, refined and improved, as well as rejected in subsequent practice. In the process, weakly defined problems, weakly established techniques and conjectural solutions may be reinforced and substituted by better-structured problems, techniques, and so forth. The 'technological' products of experiments are depicted in Figure 5.2.

Conclusion

The scrutiny of experimental results by scientists educated in other cultures and holding different beliefs fosters the autonomy of these results from the processes that generated them. This scrutiny gives rise to new problem-situations that extend knowledge production. Previously neglected courses of action can then be identified and explored. The results that are eventually accepted by the wider community of scientists are not only justified by robust three-way coherences, but they also carry new knowledge – the knowledge generated by the confrontation of a wider set of items of culture and beliefs. Because scientists and scientific communities may resist critical challenges, the social organization of science should actively promote critical interaction within and between scientific communities. The socially validated results of experiments establish new items of scientific culture. These may include new apparatuses and tools to intervene in the material world and new facts about the material world.

6 The social epistemology of experiment

This chapter concludes the social epistemology of experiment (SEE). It rounds up the various arguments developed in the previous chapters and proposes a framework to evaluate the epistemic value of the processes and products of experiment. It then applies the framework to Smith's market experiments presented in Chapter 3.

Coherences and resistances

The social epistemology of experiment selects coherence as the central principle that guides experimental practice and grounds belief in experimental knowledge. Experimental practice is conceived of as an activity that consists of forging relations of coherence among heterogeneous items of scientific culture until a three-way coherence is achieved among the components of the experimental system. The mutual support among the material procedure, the instrumental model and the phenomenal model gives experimenters' confidence in their practice and in the outcome of that practice. Achieving a three-way coherence is far from trivial. It involves the direct participation of the material world and it is socially validated by a process of critical interaction that helps scientists to avoid the partiality of beliefs framed in the context of a particular scientific culture.

Experimental coherence is worked out during knowledge production via conceptual and material manoeuvring of the experimental system until scientists succeed in making sense of the phenomenon produced. When coherence obtains, the material procedure interpreted through the instrumental model produces a phenomenon that is interpreted by the phenomenal model. Experimenters then believe they have made sense of their practices and respective outcome. When coherence is attained, inquirers no longer have the inclination to revise the elements of the system any further. The experiment ends.

The social epistemology of experiment pays special attention to scientists' disposition to obtain confirmation of prior expectations and to the enforcement of group commitments by scientific communities. The conceptualization of experimental practice as an endeavour in which scientists strive for the attainment of coherent resolutions must take into account that scientists tend to produce results that fit their conceptual frameworks and that overlook potential sources of error.

It identifies as major sources of epistemic value the direct participation of the material world in knowledge production and the social dimensions of knowledge production, whose value lies in the potential to promote the revision of scientists' prior beliefs. Participation of the material world and the social validation of experimental results carry the potential to resist scientists' intentions, which force them to revise and correct the partiality of their viewpoints.

Participation of the material world and the social dimensions of knowledge production force scientists to conceive questions they had not imagined and to provide answers they had not thought of. Insofar as the participation of the material and the social worlds in knowledge production vary, the epistemic value of experimental results varies too. The implication of this is that the epistemic appraisal of the processes and products of experiment must take into account the participation of both the material and the social worlds. That is, the epistemic appraisal of experiments requires evaluating the extent to which the material and the social worlds participated in knowledge production.

The social epistemology of experiment, then, raises questions of the kind: what is the participation of the material world in the production of experimental results? What is the degree of susceptibility of experimental systems to scientists' manipulations? Is the relevant scientific community involved? Did the processes of social validation raise the relevant questions? Were the questions raised answered? What was the contribution of these knowledge claims to the advancement of science and society? And the social epistemology of experiment provides the means to answer them – the epistemic tests of experiment are now introduced.

Epistemic tests of experiment

Epistemic tests aim at evaluating the epistemic value of experimental claims to knowledge. They do this by assessing the actual participation of the material world in knowledge production and the critical interaction of the community of scientists that produced and evaluated these claims. The *materiality test* and the *stringency test* assess the contribution of the material world, and the *social robustness test* assesses the processes of social validation of experimental results. The *technological test* assesses what happens to the products of experiment, once they have been socially validated by the relevant community.

Thus far I have been focusing on what Mary Morgan calls the 'ideal laboratory experiment', which corresponds to the stylized view of experiment presented in Chapter 2 and which has been the reference model of experiment in the previous chapters. But there are different kinds of experiment with substantially different levels of materiality. Morgan's (2002, 2003, 2005) taxonomy of experiments lends itself as a useful illustration of the different levels of materiality in various kinds of experiment. She identifies three kinds: 'mathematical model experiments', 'vicarious experiments' and 'ideal laboratory experiments'. The ideal laboratory experiment is the scientific device with the highest level of materiality, whereas the mathematical model experiment is at the lower end of a continuum of vicarious experiments.

The ideal laboratory experiment corresponds to the stylized view of experiment, which consists of the manipulation and examination of a material object under the favourable conditions of the laboratory. The level of materiality is at its highest because the object under scrutiny, the mode of control and the method of demonstration are all material. In these experiments, scientists physically interfere with the objects of study, which actively participate in knowledge production. The results obtained are the direct consequences of these interventions, which depend both on scientists' interventions and on the attributes of the objects under scrutiny. In contrast, mathematical model experiments consist of the generation of logical deductions obtained from premises about the object of study. In these experiments, the inputs, the mode of intervention, and the outputs are mathematical; control is exercised via simplifying assumptions (e.g. ceteris paribus conditions, assumptions of independence between variables, etc.) and the results obtained are the outcome of the deductive or logical manipulation of a mathematical system (e.g. models of competitive price theory). Vicarious experiments are hybrid devices that combine both 'mathematical' and 'experimental' elements.

Because the participation of the material world in experiments may vary, even in laboratory experiments that more closely approximate the ideal type, the materiality and the stringency tests are devoted to the analysis of experiments' materiality. The *materiality test* assesses the composition of the experimental system, namely the object of scrutiny, the mode of intervention and the process generating the results. The materiality of the experiment and its epistemic value is higher the more experimenters directly interfere with the object of interest and the more the results obtained are the result of the object's reactions to these manipulations. Conversely, the more experimenters use conceptual rather than material items of scientific culture the lower the epistemic value of the experimental results. The *stringency test* assesses the relevance of the materiality of a given experiment. Holding the level of materiality constant, it assesses the extent to which the results of experiments are determined by scientists' material or conceptual manipulation instead of the agency of the material world or, in other words, it assesses the actual possibility given to the objects of study to resist scientists' expectations.

The materiality and the stringency of experimental systems are positively correlated. A lower degree of materiality is necessarily associated with a lower degree of stringency. This is so because the results will be more strongly determined by scientists' conceptual manipulations than by the agency of the object under scrutiny. Thus, both the materiality and the stringency of the experimental systems decrease the more the experiment relies on conceptual resources of practice. But for a given level of materiality, the stringency of experimental systems may vary and thus the actual contribution of the material world to knowledge production.

The epistemic value of the participation of the material world is higher when experimenting with rigid experimental systems and it is lower when experimenting with plastic systems. Plastic experimental systems are amenable to a higher degree of material and conceptual manipulation, which reduces the participation, or the relevance of the participation, of the material world. Knowledge production is guided by tentative trials at implementing an operational material apparatus and by speculative ideas about the phenomenon of interest. A clash between an expectation and a result is more likely to be resolved by attempting to obtain support for prior beliefs rather than by revising them. And this may be done by further manipulating the material apparatus so as materially to eliminate the conflict, or by explaining the effect away by conceptual manoeuvring. This means that the results of plastic systems are more critically the realization of scientists' preferred solutions to the selected problem-situations. Rigid experimental systems, in contrast, delimit the range of admissible material and conceptual manoeuvrings. They employ material apparatuses for which the proper operation and purposes have already been stabilized in prior scientific practice.

The reduced epistemic value of experimental systems may, however, be overcome by conducting more experiments that improve the replicability and robustness of experimental results. New experiments can ensure that the phenomenon under scrutiny can be reproduced by different means and by different experimenters and thus that it is not a fortuitous event associated with an extravagant design and group of scientists. The reproduction of the phenomenon by substantially different means and in different social settings enhances the strength of the result, which then becomes a robust phenomenon.

It is now widely recognized that the exact reproduction of experiments is seldom realized by other scientists. Not only are experiments extremely hard to reproduce, but also, and more importantly, there is no great interest in faithfully reproducing a particular experiment, except when the experimental results are extremely controversial. Experimenters are far more interested in investigating the effect of introducing relevant modifications to the experimental set-up. Moreover, the reproduction of phenomena with different experimental systems provides stronger support for the relative autonomy of the results from the material procedures, as well as the scientists that generated them. Thus, the more a phenomenon is recalcitrant to altered conditions, the more autonomous it is from the material, conceptual and social conditions that produce it.

The *social robustness test* evaluates the processes of production and social validation of experimental results. It assesses whether these processes triggered and promoted effective or transformative criticism. The goal is to assess whether interesting and difficult questions were asked and answered, and whether scientists revised their opinions as a result of critical discussion. The more difficult and interesting the questions raised and answered, the higher the epistemic value of experimental results because it is the outcome of a process of criticism that has addressed critical charges levelled against it. In experimental science, the process of critical evaluation often suggests the design and implementation of new experiments to check whether the results are the outcome of potential backgrounds. When the community agrees that the experimental phenomenon is no artefact of the experimental procedure, it becomes a robust phenomenon. It becomes a fact supported by various three-way coherences that the various groups of researchers produced. This does not mean that all inconsistencies and disagreements have been met and addressed. It means that the community as a whole agrees that sufficient arguments have been adduced that justify belief in the newly discovered fact.

The term 'robustness' is meant to emphasize the role of social validation in improving the replicability and robustness of experimental results. It highlights that the appraisal of experimental results by scientists other than those directly involved in the production process is critical to the conduction of new experiments to test previous results. It also highlights that this collective appraisal improves the robustness of experimental results, even when it does not give rise to new experiments.

The social validation of experimental results does not require the reproduction of the experiment by third parties to verify whether the same results obtain. It may suffice that scientists are persuaded that they would obtain the same results if they had implemented the same material apparatus and followed the same procedures. The process of social validation of experimental results may therefore follow a kind of virtual experiment whereby the scientists who did not take part in the experiment evaluate whether the sequence of events described in the experimental reports conceivably yield the reported results. It is in fact this evaluation that may originate new experiments if they think that there is something wrong with the experiment.

To sum up, the collective way whereby experimental results are produced and socially validated at the community level has a critical epistemic function in experimental practice. It not only improves the replicability and robustness of experimental results by suggesting new experiments, but it also does so when it does not suggest any. This is why the inclusion of the social dimension of knowledge production in an epistemology of experiment is important. And it is this reason that justifies the title of this book. The social dimension of knowledge production constitute an important source of epistemic value, which has been overlooked in the philosophical studies of experiment.

Because the fruitfulness of research programmes can only be evaluated in future practice, the *technological test* assesses what happens to the results of experiments produced within the conceptual framework of a research programme. It evaluates the extent to which the results of past practice are used in subsequent practice, i.e. whether they have become new items of scientific culture. If so, it also examines the extent to which the new items of culture introduce new modes of intervening in the material world and suggest new phenomenal domains to explore. As new items of culture are mobilized in the forging of new coherent relations, they continue to gain autonomy from the cultural and the social context in which they were produced and established.

But they also raise the chance of being revised, modified and rejected in the course of practice. The technological test is thus a measure of the social usefulness of the products of experiment, in science and elsewhere. Figure 6.1 depicts a mature research programme and the functions and roles of the four epistemic tests applied in its appraisal.

The four tests can apply to various experimental units. The materiality test may apply to a single experiment, the stringency test may apply to a particular category of experiment, the social robustness test may apply to a particular dispute, and the technological test may apply to the relation between a particular phenomenon and a theory that explains it. When the tests are applied to a mature research programme that examines a well-circumscribed phenomenal domain, they are interdependent and feedback upon each other. In this case, the stringency test assesses the strength of the fit between the conceptual models and material procedures that produced data about the phenomenon of interest. The epistemic value of the fit increases if the participation of the material world is relevant and if it is the outcome of an effective exercise of criticism. The reliability of the procedures and robustness of the results improve further if they become new resources for scientific practice. (In the figure the arrows represent the relations that the tests evaluate.)

The social epistemology of experiment provides a normative framework to assess the replicability and robustness of experimental results. The four epistemic

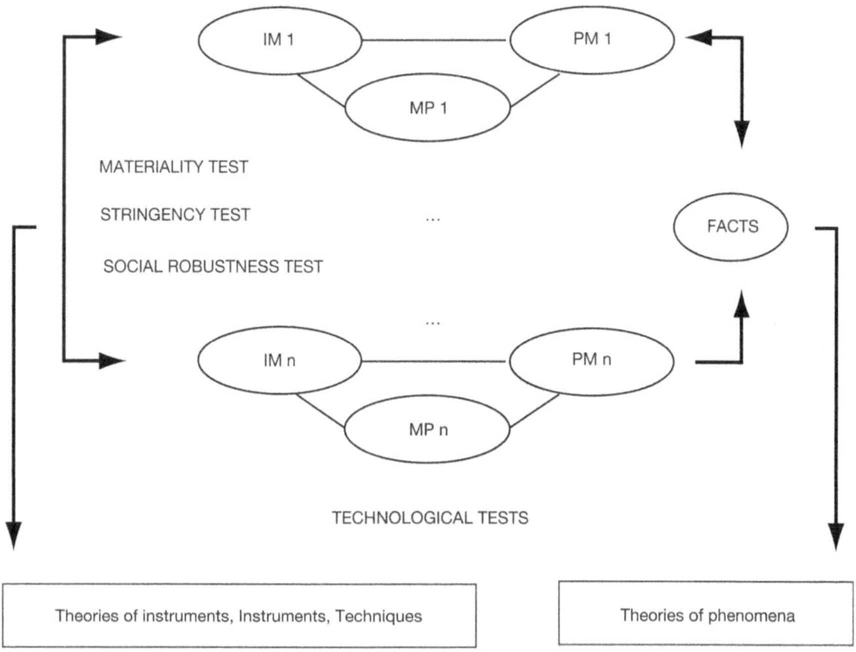

Figure 6.1 The epistemic tests of experiment

tests aim at assessing the autonomy of experimental results from the material and the social conditions of the experimental processes of knowledge production that generated them. They appraise, in particular, the effect of scientists' interventions and the sensitivity of the results to particular sets of scientific culture. Or to put it in another way, they test whether the phenomenon produced is supported by various three-way coherences.

The epistemic tests allow a fine-grained analysis of the epistemic value of experimental results, which is not comprised in the notions of replicability or robustness. The epistemic value of the three-way coherences that support a given result depends on the materiality of the experimental system and on the sociality of the experimental processes that generated it. I now illustrate the relevance of the proposed social epistemological framework by applying the four epistemic tests to Smith's market experiments.

The market experiments: the epistemic appraisal

Recall that as Smith presented it, the first market experiment was designed with the expectation that it would generate negative evidence for competitive price theory. The idea behind it was that negative evidence obtained under conditions favourable to the hypothesis under test is far more compelling than disconfirming evidence obtained under adverse conditions. But the market experiment instead produced evidence consistent with the theoretical prediction. This, then, raises the symmetrical doubt about the import of confirming evidence produced under favourable conditions to the hypothesis being tested. In order to appraise this, the four epistemic tests of experiment are applied to Smith's market experiment.

As the 'material world' of the experimental systems of economics refers to the experimental participants and to the microeconomic institution, the materiality and stringency tests evaluate their relative contribution to the experimental results.

The 'materiality' of the market experiment is low for at least two reasons. First, the experimental market, which is the object of study, is a surrogate of a 'real' market to test the predictions of competitive price theory. Second, the results obtained are substantially determined by the experimental procedures rather than by the characteristics of the trading institution. That is, the relevance of the materiality of the market experiments is low.

The experimental market is more adequately perceived as a model of competitive theory, rather than as a model of a 'real world' market. As Smith explicitly recognizes, to give the theory the best shot, the experimental market was built by reference to the theoretical market. Information about real markets was used only when the theory proved to be an insufficient guide for the design and implementation of the experimental market. In Smith's words, the experimental market was thought of as 'a good general model of received short-run supply and demand theory' that provided 'the best chance of fulfilling the conditions of an operational theory of supply and demand' (1962: 111). The experimental market deviated in significant ways from 'real' markets, and this was not taken as a problem; quite the contrary. The greater stability of the conditions of the experimental market, for example, was not problematic because stability was needed to study the equilibrium tendencies of theoretical competitive markets. As Smith puts it, theoretical equilibrium is 'a condition toward which the market would move *if* the forces of supply and demand were to remain stationary for a sufficiently long time' (p. 115, emphasis in original). And it was this concept of equilibrium that the experiment was designed to study. Even though the experimental market is more 'material' than the theoretical market because it has students performing the role of buyers and sellers and engaging in the exchange of a fictitious good, the 'materiality' of the experimental market is low. It is low because the experimental market is most adequately conceived of as a material instantiation of a theoretical market.

The materiality of the market experiments is not very relevant because the role of experimental participants in these experiments was extremely limited. On closer inspection, one notes that the market's trend to equilibrium is very strongly determined by the design set-up of the experiments. Subjects were explicitly told to behave as theoretical sellers (or buyers) by receiving explicit instructions on how to maximize their earnings (by selling at high prices or buying at low prices) and by being warned not to trade at a loss (selling below reservation prices or buying above them). In addition, the enforcement of the precepts of experimental economics gave them no reason to do otherwise. Thus, it is not surprising that subjects' behaviour conformed to the theory's predictions.

Most crucially, however, the structure of the experiment had a critical role in generating a trend towards equilibrium for reasons other than the characteristics of the market (such as the dissemination of information and multi-period trading). The trend towards equilibrium is most adequately explained by the pattern of values induced in the experimental commodities (i.e. the supply and demand functions) and the stationary repetition of market conditions at the beginning of each period. This was demonstrated by the simulation carried out by Dhananjay K. Gode and Shyam Sunder (1993) that showed that even a market with zero-intelligent traders, who were only restricted to making non-negative profits, succeeds in achieving equilibrium, a success that is explained by the parameters of the experiment (see also Holt *et al.* 1986; Banks *et al.* 1989; Holt 1995).

The structure of the experimental market significantly determines that the buyers with higher redemption values are more likely to make purchases because they more easily make profitable trades. The sellers with lower production costs are also better able to sell their goods at a profit. These two factors taken together imply that after the initial contracts, the tradable commodities remaining in the market are those with lower redemption values (which can only be bought at lower prices) and with higher production costs (which can only be sold at higher prices). Consequently, as the trading period elapses, the remaining goods are transacted at prices that approximate the equilibrium price (which is in between the remaining highest redemption values and lowest production costs). That is, as the trading period progresses, the subsequent transactions tend to be made on terms that slowly approximate the equilibrium price. The goods with the lowest redemption values and those with higher production costs are gradually excluded from the market. In this way, both price and quantity tend to move towards equilibrium levels.

Because there is stationary repetition, the transaction prices of a period tend to affect the terms of trade of subsequent periods. This effect was noted by the strong correlation between the transaction price of the last period and the first transaction prices of the subsequent period. Such correlation indicates that buyers with high redemption values learn that there are sellers willing to sell at much lower prices and so they try to transact at those prices. The low cost producers, in turn, try to sell at higher prices. The price trend is thereby extended from one trading period to another until competitive price is eventually reached (see Roth 1995a, n. 88).

To conclude, the structure of the experimental markets had a crucial role in determining the results of the experiment. The equilibrating tendencies of the experimental markets are more easily attributed to the structure of the experiments that generate the same results with both human and non-human agents. Because the materiality of the market experiments is low and not very significant, the market equilibrium does not provide strong supporting evidence to competitive market theory.

The experiments produced conclusive results, however. The market experiments easily discriminate between the two alternative phenomenal models in confrontation: equilibrium v. non-equilibrium. Even though the equilibrium was a surprising result from the viewpoint of Smith's expectations, as he expressed them, there is no doubt that this was the resulting phenomenal model. This outcome is reinforced by the robustness of the results to modifications introduced to the experimental system. This provides further evidence for the extremely high level of Smith's intervention that, as I argued, substantially determined the experiments' results. This, thus, points to the importance of assessing both the materiality and stringency of experimental systems.

Economic experiments are in general amenable to the scrutiny of a wide and varied audience. In contrast to complex experiments in physics, such as in high-energy physics, where public appraisal of experimental results cannot extend much beyond the community of specialists, in economics both the practice and its outcome are accessible to other experimenters, non-experimenters and non-economists alike. The reason for this derives from the simplicity of economic experiments that must be easily understood by experimental subjects and the fairly complete description of experimental procedures in the published reports of experiments, as we have seen in Chapter 3. These two factors together render both the practice and the outcome of practice suitable to the scrutiny of a wide and heterogeneous community of researchers. (In fact, this feature is what has made the present work possible.)

Where market experiments are concerned, we have seen that the hostile environment to the use of the experimental method in economics forced Smith to adduce a varied set of arguments in support of both the market experiments and the experimental method. Future research on market experiments, as we will see in the next section, introduced successive revisions to the conceptual understanding of the purposes and functions of experimental markets, as well as of other economics experiments. Thus, market experimentation proved to be a socially robust research programme.

We will also see in the next section that market experimentation proved to be very successful technologically. The market experiments became tools for subsequent practice as well as for policy-making. This is explained by the low levels of materiality and stringency, or the high degree of control economists learned to exercise over the actions of experimental subjects, and later on those of the economic agents. The technological success of market experiments is also explained by their high level of social robustness. The experimental markets became well-understood microeconomic systems that could control human behaviour for specified goals.

The technological success of market experiments: from test-devices to 'testbeds'

The conceptual understanding of the first market experiments evolved with Smith's experimental practice and that of others. As we have seen, the first experiments were inadequate tools to test competitive price theory. But in the course of practice its applications extended until it became a device for the design of market institutions.

The first motivation of the market experiments was to test competitive price theory. Confronted with confirming evidence, Smith focused on testing the robustness of market equilibrium, which proved robust to modifications to the shapes of demand and supply curves and to the distribution of surplus between buyers and sellers (Smith 1964, 1965). Having established the robustness of equilibrium in the double-auctions, Smith set out to investigate other markets and their relative performances (Smith 1967, 1976b, 1980a; Plott and Smith 1978; Smith *et al.* 1982; Smith and Williams 1983; Miller, Plott and Smith 1977). Having found that the double-auction is the most efficient institution, Smith started to take the double-auction experiment as a proxy for the competitive market which could then be used as a benchmark, i.e. a reference against which other market institutions could be designed and compared in the laboratory. In Smith's words:

> The motivation for selecting the double auction for extensive experimental study … was based on the conjecture that this institution was the one under which classical supply and demand theory had the best chance of being validated. However, I did not seriously expect competitive price theory to be supported by these initial probes … But if competitive

> theory had validity under the double auction, this would provide the 'control case' or reference institution against which other forms of market organization could be compared.
>
> (Smith 1976b: 47)

In the course of practice, experimentation with markets became a field of experimental economics in its own right, which may now be decomposed into three main sub-areas of research.[1] The field of *auctions* studies the comparative efficiency of auction mechanisms for the transaction of special goods (e.g. Smith 1967, 1976b, 1980b). The field of *industrial organization* studies factors that affect competition and that give rise to antitrust phenomena such as predatory pricing or collusion (e.g. Smith 1981a, 1981b; Coursey, Isaac and Smith 1984; Isaac and Smith 1985). Finally, the field of *capital and asset markets* addresses the specificities of the financial markets and related phenomena, such as for example the formation of market bubbles (e.g. Smith *et al.* 1988).

The experimental market gradually became a resource of practice of wider application. It also became instrumental for theoretical development. It became a tool that could provide 'a rigorous testing of our ability to model elementary behavior before confronting such models with field data' (Smith 1976b: 62). These tests had the important advantage of guaranteeing independence of theories from field-data during theoretical construction and prior to their submission to testing with field-data. In contrast with field-data, the main advantage was that 'it is never tautological to modify the model in ways suggested by the results of the last experiment' (Smith 1976a: 274). This is the case because there is always the possibility of conceiving another experiment to test the modified model before the model is finally confronted with field-data.

As the results of experiments accumulated and found increasing support, they became the field's 'stylized facts', i.e. empirical propositions well confirmed in the laboratory. The first market experiment became the double-auction experiment that generated the stylized fact that 'allocations and prices converge to levels near the competitive equilibrium … prediction. This convergence is rapid, occurring in three to four trading periods or less when subjects are experienced with the institution' (1982: 943–52).

In the course of experimental practice, early experiments thus became well-understood devices that could be identified by their designs (e.g. *the* Double Auction, *the* English Auction, etc.). And each experiment became associated with a set of stylized and significant facts (e.g. the First-Price Sealed Bid Auction generates higher prices than the Dutch Auction).[2] In short, they became the fields' items of scientific culture.

As understanding of the new method grew, experimenters began to conceive of the use of market experiments for applications beyond academic purposes. Experiments became policy tools that could provide 'empirical justification and preliminary experience for the design of field experiments' and means of 'exploring the policy implications of new institutions, or alterations in existing institutional rules' (1976b: 62).

The adoption of the market experiment as a policy tool was stimulated by the context of increasing market deregulation in the 1980s and the resulting need of conceiving new market arrangements for a number of sectors in restructuration. At first, experimental studies were commissioned to give policy recommendations on the institutional make-up of special industries. For example, the American Civil Aeronautics Board commissioned an experimental study from David M. Grether, R. Mark Isaac and Charles R. Plott (1989) to evaluate the overall impact of intensifying competition and deregulation on the aviation industry. The aim was to offer policy guidance on how to adjust use of airport capacity to the overall contextual tendencies of growth, competition and deregulation. The Federal Energy Regulatory Commission and the Energy Information Administration, to give other example, hired Kevin McCabe, Stephen J. Rassenti and Vernon L. Smith (1989) to investigate the properties of an auction market for the sale and transportation of natural gas. These commissioned reports, however, only provided recommendations for the patrons, which could be used at their discretion.

Only recently have experiments been used as 'testbeds' of market mechanisms, i.e. of 'a working prototype of a process that is going to be employed in a complex environment' (Plott 1997: 605). That is, they became tools for the design and test of auction mechanisms before they were implemented in the field. This was the case of the bid-auction commissioned by the Federal Communication Commission to allocate licenses for wireless Personal Communication Systems, which is analyzed in detail in Chapter 10.

A final use of market experiments is to shed light on real world phenomena. The 'winner's curse' is a famous phenomenon identified in 1971 by the Atlantic Richfield Company that claimed that the exploitation of oil leases in the Gulf of Mexico was informed by this curse. The curse was that the winning bidder was the trader who mostly overestimated the value of the oil tract and therefore was prone to incur high losses (cf. Capen *et al.* 1971). This curse occurred, it was argued, because the leases were transacted at an auction (a common value auction) where the values of the items transacted were unknown at the time of the sale. Because bidders could only resort to their private estimates for that value, the winner of the auction was the trader who possessed the highest estimate, an excessively optimistic one.

The claim that the winner's curse was occurring in the Gulf of Mexico could not be settled by non-experimental means. Economic theory predicted that winning bidders are able to make normal profits because they can take into account their high private estimates.[3] On the other hand, field data from common value auctions were inconclusive because the private valuations of the items could not be known. In addition, the company had an interest in convincing other companies to act as a cartel (by reducing their bids), which damaged its credibility. In the face of such controversy, John H. Kagel and Dan Levin (1986) ran an experiment to test the hypothesis put forward by the

Atlantic Richfield Company, which indeed reproduced the phenomenon in the lab and provided evidence supporting the conjecture that the losses incurred could be attributed to the characteristics of the licenses.

In conclusion, the field of market experimentation possesses a high degree of *technological success*. After two decades of practice, market experiments proved to be a useful tool for solving various problem-situations. These ranged from the testing of theories and the explanation of real world phenomena to 'market engineering'. This technological success stems from the possibility of exercising a high level of control over human behaviour and hence of reproducing in the economy the stable phenomena created in the lab. (This topic is addressed in detail in Chapter 10.)

Conclusion

The social epistemological framework for the descriptive and normative analysis of experiments is now in place. The framework accounts for the processes whereby experimenters produce and justify their claims to knowledge and proposes four tests to assess the epistemic value of these claims.

They aim to assess the contribution of the two major sources of epistemic value of experiments: the participation of the material world in knowledge production and the process of social validation of experimental results. The epistemic value of experiments resides in their potential to put unconsciously held beliefs to the test and thereby enhance the autonomy of the results of experiments from the processes and contexts that generated them. The four epistemic tests may apply to various units of scientific experimentation: experiments, research programmes, stylized facts, instruments, social processes and so forth.

In this chapter the epistemic tests were applied to market experiments. They showed that this category of experiments is characterized by a low level of materiality, a low level of stringency, a high level of social robustness that together contributed to a high level of technological applicability. They also showed that, as products of experiments are employed in future practice, the conception of previous experiments may be substantially revised. The use of the products of experiments for non-scientific goals is an expressive demonstration of the relevance and fruitfulness of past scientific practice. The field of market experiments, as a whole, brought to the fore the relevance of market institutions and established experimental economics as a relevant tool for market (re)design.

In the second part of this book, SEE is devoted to the close scrutiny of the method, arguments, social processes, single experiments and series of experiments of economics. This application will allow us to make a more complete assessment of the field of experimental economics, while at the same time supplying a test for the relevance and significance of the social epistemology of experiment proposed here.

Part II

The social epistemology of experimental economics

7 The foundation of experimental economics

Vernon Smith is the field's prominent practitioner who has most contributed to the establishment of experimental economics. He has in fact won the Bank of Sweden Nobel Memorial Prize for having done so. This chapter presents a historical account of the experimental field of economics. It examines the path that Vernon Smith traced in his attempt to win the profession's recognition for the relevance of the experimental method, as well as the overall context that favoured it. Smith's trajectory is particularly illustrative in showing the difficulties scientists face when exploring new areas of research. Their establishment involves a long process of knowledge production until the significance of the results stabilizes and arguments can finally be presented to justify them. This is not to say that Smith was and has been a lone explorer. Smith's journey was certainly not a solitary one. As will become apparent from the historical account, Smith's contribution was as informed by the work of those who preceded him as by the work of those who collaborated with him, and perhaps most importantly, by the resistance of those who created obstacles on his way to establishing the experimental field in economics.

Economics, an experimental science

The experimental field of economics is an achievement of the second half of the twentieth century that only recently gained the discipline's recognition. Economics was considered a non-experimental discipline at least until 1985. In this year, Paul Samuelson and William Nordhaus still presented economics as a non-laboratory science in their best-selling textbook *Economics* and comforted economists to 'be content largely to observe' (p. 8).

The evolution of the discipline was by and large affected by this consensual shortcoming and by attempts to overcome or attenuate it. Economists, in their efforts to make economics a scientific discipline, tried to make do with other methods and techniques. Methodologically concerned economists recommended, for instance, the construction of theories to be built up deductively from assumed premises about the behaviour of economic agents, which could then be applied to their domain of inquiry after including specific allowances (e.g. Mill 1874 [1844]). More recent methodological proposals have recommended that economists should instead concentrate on developing theories capable of generating testable predictions to be submitted to empirical testing (Friedman 1953). Empirical testing in turn relied on data obtained from 'naturally occurring processes'. Econometrics and statistics were the empirical methods *par excellence* to bring data to bear on the theoretical issues of interest. Other economists, taking as a starting point the specificity of economics as a social science, proposed instead approaches that took into account the historical contingency of human action and its relationship with the social structures that guide it (Lawson 1997). But the profession at large continued to try to emulate the natural sciences, and economics eventually became an experimental science.

Experimental work in economics took off in the 1980s. A large and increasing community of economists now conducts experiments in laboratories, whose numbers keep growing everywhere around the globe. The community of experimenters present and discuss their work under the auspices of its official association, the Economic Science Association, founded in 1986. Reports of experiments are published in top journals such as *Econometrica*, *The American Economic Review* and the *Economic Journal*, and since 1998 also in the specialized journal *Experimental Economics.* Experimental Economics is now part of the curricula of undergraduate and graduate courses and it is a field with one recipient of the Bank of Sweden Nobel Memorial Prize, awarded in 2002 to Vernon Smith 'for having established laboratory experiments as a tool in empirical economic analysis, especially in the study of alternative market mechanisms'. This prize was jointly awarded to the psychologist Daniel Kahneman 'for having integrated insights from psychological research into economic science, especially concerning human judgment and decision-making under uncertainty'.[1] The success of the field has been such that it has also given rise to a new industry in the business of consultancy services, particularly in the design of market mechanisms. In short, economics has become an experimental science.

The field of experimental economics

Experimental Economics has grown to maturity and now has a consolidated basis for knowledge production. It already possesses a fairly stable set of methodological principles, procedures, benchmarks and stylized facts that are being passed on to new generations of economists through the field's textbooks (Davis and Holt 1993; Friedman and Sunder 1994; Friedman and Cassar 2004). The new generations of economists know which problem-situations are worth pursuing and which tools they can use to solve them. This is indeed what explains its rapid growth in recent years.

In the first part of this book we have seen that to experiment in economics is to create a microeconomy in the laboratory for the purpose of observing and measuring variables that are relevant to the study of economic institutions and individual behaviour. And that economists create experimental microeconomies to address many different problems. So far we have focused on *market experiments*, the research programme Smith most contributed to. In these experiments, subjects perform the roles of buyers or sellers (or producers and consumers) in the exchange (or production) of a particular good to allow the study of market institutions. Started to test competitive price theory, research on experimental markets has expanded considerably. As we have seen in the previous chapter, market experiments evolved from test-devices to 'test-beds'. And they have been used to study various market-related issues, such as for example market allocation mechanisms, antitrust phenomena such as predatory pricing or collusion, and the formation of bubbles in asset markets.[2]

Game theory experiments are devoted to the study of models of social interaction that do not necessarily have the market as the privileged context of interaction. Famous games include the dictator game, the public goods game, and the ultimatum games (which we will see in detail in Chapters 10 and 11). The major difference between market experiments and game experiments is that the former focus on the performance of market institutions, whereas the latter focus on individuals' decisions in particularly interesting strategic or coordination problems. Or to put it in another way, while the former focuses on the study of microeconomic institutions, the latter focuses on the study of microeconomic environments. But in both kinds of experiment individual and aggregate outcomes are determined by the joint effect of the set of rules and subjects' interactions with other individuals. There are also hybrid experiments that combine aspects of both kinds of experiments that focus, say, on the strategic structure of particular markets (e.g. bargaining in bilateral monopoly).

Finally, the third grand umbrella of economics experiments is *individual decision-making* that focuses on simpler problems where the outcome of decision-making for the individual depends only on his/her own decisions. They may also depend on the states of the world that emerge after the decisions were made if the experiments involve problems of risk and uncertainty. These experiments have been designed, for example, to test the axioms of expected utility theory (e.g. transitivity) or to measure individual attitudes towards risk (e.g. risk aversion). Chapter 12 focuses on one research programme in this field, the preference reversals research programme.

Arguing for the experimental method

Smith's first incursion in the field dates back to 1956 when, at Purdue, he ran the first market experiments in the classroom. During these formative years, as Smith recounts, he faced a great deal of resistance from fellow economists when he presented the results of his market experiments, in informal discussions with his peers or in more formal settings such as at faculty seminars and workshops. This scepticism challenged not only the results but also the whole experimental enterprise. Economists simply could not see the purpose and significance of laboratory experiments for economics: 'People had been skeptical that there was a trick, some people reason why the experiments worked that had *nothing* to do with economics or theory or that overused, undefined thing that economists call the "real world"' (1991: 372, emphasis in original).

The resistance encountered was so strong that Smith was compelled to combine his experimental practice with what could be considered more 'credible' work. In this regard, it is worthwhile to provide Smith's first-hand accounts of this resistance as he experienced it:

> In the meantime I had to make a living and during these formative years I was writing and publishing on other topics – capital and investment theory, corporate finance theory and the economics of uncertainty, and natural resource economics. Compared with the experimental work, this other research was much easier to do and easier to publish … The profession was hungry for new theory in these areas, indeed any area that employed recognizable methods; it was not hungry for evidence, and certainly not laboratory evidence, because theory provided all the requisite understanding.
>
> (Smith 1991: 3–4)

Along with his experimental work, Smith had to gather arguments that could justify the use and relevance of the experimental method in economics:

> Why do we do what we do in the ways that we do it? None of my research outside of experimental economics required me to come to terms with this question. When you do mainstream research everyone takes for granted your right to do it. In confronting these issues I was led to write about them … This sort of writing seems inevitable if you want to convey some appreciation for the role of experiments in increasing economic understanding. It is not enough to just do experiments, and to report them, because they are not part of the culture of your audience.
>
> (Smith 1990: 5)

It would take him two decades until Smith was finally able to justify the role of experiments in increasing economic understanding, which he did, in 1982, in the seminal article 'Microeconomic Systems as an Experimental Science', published in *The American Economic Review*. Here Smith provides the first comprehensive depiction of the experimental field of economics (reviewed in Chapter 3), which at the time counted only on a few and partial attempts at doing so. In Smith's words:

> It is appropriate for this effort to have been modest, since it has been more important for experimentalists to present a rich variety of examples of their work than abstract explanations of why one might perform experiments. … This seems to be the time and place to attempt a more

complete description of the methodology and function of experiments in microeconomics.

(Smith 1982: 923)

But Smith started arguing for the experimental method of economics when he first reported his market experiments. In his first experimental article, Smith (1962) built a coherent line of argumentation in support of both experimental results and the experimental method (as shown in Chapter 3). Eleven experiments were reported, not only to demonstrate that sufficient evidence had been collected to support the main result, but also to argue for the legitimacy of the experimental method. The market experiments and the experimental method were simultaneously grounded on a *three-way coherence* supported by different experimental designs, each of which yielded the same result: convergence of the experimental market to equilibrium.

The resistance encountered had nothing to do with the controversy surrounding the experimental results. The results obtained provided supporting evidence for a well-established theory. The problem was that the experimental data were not considered valid. The idea of an economics experiment was simply foreign to the whole profession. But even if economists had been willing to consider the experimental method, Smith's results would have been deemed uninteresting. They provided empirical support for a theory that was widely shared. The first published report of market experiments can, therefore, be more adequately perceived as a first attempt at justifying the use of the experimental method in economics, rather than an empirical test of competitive price theory.

Smith was cautious in deriving implications from his first set of experiments. The market experiments were presented as tentative testing devices, which needed further experimental work. The experimental market was described as a 'simulation' that attempted to capture essential aspects of real markets. The data generated constituted evidence for the success of competitive price theory in predicting equilibrium in experimental markets and in these markets only. No further implications were derived. The theory simply predicts well therein.

Smith was more concerned with explaining the concept of an economics experiment. To that end, the experimental design and procedure were carefully described with the help of the conventional supply and demand charts depicting the crucial aspects of the experiments. The experimental data (i.e. the experimental contract prices for each trading period) were presented with the use of diagrams. This was rhetorically ingenious. After all, Smith's experiments are all about markets, supply and demand curves, and equilibria – the key concepts of economics!

This strategy was followed in subsequent market experiments where Smith provided careful reports of his experiments that continued to argue for the validity of previous results, the experimental method and competitive price theory (Smith 1964, 1965, 1967). Only gradually did Smith start compiling arguments that justified the use of the experimental method in economics.

Being the hallmark of the experimental method, it is not surprising that control was the first methodological issue Smith addressed. In his 'Induced Value Theory' (1976a), Smith identifies a set of sufficient conditions for experimental control, namely for controlling the motives of the experimental subjects. The key idea is that experimenters can ensure that subjects have the right motives with the proper design of a reward structure that induces prescribed monetary value on experimental variables and that gives the property right over the monetary outcomes of the actions taken during the experiment. Having addressed the central methodological question of economic experiments, Smith then began to answer the criticisms of sceptics who claimed that 'experimental markets have nothing to do with real economies'. How Smith dealt with these criticisms is the topic of the next chapter, for now I will take a closer look at how Smith presented his 'complete description of the methodology and function of experiments in microeconomics' that rounds up the arguments available circa 1982.

Given that the experimental method had been non-existent in economics, its justification had to have recourse to items of scientific culture with which economists were familiar. Welfare economics was an important and obvious persuasive argument in this respect. Moreover, welfare economists, were they persuadable, could be important allies at the time, given their influence in the profession. As we will see below, the founders of Welfare Economics, such as Kenneth Arrow, Jacob Marschak, Tjalling Koopmans, and Leonid Hurwicz, were all research associates at the Cowles Commission who had direct contact with other pioneers of the experimental method who were members of the RAND Corporation.

Mechanism design theory lent itself as an obvious resource in that it could be easily presented as the theoretical counterpart of experimental economics. The justification of the new experimental field relied on what Stanley Reiter (1977) called '(New)^2 Welfare Economics' and, in particular, on Leonid Hurwicz's 'Informational Efficiency of Resource Allocation Mechanisms' (1960). The main difference between (New)^2 Welfare Economics and received Welfare Economics was that the latter had been focusing on the conditions characterizing Pareto optimality and on demonstrations that the equilibria of competitive mechanisms meet these conditions. The new approach aimed instead to focus on the evaluation of alternative mechanisms, using as criteria not only the efficiency of resulting allocations, but also the system's administrative feasibility, compatibility with private incentives, the costs of operating with it, and so forth (Reiter 1977: 226).

(New)^2 Welfare Economics, therefore, provided a formal framework for the comparative appraisal of alternative allocation mechanisms, which became 'the unknown of the problem, rather than a datum' (Hurwicz 1960: 28). The similarity between (New)^2 Welfare Economics and experimental economics is striking. Whereas the new field of welfare economics provides a theoretical framework for the design and evaluation of resource allocation mechanisms, experimental economics provides an experimental framework to the same effect.

Not only did the new approach to welfare economics give experimental economics a recognizable framework that could be used to present and justify the goals of experimental economics, it also suggested potential allies who could be easily persuaded. Smith indeed attempted to attract the interest of mechanism design theorists, who could more easily understand the interest of the experimental method to test market mechanisms. This is very clear in Smith's article co-authored with Charles Plott (1978), in which both research programmes are presented as being concerned with 'the analysis of information and organization in decentralized price adjustment processes'. The experimental method, in particular, was presented as 'a "proving ground" for theories' (p. 133) and 'an empirical challenge for those interested in price adjustment processes' (p. 147). The appeal to mechanism design theorists continues as Smith (1980b) proposes to 'develop a foundation for the study of resource allocation mechanisms' (p. 345) in an article with the expressive title 'Relevance of Laboratory Experiments to Testing Resource Allocation Theory'. But welfare economists did not seem to have responded to the challenge.[3]

(New)^2 Welfare Economics was, however, a valuable theoretical resource that helped experimenters to justify the function and role of experiments in economics and that was first mobilized by Louis Wilde (1981). It was Wilde who presented experimental economics as the experimental counterpart of the new approach to welfare economics. It was Wilde who first stated that 'a laboratory experiment in economics attempts to create and study a small-scale microeconomic environment ... [whose] purpose is to uncover systematic relationships between individual preferences, institutional parameters, and outcomes' (p. 139). Wilde therefore played a very important role in bringing together the relevant items of scientific culture to construct an articulated framework that justified the use of experiments in economics. From Wilde (1981) it was only a small step for Smith to round up the extant contributions and put forward a theory of laboratory experiments, as he did in his 'Microeconomic Systems as an Experimental Science'.

The early arguments Smith put forward in defence of experimental economics therefore relied on the persuasive force of a coherent association between an emerging and well-received theoretical research programme and the contested experimental method. The point was simply that experimenters are only doing what theoreticians do by different means.

Besides the coherent relation established with an emerging field of theoretical research, Smith also mobilized non-economic items of scientific culture to argue for the relevance of the experimental method. Of particular interest is the evocation of the similarity between economics and other sciences, such as astronomy and meteorology, neither of which could interfere with their macro-objects of interest (e.g. climate), but could bring micro-scale experiments (e.g. on the thermodynamics properties of gases) to bear on macro-scale phenomena (1982: 936). From the philosophy of science, Smith adopts the Kaplan taxonomy to present the methodological uses of laboratory experiments (1982: 940). Finally, Smith mobilizes the falsificationist rhetoric, quite popular among economists at that time (Blaug 1992 [1980]), to stress the importance of submitting theories to the test and the role of experiments to that end.

It is easy to see that Smith adopted a rather conservative strategy. He appealed to scientific worldviews, economic theories, and philosophical and methodological principles, as well as discursive practices that the community of economists could find persuasive at the time. The evolution of the experimental study of market mechanisms shows, however, that the strategy was not very effective. Experimental economics continued to be a largely autonomous practice with a 'life of its own'.

But Smith succeeded in attracting the interest of young researchers who could foresee the potential of the experimental method. One important collaborator was Charles Plott, a young colleague who arrived at Purdue in the late 1960s, and who would later give an important contribution to the field. Plott not only joined Smith in dealing with the first wave of criticisms targeted at the experimental method, as we shall see in the next chapter, but he also helped expand the domain of application of the experimental method to other areas such as social choice theory, public economics and much of political science (Plott 1979; Fiorina and Plott 1978; Plott and Levine 1978). Other important collaborators were Arlington Williams, James Cox, Kevin McCabe and Stephen Rassenti, among many others, with whom Smith established new partnerships when he moved to the University of Arizona in 1975. In 2001, Smith finally expanded his network of co-practitioners to George Mason University. But by this time the experimental method had become an established field of economics. He no longer had to justify why he carried out market experiments.[4]

The early beginnings of experimental economics

The branch of market experimentation initiated by Chamberlin in 1948 and then taken up by Vernon Smith was critical to define and establish the standards for experimental practice in economics. But it is remarkable that the three grand categories of economic experiments emerged with equivalent expression at about the same time, notwithstanding some earlier dispersed breakthroughs. It is no coincidence, however, that *individual decision-making experiments* and *game theory experiments* came out at the same time and grew in tandem. The reason is that they share a major theoretical breakthrough: John von Neumann's and Oskar Morgenstern's *Theory of Games and Economic Behavior* (1944), which gave economists a theory that generated an array of new predictions that were suitable for experimental research.

The first incursions in the field of *individual decision-making experiments* indeed aimed at testing the axioms of expected utility theory developed by von Neumann and Morgenstern in their *Theory of Games and Economic Behavior* and further developed by Savage (1954). An important contributor associated with the origins of this branch of research is Maurice Allais (1953), whose name became associated with probably the best known 'anomaly' to expected utility theory – the Allais paradox[5] – which caught the interest of economists for the experimental study of the violations of expected utility theory. Ever since, individual choice experiments have been prolific in collecting 'anomalies' and a most inspiring field for the development of new theories.[6] Earlier references of *game theory experiments* include Melvin Dresher and Merrill Flood's test of what subsequently came to be famously known as the prisoner's dilemma (Flood 1958), the n-person games by Gerhard K. Kalisch, John W. Milnor, John F. Nash, and E. D. Nering (1954) and the coordination games by Thomas Schelling (1957).

In the historical recollections of the field, it emerges that the development of game theory and the openness of game theorists to cross-disciplinary collaboration were two critical factors in the development of experimental economics (Friedman and Sunder 1994; Roth 1995a; Dimand 2005; Rizvi 2005). Game theory is deemed to have had a crucial role in making economics experimental because its variables were particularly suited to experimental control. Indeed, games define decision problems with a relatively simple structure and precise assumptions about the behaviour of individuals, which are easily implemented in the lab. For example, the ultimatum game is a very simple problem that consists of the partition of a particular sum of money between two individuals where one individual proposes a division of the amount and the other either accepts or, by rejecting, determines zero gains for both of them. Moreover, game theory urgently needed new tools for choosing among competing principles. Finally, game theorists are praised for having been more open to new approaches, as they were more used to doing interdisciplinary work, and thus for envisioning the potential of the interplay between experiment and theory.

An important factor that contributed to the birth of this symbiotic relationship between game theory and experimental economics is the broader context of research carried out under the banner of the RAND Corporation.[7] In the late 1940s, right after the Second World War, the RAND Corporation re-oriented its research to peacetime, selecting the field of 'cybernetics' as its privileged area of investigation. The goal was to further the application of mathematics to a wider range of human affairs. It included computer science, artificial intelligence, information theory, mathematical economics, mathematical learning theory, game theory, automata theory and operations research. This context was important for the development of experimental economics because it provided a favourable environment in which to do cross-disciplinary work, and, especially, it gave game theorists and economists the opportunity to acquaint themselves with experimental methods in other social sciences, namely in experimental psychology.

But the initial interest in introducing empirical techniques into economics did not come from game theorists, as Herbert Simon, a privileged observer, explicitly put it:

> I do not think that the impetus for experimentation within a game-theoretical framework initially came from economists, but rather from psychologists

> (particularly those who had begun to build mathematical learning theory), statisticians, and interdisciplinary types close to cybernetics and management science ... Experiments, of course, came naturally to psychologists – that is the way they learned to do science.
>
> (Simon quoted in Smith 1992: 253–54)

Game theory, however, played the critical role of bringing game theorists into close contact with scientists interested in the same matters and with backgrounds in various areas of empirical science (Dimand 2005). This explains the fact that the early contributions to game theory and experimental economics mentioned above were researchers or consultants at the RAND Corporation or had contact with its researchers through various means, such as in seminars and conferences.

The 1952 Santa Monica Seminar, eloquently entitled 'The Design of Experiments in Decision Processes', is exemplary in this respect. It aimed to provide a forum that would stimulate empirical research and further theoretical development. It represented the first relevant exchange of experimental research on a larger scale. It brought together RAND researchers, researchers from Princeton and Michigan, which were at the time two leading universities in game theory (Howard Raiffa, Oskar Morgenstern, John Nash, John von Neumann, Lloyd Shapley and Martin Shubik), and researchers from the Cowles Commission in Chicago (Kenneth Arrow, Gerard Debreu, Leonid Hurwicz, Tjalling Koopmans, Jacob Marschak and Herbert Simon) (Dimand 2005).[8] Its success was modest, however (Smith 1992). The conference proceedings, *Decision Processes* (Thrall *et al.* 1954), contained only five experimental papers out of the nineteen papers contributed. Interest in game theory at RAND subsided in the late 1950s because it no longer seemed fruitful for military research. But it nonetheless marked the subsequent evolution of the experimental field of research.

Philip Mirowski (2002: 545–51), for instance, takes Smith's market experiments as a product of the 'cyborg science' practised at the RAND Corporation. The marks of cyborg science are present, in his view, in the treatment of social interactions as games between isolated asocial subjects and in their study through the mediation of computers and simulations. It is also present in the methodological principles of experimental economics that imposes 'mechanical rationality' on experimental subjects whose exchanges occur in 'machine-like' market institutions.

The methodological principles of experimental economics were in fact stabilized around this time. The joint work of the economist Lawrence Fouraker and the psychologist Sidney Siegel, of Pennsylvania State University, was, in this regard, of particular importance even though this collaboration did not last long due to Siegel's early death. But their early work on bargaining in bilateral monopoly and oligopoly (Siegel and Fouraker 1960; Fouraker and Siegel 1963) did contribute to set the basic principles of experimental economics that still characterize current practice: the careful design of instructions and their inclusion in research reports; the enforcement of anonymity; and the use of monetary incentives (Smith 1992: 247).[9]

The symbiotic relation between game theory and experimental economics is further supported by their simultaneous recognition in the 1980s. As, S. Abu Turab Rizvi (2005) argues, economists only took experimentation seriously when the influence of general equilibrium theory subsided. The reason for this was that experimentation did not fit within the framework of general equilibrium theory, which had dominated economics until then, and which already had an empirical method of its own, econometrics. Theories were to be constructed deductively from basic axioms and theoretical conclusions tested with field data.

Experimental economics and other fields became important during the late 1970s and early 1980s, when new approaches started to be developed. By this time game theory already provided a theoretical framework on which theory and experiment could interact and inspire each other. Game theory experiments have since uncovered systematic violations of theory and have been also an important source of theoretical development. Theories of other-regarding behaviour that incorporate 'non-economic' factors such as fairness considerations and the evolutionary models of learning and adaptive behaviour are among some such examples, as we shall see in Chapter 10.

Experimental work in economics also has a 'life of its own'. This is well illustrated by market experiments (Chapter 6). Smith's first market experiments led to a whole research programme devoted to the study of market institutions. As we have seen, this research programme has produced its own resources for practice. It stabilized experimental principles and procedures, benchmarks and stylized facts, which became the scientific culture of the field of research.

The focus of this chapter has been on Smith's trajectory and its context. But before concluding, it should be mentioned that the foundation of experimental economics is not an American historical episode. Early incursions of experimental research in economics also took place in Europe and at about the same time. A key reference is the seminal work by Reinhard Selten, who started his experimental practice in the 1960s and was the leading figure of the first European laboratory set up in Bonn in 1986. Research in Europe took quite a different path, however. It was more oriented towards understanding behavioural processes, rather than individual or aggregate outcomes (Friedman and Sunder 1994: 127–28). It focused on individual decision-making and, especially, on Simon's approach to bounded rationality. This geographical demarcation has become blurred in recent years, as new experimental labs have been opening in Europe and elsewhere. The growth of the field of Behavioural Economics in recent years also testifies to the wider recognition of the relevance of behavioural studies to economics (more on this in Chapter 11).

Conclusion

The historical incursion into the birth of laboratory experimentation in economics shows that the post-war period provided particularly favourable conditions for its emergence. It favoured interdisciplinary work that could be carried out under the auspices of well-organized institutions. But it not only promoted interdisciplinary work, it also promoted work of a particular kind. It brought mathematically minded scientists into close contact with researchers with an empirical background for whom experimentation was the natural way to do science. This, then, explains the characteristics of a significant branch of experimental economics.

The foundation of the field of experimental research in economics has also been a long, collective endeavour. Experimenters had to become full experts in the new method before they were able to justify and build the methodological foundations for it. Three decades of research were needed to stabilize the fields' aims, standards, and conceptual and instrumental tools, which would assist economists in evaluative judgments about the experimental procedures used to elicit interesting economic phenomena, and thus determine the status of the phenomena as facts or artefacts. Experimental economists also had to wait for the opportunity to fill the space left open by the dominant theoretical and empirical research programmes.

The development of experimental economics owes a debt too to the social processes of criticism and to the scepticism encountered. It was this scepticism that motivated Smith to produce robust results that could face up to the criticism of the sceptics and ultimately to present an articulated theory of experimentation in economics. The methodological foundations of experimental economics, as put forward by Vernon Smith in his 1982 seminal paper, are the result of coherent achievements that articulate his experience and that of others. At the same time, Smith appealed to what he perceived as the dominant values of potential allies. Not all arguments were found persuasive, however. Various research programmes are now carried out by different subspecialities, each of which pursues its own research agenda. The experimental method has thus become a tool for research assuring wider application. In the next chapter we will see how Smith and his collaborators responded to the charge that economics experiments have nothing to do with the 'real world'.

8 Early methodological debate in experimental economics

The social epistemology of experiment (SEE) identifies as the main sources of epistemic value of any experiment the direct participation of its subject matter and the collaborative nature of knowledge production. These two factors create possibilities for the manifestation of both 'material' and 'social' resistances that force experimenters to conceive of and answer relevant questions, and thereby produce more reliable and robust experimental results.

In this chapter I spell out the contribution of each factor to experimental economics and mobilize them to examine early methodological debates. I focus in particular on the debates that questioned the relevance of experiments and the arguments put forward to justify the adequacy of economics experiments to test theories. I show that the discussion carried out by the experimenters themselves failed to provide full-blown arguments. They were instead defensive responses that did not satisfactorily answer the critical charges.

Control and the participation of subjects in experiments

We have seen that control is the defining feature of scientific experimentation. It allows for producing data with a more direct bearing on the problems in which scientists are interested. In economics, experiments allow the creation of a manageable microeconomic system in the laboratory to study the fourfold relationship 'environment (e) – institution (I) – behaviour (m) – outcomes (X)', which has for long been central to economic analysis but which was largely unobservable and undetectable by non-experimental means (cf. Figure 3.1). This means that economics experiments allow for studying the relation among the attributes of economic agents, the set of rules of communication and exchange whereby they interact with one another, the actions they take under those rules, and the performance of microeconomic systems.

The measurement of environmental variables, namely of individual preferences, knowledge and technological endowments, could not be rigorously measured with field data. This is so because the use of field data is highly sensitive to the specifications of econometric models, and thus 'the particular model chosen inevitably must be influenced partly by the technical requirements of the methodology and not only by the scientific objectives of the exercise' (Smith 1982: 929).[1]

Moreover, the work required to convert non-experimental data into useful information on the problem at hand is highly sensitive to scientists' prior beliefs. In the face of ambiguous results, there is a high likelihood that economists improve the model's fit with 'reasonable expectations'. As a result, 'the whole process becomes an exercise in fitting a particular belief system to field data by manipulating model specifications and perhaps estimation methods' (Smith 1982: 929, n. 8).[2]

The study of the relation 'environment (e) – institution (I) – behaviour (m) – outcomes (X)' is possible due to the exercise of a high level of control over the institution and the environment. We have seen that economists control the institution by designing and enforcing the rules of communication and exchange that define the experimental task and how it is to be carried out. They control subjects' preferences by paying subjects in accordance to the outcomes of the actions they take during the experiment in a context of relative anonymity. In this way experimenters induce self-interested reward-maximizing motives onto experimental subjects. A controlled experiment in economics hence elicits behaviour that can be interpreted in the light of motives induced by the reward structure and the institution that organizes subjects' interactions. Experimenters can then understand how the environment and the institution translate into individual behaviour and how this, in turn, affects the performance of the microeconomy.

The direct participation of human subjects is the major source of epistemic value of economics experiments. It is this participation that makes it difficult to 'fit a particular belief system' to experimental data. Participants in economics experiments may behave differently from the behaviour postulated by economic theory and induced in the laboratory. They may 'resist' economists' expectations and thereby prevent experimental results from being exclusively determined by their material and conceptual interventions in the experimental microeconomic systems. The tight control exercised over subjects' preferences (via the reward structure) and subjects' actions (via the microeconomic institution) substantially reduces the 'resistance' of the participants in experiments (recall Smith's double-auction experiment in Chapter 6). But it does not follow from this that participants cannot resist or that the epistemic value of economic experiments calls for a different explanation.

Strict adherence to the methodological prescriptions of experimental economics does not ensure that individuals are self-interested income-maximizers, that they succeed in taking the course of action that best suits their interests, or that some desired social goal is reached. For one thing, subjects' motivations are multiple and not always effectively controlled by the experimenters. In addition, the cognitive limitations of individuals and the complexity of the decision-making process may prevent them from perceiving and pursuing the best course of action. And even when perceived and pursued, the best courses of action may produce undesirable collective outcomes. That is, experimental participants may behave in a non-self-interested manner and thus fail to maximize the experimental pay-off, or by behaving self-interestedly they may produce socially undesirable outcomes. It is precisely this potential mismatch between individual preferences and individual actions (e.g. Allais paradox), or between individual actions and aggregate outcomes (e.g. antitrust phenomena), where the relevance of microeconomic experiments lies. The goal of experimenting with microeconomic systems is precisely to study the factors that affect the alignment between individual preferences, individual actions and some desired social goal. Not to mention that an economics experiment may also have as a goal learning how to control human behaviour for certain purposes. In this case, the purpose of the experiment is to learn how to align individual preferences and individual actions to attain some desired social end (e.g. market design).

To conclude, the participation of experimental subjects is the main source of epistemic value of an economics experiment. It is the major factor that causes 'resistances' to economists' expectations and thereby contributes to the production of knowledge of human behaviour in particular socioeconomic contexts. Insofar as experimenters control human behaviour by inducing self-interest and income-maximizing behaviour, the participation of subjects in economics experiments allows for the identification of the circumstances that affect the manifestation of this behaviour.

The social dimension of experimental economics

Experimental work in economics is now part of 'normal science'. Economists know how to do work that can be recognized as legitimate in the field. They know which problems to select and how to solve them, and professional judgment is made in a relatively consensual way by means of fairly stable and shared criteria. This means, however, that the scope of the experimental method of economics is fairly circumscribed to problem-situations that can be framed within its overarching 'paradigm', that is, problem-situations that can be conceptualized within the framework of a microeconomic experiment and the fourfold relationship mentioned above (cf. Chapter 3).

Besides the enforcement of the socially established practices by the relevant institutions, of particular relevance to the present purposes is the examination of the collective nature of knowledge production in experimental economics. In economics, experimental claims to knowledge are generated in a fundamentally interactive way by series of experiments through which economists build upon one another's results. The adoption and adapting of previous experiments is thus a pervasive practice in the design of new experiments, which perhaps finds no parallel in other experimental disciplines or in other economics methods.

Two factors explain this characteristic of experimental economics: (1) the fact that practitioners share a fairly stable and consolidated basis for knowledge production, and (2) the high degree of exposure of the process of knowledge production to public scrutiny. This exposure is facilitated by the complete reporting of economics experiments in scientific journals and the shared norm of rendering relevant information available upon request (cf. Davis and Holt 1993: 22). Thus, in addition to the instructions given to subjects, experimenters may also have access to information regarding the recruitment of subjects, the implementation of trial tests, the composition of the subject pool and subjects' experience level, the procedures used for matching subjects to roles, the use of computers and other devices, experimental data, and so forth.

The most adequate unit of analysis in experimental economics should, then, be series of experiments that define a given research area, rather than the single experiment. The incremental way in which knowledge is produced by series of experiments emerges very clearly in surveys of the field (e.g. Kagel and Roth 1995). It is therefore not surprising that its epistemic value is explicitly stressed by experimental economists. Here is how Alvin E. Roth, an experienced experimenter and surveyor of experimental economics, presents it:

> For the first time [in the 1950s], there began to be a wide variety of areas in which different groups of experimenters began to study the same issues from different points of view. This meant that there began to be series of experiments in which investigators with different hypotheses responded to one another's experiments, critically examining earlier conclusions. It is this process, in which experimental results suggest new experiments and in which different points of view suggest different experiments to different groups of experimenters, that allows us to begin to look back on experimental economics as a cumulative process. *This kind of dialogue is one of the great sources of strength of the experimental method.*
>
> (Roth 1995a: 21, emphasis added)

The incremental way whereby experimental knowledge is produced follows a well-defined pattern. In the early stages of a research programme, not much is known about the means and the results of experimental practice, and as a result, there is ample room for disagreement. At first, follow-up experiments investigate whether or not the experimental phenomenon is to be attributed to an artefact of the experimental procedure. This normally calls for the re-examination of the standard procedures of experimental economics, especially so if the phenomenon seems to disconfirm a well-established theory. Experimenters then check instructions for lack of clarity, subjects' inexperience, adequacy of the reward structure, and other familiar sources of 'error'. If the phenomenon remains recalcitrant, attention is directed to investigating its causal factors. Only at a later stage, when the results are better understood, do experimenters try to put forward and test tentative explanatory hypotheses. Earlier results may then be reinterpreted, areas of disagreement narrowed down, and what were apparently conflicting results may eventually be integrated into a more general and complete account. Or, on the contrary, the conditions under which the phenomenon occurs may be more narrowly defined and earlier conclusions may be entirely reinterpreted. At any rate, series of experiments eventually lead to more robust and socially validated conclusions. (In Chapter 12 this pattern is illustrated in more detail, with the preference reversals programme.)

Not only is experimental economics an intrinsically social process of knowledge production, as I have just described, but also the collective nature of knowledge production and assessment also performs the epistemic role of controlling the effect of 'background beliefs'. Again, this is explicitly noted by experimenters. As Roth notes,

> [s]ince decisions made in the design of the experiment cannot be regarded as random samples from the space of possible design choices, *there is room for an experimenter's prior beliefs about the likely outcome of the experiment to influence the outcome, through these design decisions* ... The reason is that the designer of an experiment may have to make many particular decisions, and choose the level of many parameters that may affect the phenomena under study. If there is reason to believe that the resulting observations depend in important ways on some of these choices, variations may be incorporated into the experimental design, or into subsequent experiments, to see if this is the case.
>
> (Roth 1988: 1023, emphasis added)

The effect of experimenters' prior beliefs is not as problematic in experimental economics because it can be identified and checked by other experimenters. If there is the suspicion that a given result is caused by some arbitrary decision, this suspicion can be clarified by the design of more experiments. By conducting series of experiments, experimenters can clarify the points of contention and build up collectively confidence in their experimental claims to knowledge.

Not only does subjective belief not jeopardize the experimental enterprise, it can also be an epistemic asset if it promotes the scrutiny of experiments conducted by others. This requires a critical community of economists, which depends greatly on the community's pool of prior commitments. As Roth puts it, 'experimentation is well served by skeptical readers and particularly by experimenters with different theoretical predispositions' (1988: 1024).

To conclude, the epistemic value of experiments stems from the participation of experimental subjects and from the high degree of exposure of experiments to critical scrutiny. The participation of experimental subjects allows for more direct measurement of variables pertaining to individual preferences, technology and commodity endowments, and thus the study of the relation among individual attributes, institutions and behaviour. The exposure of experiments to critical scrutiny favours the identification of conscious and unconsciously held beliefs and the arbitrariness of decisions taken in the course of experiment. In so doing, it promotes the autonomy of the results from particular sets of beliefs and practices and thereby promotes the replicability and robustness of experimental results. But we have not yet discussed for what purposes experimenters create microeconomic systems in the lab. This is the issue to which I now turn.

The roles of experiment

Even though different taxonomies have been proposed to classify experiments according to their role and function in economics, the main purposes of experiments are: (1) to test economic theory, (2) to produce stylized facts, (3) to provide understanding of the real world, and (4) to produce proposals for policy-making.

Borrowing Kaplan's taxonomy, Smith's (1982) classification draws a distinction between experimental work that can be framed within a well-established theory, a known phenomenal domain or standard methodological procedures, and marginal experimental work. The former kind of research includes *nomothetic experiments,* which establish the 'laws' of behaviour suggested by theory or by observed empirical regularities in the field, and *boundary experiments,* which establish the limits of generality of a theory and identify important extensions in theory (p. 942). *Heuristic experiments* explore new topics of inquiry. The main difference between heuristic experiments and the other experiments is that only the latter employ 'replication and rigorous control to reduce error', and thus 'provide the most compelling and objective means by which each of us, as scientists, comes to see what others see, and by which, together, we become sure of what it is that we think that we know' (p. 940). Heuristic experiments are, on the contrary, less likely to follow a rigorous design pattern. This is so because 'the objectives may not be as sharply defined by theory or by a hypothesized pattern which is thought to characterize previous experiments' or 'the procedural mechanics of the experiment may be new and untested' (pp. 941–42). These experiments may, however, be an important source of new discoveries because '[it] is through exploratory probes of new phenomena that attention may be redirected, old belief systems may be re-examined, and new scientific questions may be asked' (p. 942).

Based on the experiments' intended audience, Roth (1995a: 21–23), for example, classifies three kinds of experiment: 'speaking to theorists', 'searching for facts' and 'whispering in the ears of princes'. Experiments that speak to theorists produce results that aim to feedback into theoretical research. Experiments that search for facts explore unknown and badly understood phenomena about which existing theory is silent. Thus, whereas 'speaking to theorists' experiments engage experimental and theoretical economists, 'searching for facts' experiments 'are part of the dialogue that experimenters carry on with one another' (p. 22). Finally, the experiments that 'whisper in the ears of princes' address relevant issues for policy-making. According to Roth, '[t]heir characteristic feature is that the experimental environment is designed to closely resemble, in certain respects, the naturally occurring environment that is the focus of interest for the policy purposes at hand' (p. 22).

Similarly, Douglas D. Davis and Charles A. Holt (1993) distinguishes among the theoretically oriented tests of behavioural hypotheses, the search for empirical regularities, the theory stress tests that try to bridge 'the gap between laboratory and naturally occurring markets' (p. 19–20). Daniel Friedman and Shyam Sunder

(1994), along the same lines, identify as purposes of experiments the discovery of empirical regularities in areas where there is no theory, the testing of theories, the measurement of individual attributes, and 'test-bed experiments' as a new instrument of institutional engineering (pp. 7–9).

The various taxonomies thus evoke either the relation between experiment and theory or the relation between experiment and the real world. In the remainder of the chapter we will see how experimenters have justified the use of experiments to test theories. The relation between experiment and reality is addressed in the next chapter.

Experiment versus theory

Chapter 3 presented Smith's (1962) first market experiments that aimed to test competitive price theory. The experimental market was presented as an operational model of a competitive market that was used to check whether it converged to equilibrium. Because convergence was observed, Smith concluded that the theory predicts well therein. No arguments were presented to justify the adequacy of the experiment to perform the empirical testing of theories. Twenty years later, he presented the microeconomic experiment as a falsifying tool, which, a further twenty years later, became a more modest instrument for theoretical construction and development (Smith 1982, 2002). In the process, new arguments were adduced and presented to justify the relation between experiment and theory.

Falsificationism (Popper 1959 [1934], 1965 [1963]) has been a very popular methodology among economists.[3] It is, therefore, not surprising that experimental economists also mobilized falsificationist arguments to justify the use of experiments. Falsificationism depicts good scientific practice as consisting of the proposal of 'bold conjectures' and their submission to 'severe testing'. This means that economists should propose hypotheses that make low-probability predictions about the world and then deliberately attempt to produce evidence that falsifies the theory. If the test generates negative evidence, the theory is refuted and, as a result, it should be discarded and replaced by a new one. If the hypothesis survives the test, the theory is corroborated by experience, which means that the theory has thus far resisted attempts at falsification.

But Smith does not elaborate on how economics experiments can work as falsifying tools. Smith merely alludes to the falsifying power of economic experiments. He simply asserts that experimental microeconomies are adequate testing devices because they carry the potential for falsifying theories. Underlying the falsifying power of economics experiments seems to be the participation of the experimental subjects. He says:

> Microeconomic theory abstracts from a rich variety of human activities which are postulated not to be of relevance to human economic behavior. The experimental laboratory, precisely because it uses reward-motivated individuals drawn from the population of economic agents in the socio-economic system, consists of a far *richer* and more *complex* set of

> circumstances than is parameterized in our theories. Since the *abstractions* of the laboratory are orders of magnitude smaller than those of economic theory, there can be no question that *the laboratory provides ample possibilities for falsifying any theory we might wish to test.*
>
> (Smith 1982: 935–36, emphasis added)

The falsifying potential of experiments is, in Smith's view, due to the participation of experimental subjects who bring to the lab the richness and complexity that is characteristic of socioeconomic systems but which is absent in economics theories. The participation of experimental subjects renders experiments 'real' systems in that in the laboratory '*real* economic agents exchange *real* messages through *real* property right institutions that yield outcomes redeemable in *real* money' (1982: 935 emphasis added).

The mere evocation of the word 'real', or the increased levels of complexity of the laboratory relative to the theories under test, does not suffice to justify the adequacy of experiments as falsifying devices. It does not do the trick if it simply means the creation of a context wherein 'real rules' by way of 'real profits' induce in 'real people' the behaviour postulated by economic theory; as it did not in Smith's market experiments.

Smith does not spell out how and to what extent the 'reality' of microeconomic systems enhances the falsifying conditions of the experimental system. But from what has been discussed thus far, it is not difficult to see that the falsifying possibilities of experimental systems derive from the participation of experimental subjects whose behaviour may deviate from the behaviour postulated by economic theory. That is, the falsifying conditions of an economics experiment depend on the 'resistances' experimental participants pose to economists' expectations.

But underlying Smith's falsificationist rhetoric seems to be the idea that the mere participation of experimental subjects provides sufficient falsifying conditions to test economic theory. But it does not. To be a good falsifying tool, on Popper's terms, the experiment must constitute a genuine attempt at falsifying the theory under test. That is, the design of the experiment not only must allow, but it must also trigger falsifying behaviour. Only then can an experiment be considered a 'severe test'. A microeconomic experiment is certainly not an adequate test if it constrains the participation of experimental subjects in such a way that it renders virtually impossible the manifestation of falsifying behaviour. As we have seen, this was the case of Smith's early market experiments (Chapter 6). As a result, the experimental data did not even constitute compelling corroborating evidence.

Following recent philosophies of confirmation, Francesco Guala (2005a) synthesizes the conditions for the strength of inductive inferences from experimental evidence (e) to hypothesis (H) in the following way:

> A hypothesis H should be considered indicated (qualitatively) by the evidence e only if the test that produced e is such that there is a high

> probability of observing *e* if the hypothesis is true, and a low probability of observing *e* if it is false.
>
> (Guala 2005a: 117)

The strength of inductive inference hinges, in particular, on ensuring that the evidence obtained is not due to some background factor that 'interferes' to create the illusion of a phenomenon that does not exist.

The assessment of the strength of inductive inferences from experimental evidence brings to the fore the well-known problem of underdetermination, or the Duhem-Quine thesis, in philosophy of science, which spotlights the fact that the relation between an observational statement and a theoretical hypothesis is not of a deductive kind. The test of an empirical hypothesis is always a conjoint test of a target hypothesis (e.g. a competitive market tends to equilibrium) together with a variety of auxiliary hypotheses (e.g. the experimental subjects understood the task at hand). Thus, when experimenters obtain negative data for the hypothesis under test they do not know which hypothesis(es) is(are) falsified. Conversely, a positive result does not provide strong corroborative support for the target hypothesis. To put it in another way, evidence is as fallible as theory is, and therefore a clash between theory and evidence does not have sufficient disproving force, especially if the theory is well established. Consequently, when experimental data conflict with ingrained and expected beliefs, scientists question empirical results instead.

The problem of underdetermination was not unknown to experimental economists. In subsequent work, Smith shows he is fully aware of it:

> When the data are consistent with the predictions of a theory, it is sometimes said that the results are not interesting because they merely confirm what economists already knew ... which seems to suggest that "truly" authoritative theory cannot be doubted seriously. When the data are inconsistent with the predictions of theory it is not uncommon to assert that there must be "something" wrong with the experiments. ... questions about experimental procedure are more likely to be raised when the results appear to disconfirm accepted theory than when they appear to confirm such theory.
>
> (Smith 1989: 167–68)

Awareness that falsificationism did not provide the most adequate methodology to account for and guide experimental practice is noticeable in Smith's later writings. From a falsifying instrument, the microeconomic experiment then became a tool for theoretical 'extension' with increased 'empirical content' within the realm of a given research programme. The Lakatosian methodology of scientific research programmes (Lakatos 1970) hence became the new model of good scientific practice:

> In any confrontation between theory and observation the theory may work or fail to work ... when it works, you lean mightily upon the theory

> with more challenging 'boundary' experiments designed to uncover the edges of validity of the theory where certainty gives way to uncertainty and thereby lays the basis for extensions in the theory that increase its empirical content. … When the theory fails to work in initial tests, the research program is essentially the same. This is because all theories can be expected to be more or less improvable, and statistical tests of theories, whether the results are initially "falsifying" or not, are simply the means to motivate extensions in theory. Better theory that narrows the distance between theory and observation is always welcome.
>
> (Smith 1989: 152)

Not only could the more tenable methodology of scientific research programmes better account for the practice of economists, who do not really reject theories on the basis of experimental data, but it could also make the more reasonable claim that experimental economics has been part of progressive research programmes and that experimenters do what can be expected of them. Whatever the results of experiments, the ultimate goal is to increase the theory's empirical content. This can be done either by pushing the edge of the theory's validity when it resists falsification or by modifying the theory in the light of refuting evidence.

In the course of his methodological reflections, Smith finally acknowledges the social dimension of experimentation in economics. He explicitly states that the underdetermination problem is resolved collectively by series of experiments. Experimenters' 'natural instincts and lively professional interactions lead them perpetually to design new experiments that examine the right questions' (2002: 91). He says:

> [e]xperimentalists design new experiments with the intention of confronting the issues in the controversy, and in the conflicting views that have arisen in interpreting the previous results. This leads to new experimental knowledge of how results are influenced, or not, by changes in procedures, context, instructions and control protocols … This process is driven by the D-Q problem, but practitioners need have no knowledge of the philosophy of science literature to take the right next local steps in the laboratory. Myopia here is not a handicap. … The bottom line is that good-enough solutions emerge to the baffling infinity of possibilities, as new measuring systems emerge, experimental tool kits are updated, and understanding is sharpened.
>
> (Smith 2002: 103–4)

Even though the arguments for the use of experiments as testing tools have been superficial, they are based on the two epistemic factors of experiments. The social epistemology of experiment can now assist in providing a more articulated justification.

Economics experiments can provide good testing conditions for economic theories because they are controllable systems that can be made to bear on theoretical hypotheses. The transparency of experimental systems and their exposure to critical scrutiny facilitate the identification and check of auxiliary hypotheses. Alternative interpretations of results can be examined and discriminated by the design of new experiments. Participation of experimental subjects in turn conveys epistemic value to the results obtained. Experimental subjects can behave differently from the behaviour postulated by economic theories and thereby produce results that disconfirm theoretical predictions. The design of the experiment, however, should not constrain participants' actions to the extent that it prevents observing the behaviour that is being tested. The strength of both negative and positive evidence for a given hypothesis depends on the extent to which experimental results were generated by the actions of the experimental subjects rather than those of the experimenters (this topic is developed extensively in Chapters 10 and 11).

The 'simplicity' and the 'artificiality' criticisms

The relation between theory and experiment has also been discussed in debates that do not directly address the purposes of experiments. It has appeared in the more radical discussions about the relevance of economics experiments. Initially, the community of economists doubted that experiments can provide any relevant knowledge. The doubts and criticisms were varied and they carry different implications, but they all point to the distance between the laboratory and the 'real world'. To simplify, they are here organized under the labels of the *simplicity* and the *artificiality* criticisms. Whereas the former targets the simplicity of the laboratory and its failure to capture the complexity of 'real world' environments, the latter denies at the outset the possibility of generating any meaningful knowledge in the artificial conditions of the laboratory.

These debates have, however, been rather asymmetrical in that the critiques levelled against the experimental method of economics have not been translated into fully articulated and published arguments. The criticisms appear only implicitly in experimenters' written responses to them.

The simplicity criticism is less damaging to experimental economics. Two versions can be identified. One version argues that the experimental situation can never capture the complexity of real-world situations. The experimental microeconomy is a simple and neutral context of interaction in which subjects guided by self-interest and reward-maximizing motivations make fairly abstract decisions. In real-world contexts, in contrast, human motivations are heterogeneous and dependent on the specificity of the situations. The attention experimenters dedicate to the design of the experiment testifies for this. They are devoted to controlling human motivations, which are multiple and context-dependent. Given the analogy of this criticism with heterodox critiques to mainstream economic theories, this is dubbed the *'heterodox' simplicity criticism*.[4]

A second version of the simplicity criticism argues that the experimental context does not create the necessary conditions to generate self-interested motivations and maximizing behaviour, which are deemed to characterize experienced economic agents of the real world. Because this criticism may be voiced by economists when confronted with evidence refuting mainstream economic theory, it is dubbed here as the *'orthodox' simplicity criticism*. Graham Loomes provides a very eloquent depiction of this criticism by a fictional sceptic, which is worth quoting at length:

> You take a group of people – whatever people come most readily to hand – and trust them into an artificial and unfamiliar situation. You then describe the experiment, perhaps getting them to read through several pages of instructions, followed by some test questions and/or a few minutes of "practice time". Then you set them going, with no real opportunity to acclimatize to the situation or think things through, still less to take advice and plan some course(s) of action. Instead, they have to go straight into action. ... But the real world differs from your experimental environment in certain important ways. If I'm going to enter into negotiations about something that matters to me, I'll think out my strategy and tactics carefully in advance. If I'm searching for a job, a house, a car or some other major item of expenditure, I'll engage in a rather more varied and sophisticated search procedure than your experimenters allow ... I'll lay out the alternatives carefully, think about the possible consequences, take advice if necessary, and weigh up the pros and cons until I reach a considered balanced judgment.
>
> (Loomes 1991: 598)

The *artificiality criticism* presents a more damaging attack to economics experiments. The problem, in this view, is not that experimental subjects behave or fail to behave as economic agents in the lab; it is rather that the behaviour elicited in the lab is substantially different from behaviour in 'real world' situations. This is so because human behaviour is highly sensitive to context and the lab is a very special one. Nikos Siakantaris, for example, argued that the 'laboratory is not a socially neutral context, but is itself an institution with its own formal or informal, explicit or tacit rules' and therefore 'the laboratory is itself a special kind of society' and one distorted by 'the idea of experimenting with humans' (2000: 274–75). To use again the words of a fictitious sceptic, artificial criticism can go like this:

> They know that you're running an experiment, and so they know you're looking for something. Despite your protestations, they may believe there is *a* right answer which will be rewarded. Or they may want to please you, or create a favourable impression of themselves. Or they may simply feel pressure to do *something*, and so they look for cues, and seize upon whatever the experimental design (consciously or unconsciously) suggests

> to them. At best, their behavior is a first approximation, vulnerable to all kinds of biases from extraneous sources and from the way the experiment is set up and the way the decision problems are framed.
>
> (Loomes 1991: 598, emphasis in original)

The artificiality criticism hinges on an important distinction between the natural and the human sciences. In the human sciences scientific experimentation involves human beings who are conscious individuals whose behaviour depends on how they perceive the situation they are in and how they more or less consciously behave in it. Consequently, the artificial context in which subjects interact has a non-negligible impact on subjects' actions.

To conclude, one can say that, whereas the *simplicity criticism* targets the 'material' quality of economics experiments, i.e. their human and socioeconomic 'richness' or 'complexity' to use Smith's terms, the *artificiality criticism* targets the relevance of the 'material' component of economic experiments. The former argues that the agency of experimental subjects cannot manifest itself to its full extent, and thus may concede that it is useful for more modest purposes. The latter argues that the participation of experimental subjects is not and never can be meaningful.

The experimenters' responses

Experimenters have dismissed the artificiality criticism straight on by stressing that the experimental microeconomic system is as 'real' as a natural socio-economic system because therein 'real' people make 'real' profits within the context of 'real' rules and, hence, the principles of economics that apply to the natural contexts also apply to the laboratory. They acknowledge, however, that experiments are simple systems.

> [e]conomies created in the laboratories might be very *simple* relative to those found in *nature*, but they are just as *real*. *Real* people motivated by *real* money make *real* decisions, *real* mistakes and suffer *real* frustrations and delights because of their *real* talents and *real* limitations. Simplicity should not be confused with reality. Since the laboratory economies are *real*, the general principles and models that exist in the literature should be expected to apply with the same force to these laboratory economies as to those economies found in the field.
>
> (Plott 1991: 905, emphasis added)

The repetitive use of the word 'real' does not make this an adequate response. The distinction between the natural and the social sciences, on which the artificiality criticism hinges, is not addressed. Real experimental subjects may behave differently in the lab. But the mere invocation of this distinction, as I will argue in the next chapter, does not suffice to condemn experiments to irrelevance, either.

The response to the simplicity criticism is more elaborate. It introduces a distinction between the goals of economics experiments, which attempts to neutralize the criticism for theory-testing. But it acknowledges its relevance when experiments are meant to bear on some real-world situation (Plott 1979, 1982, 1987, 1991; Plott and Smith 1978; Smith 1980b, 1982; Wilde 1981). The argument goes as follows: as long as an experiment aims at testing a theory, or at discriminating between alternative theories, it does not need to reproduce, and no presumption need be made about its connection with the more complex 'real-world' context. It only needs to include the parameters relevant to the theory or theories being tested. The comparative advantage of an experiment is precisely to study interesting relations confounded in nature. In Smith's words:

> What is important about an experiment is that it be relevant to its purpose, not that it be realistic in the sense that it be 'real-world-like' in some subjective sense. Indeed, the best experiment is the crucial experiment whose outcome clearly distinguishes between competing theories. But the conditions of the crucial experiment may rarely, if ever, occur in nature.
>
> (Smith 1980b: 350)

Rather than being a problem, the simplicity of experiments is instead a methodological asset. It allows for designing crucial experiments that discriminate between competing theories. This response, however, makes experiment subservient to theory. In so doing, it passes the critical charges on to the theoreticians.

> Experiments are sometimes criticized for not being "realistic" … There are two appropriate responses to this criticism: First, if the purpose of the experiment is to test a theory, are the elements of alleged unrealism in the experiment parameters of the theory? If not, then the criticism must be directed to the theory as much as to the experiment. Laboratory experiments are normally as "rich" as the theories they test. Second, are there field data to support criticism, i.e. data suggesting that there may be differences between laboratory and field behavior. If not, then the criticism is pure speculation; if so, then it is important to parameterize the theory to include the behavior in question.
>
> (Smith 1980b: 350)

Smith suggests that an experiment is at least as 'realistic' as the theory being tested, therefore charges of 'unrealisticness' compromise the theory rather than the experiment. If empirically grounded, these charges spotlight a failure of the theory that should then be revised.[5]

The strategy of directing the burden of responding to the simplicity criticism at theoreticians does not constitute a good critical response. This is, in fact, an overly defensive attitude that does not promote the examination of what is at stake – the simple contexts of social interaction in the laboratory. Moreover, experimenters should be able to justify their interest in carrying out these simple tests. An experimenter is not a mere technician who waits for the theoreticians' testable hypotheses. At any rate, this is not the practice of experimentation in economics. Experiments possess a high degree of autonomy from theory, even in empirical testing. Various reasons can be provided. For one thing, theories do not come with testing instructions that specify what is to be tested and what a satisfactory test is; in fact, any single theory may give rise to various experimental tests. Furthermore, the justification of experiments should not depend on the endorsement of a particular conception of economic theory (i.e. realist), which may not even be shared by the theoretical economists. Besides, different conceptions of what constitutes a good economic theory may be compatible with the experimental method. Finally, these responses leave unexplained the role of simple experiments for other purposes. To conclude, experimenters should be able to provide independent arguments that justify the simplicity of experiments.

Plott (1991) introduces a further twist. He argues that simple laboratory microeconomies are good test devices of general theories. General theories depict economies 'found in the wild' by representing their structure and by using 'basic principles intended to have applicability independent of time and location' (p. 905). The simplified experimental microeconomies provide good testing conditions for these general models because general models must also apply to simple special cases. If the theory fails in these special cases, then it also fails in the complex economies found in the wild. Plott insists that 'experiment should be judged by the lessons it teaches about theory and not by its similarity with what nature might happen to have created' (p. 906).

Plott presents the simplified nature of economics experiments as an interesting characteristic for testing theories of a particular kind. Rather than being a handicap of the experimental method, simple experiments reinforce the epistemic weight of negative evidence for general theories. If the theory does not predict well in simple environments, then it should be discarded or modified. But Plott's views incur in the same problems noted above. They also make experimentation subservient to theory, and to a particular kind of theory. Moreover, a preference for general theories in the profession is not at all clear, as Plott defines them (Hausman 1992; Guala 2005b). Nor is it easily ascertained what are the general theories of economics. Moreover, most economic theories do not have explicit domains (Lipsey and Chrystal 1995: 31). The interest of experimental economics is also to test the edges of validity of theories, models and conjectural hypotheses. Experimental practice would be a very limited enterprise if it only tested theories in the domains where they were already expected to apply (Cubitt 2005). And again, this argument leaves the use of experiments for other purposes unjustified.

Smith's and Plott's evasive responses reveal more than they attempt to hide. There transpires a genuine difficulty in justifying the capability of experiments to provide understanding about real world economies and human behaviour therein.

Plott's defence of experiments as tests of general theories is affected by his scepticism regarding the generalization of experimental results. He is very explicit in clarifying that the full understanding of the 'simple' microeconomic system does not allow the extrapolation of the results yielded to the more 'complex' cases. The reason is that '[b]ehavior in very complex environments may follow different laws than those which govern behavior in relatively simple situations' (Plott 1982: 1522–23). Plott reiterates this view in later work. He says that '[e]conomies found in the wild can only be understood by studying them in the wild' (Plott 1991: 918). Experiments are simply an additional source of data that add to other empirical data when trying to understand real world economies.

Smith is more optimistic. He believes the results of experiments can also be applied to real world contexts. According to Smith, the generalization of propositions about experimental microeconomic systems to other contexts simply requires that a fifth precept – parallelism – must be satisfied. Parallelism asserts that '[p]ropositions about the behavior of individuals and the performance of institutions that have been tested in laboratory microeconomies apply also to nonlaboratory microeconomies where similar *ceteris paribus* conditions hold'. In the context of market experiments, parallelism concerns the possibility of generalizing the propositions about experimental market institutions to real world markets. For example, the propositions that 'rule A produces lower bids than rule B' in the experimental market can be generalized to other markets where similar *ceteris paribus* conditions hold (1982: 936). In Smith's view, the claim to generality is first and foremost a qualitative claim that pertains to the relation between the environment, the institution and the performance of the system. For more quantitative results, parallelism would require a tighter correspondence between the laboratory and the non-laboratory environments (p. 937). In any case, parallelism is an empirical matter that demands further empirical work. But Smith does not elaborate on what it takes to make this kind of inference. This is the topic of the next chapter.

Conclusion

This chapter shows that early methodological debate was characterized by an overly defensive attitude on the part of experimenters. This may be somehow understandable, given that experimental economics was at the time perceived with suspicion. The profession in general was sceptical about the relevance of experiments to economics. Experimenters perhaps feared to acknowledge some of the sources of these doubts. As experimental economics became more established, in the 1990s, experimenters gradually and more explicitly came to recognize some of the limits of economics experiments.

The early methodological debate did not generate satisfactory answers to the critical charges that challenged the relevance of economics experiments. Responses were guided by an ill-informed view of experiment (especially regarding its subservient relation to theory), which did not take fully into account the two epistemic factors of economics experiments and their specific roles therein.

The insufficiency of the responses may be attributed to a genuine difficulty on the part of experimental economists to come up with full-blown methodological arguments. This difficulty, shared in the economics profession, has many interrelated causes, as for example the framing of methodological discussions within inadequate philosophies of science that could not illuminate the experimental method (e.g. falsificationism and the methodology of scientific research programmes) and the methodological debate centred on theory-related issues (e.g. realisticness).

Both experimenters and the detractors of experiments have appraised experiments having theory as a reference model, and therefore they have focused too much on the representational attributes of experiments. When transposing this debate to experimentation, experimenters themselves internalized that an experiment must also be an adequate representation of some existing real-world situation. But an experiment can never fulfil this expectation. It is always an artificial and simple context. As a result, experimenters failed to take into account and use in their responses the methodological and epistemic features of experiment.

Nonetheless, experimenters have referred to the role of the participation of human subjects, and the cooperative nature of experimental economics, in their discussions on theory testing. The first was evoked in regard to the falsifying conditions of experiments, the second more recently when addressing the underdetermination problem. But these two factors must not be taken for granted. Experimental subjects must be able to disconfirm theories, and the community of experimenters must engage in effective criticism.

The most relevant element in the analysis of experiments is the participation of human subjects. This participation introduces an important distinction between theory and experiment. An economic experiment is itself a socio-economic context, the results of which must be interpreted in this light. This is the topic I turn to in the next chapter where a more complete answer to the various criticisms is provided.

9 Economics experiments and the real world

In the previous chapter, we saw that early methodological discussion about the relevance of economics experiments did not follow a process of effective criticism. Experimenters evaded the methodological and epistemic issues at stake. They were particularly unable to put forward arguments that justified the possibility of generalizing experimental results to real-world situations. The generalization of experimental results has been recently addressed by the philosopher of science Francesco Guala. In this chapter I first present the contribution of Guala to the analysis of the relation between experiments and real-world contexts, or the external validity of experimental results. I then argue that the appraisal of the epistemic value of experiments is still incomplete. It leaves unexplained a significant bulk of experimental work that does not have a specific real world target as a reference. In order to fill the gap, I introduce the notion of generic inference.

The external validity of economics experiments

The generalization of experimental results to non-laboratory contexts is the most challenging issue with which experimenters are confronted. We have seen that pioneers of experimental economics failed to provide an articulated argument that could justify the relevance of economics experiments to provide meaningful knowledge about real-world situations. Generalizing experimental results to non-laboratory contexts has, however, been addressed quite extensively by the philosopher Francesco Guala (1998, 1999, 2001, 2002, 2003, 2005a), who offers a valuable contribution to clarify what is at stake.

Guala frames the generalization of experimental results to real-world contexts as an external validity issue that requires determining whether the internally valid inferences within a given experimental system apply to other contexts. He says:

> *Internal* validity is achieved when some particular aspect of a laboratory system (a cause-effect relation, the way in which certain factors interact, or the phenomena they bring about) has been properly understood by the experimenter. For example: the result of an experiment E is internally

> valid if the experimenter attributes the production of an effect *Y* to a factor (or set of factors) *X*, and *X* really is a cause of *Y* in *E*. Furthermore, it is *externally* valid if *X* causes *Y* not only in *E*, but also in a set of other circumstances of interest, *F*, *G*, *H*.
>
> (Guala 2005a: 142, emphasis in original)

According to Guala, an external validity hypothesis conjectures that the similar, observable features of the experimental system and of its target, i.e. the concrete situation in the real world to which experimental results are to be applied, are generated by similar data-generating processes. Specifically, it conjectures that:

> 1 If all the directly observable features of the target and the experimental system are similar in structure.
> 2 If all the indirectly observable features have been adequately controlled in the laboratory.
> 3 If there is no reason to believe that they differ in the target system.
> 4 And if the outcome of the two systems at work (the data) is similar.
> 5 Then, the experimental and target systems are likely to be structurally similar mechanisms (or data-generating processes).
>
> (Guala 2005a: 180)

The external validation of experimental results is an empirical endeavour that requires the close scrutiny of both target and experimental system. It requires adducing experimental and field evidence that demonstrates that the similar observed features of the two systems are generated by similar processes. Guala stresses that the mere 'replication' of 'elements, changes and outcomes' does not suffice to demonstrate the external validity of experimental results. The problem of 'causal underdetermination', i.e. the possibility that the same data may be generated by different causal processes, requires an extra step: 'one has to show that the system constructed in the laboratory is the same as the one at work in the real world' and thereby ensure that 'the similarity between "artificial" results and "real" phenomena is not illusory'(1998: 906). According to Guala, the experimental system must fulfil three requirements. First, the materials used must 'resemble as closely as possible those of which the parts of the target system are made'. Second, their components must be 'put together just like those of the target'. And, third, it must be demonstrated 'that nothing else is interfering' both in the experimental and target systems (Guala 2002: 70).

Following the eliminative induction approach, this means that it must be demonstrated that the probability of observing the similarity between the target and the experimental system is low, if the systems are not similar data-generating processes. In order to do this, every reason that could account for the correspondence between the two systems other than their causal similarity must be eliminated. As Guala briefly puts it: 'If you want to generalize from *A* to *B*, you should make sure that *A* and *B* are as similar as possible' (2005a: 197).

From this it follows that externally valid inferences are fairly circumscribed achievements, whose 'viability depends on how much we are allowed to intervene and shape reality to fit our experimental prototypes' or, vice-versa, on how much the relevant aspects of the real world can be 'imported into the lab' (2005a: 187–89). That 'exporting the lab' is the 'safest' way to obtain externally valid inferences should not be surprising. As we have seen, control is a key feature of scientific experimentation. It is only under the controlled conditions of the laboratory that experimenters achieve internally valid inferences. Exporting these results from the lab to the real world requires that the target system also be a fairly controlled system. If not, it hardly reproduces the same outcomes. Not only must the two systems be very similar, but they must also exist in relative isolation and thus be uninfluenced by other factors.

Indeed, the examples Guala uses to illustrate external validity refer either to phenomena that occur in relatively isolated systems in the real world, which experimenters can more easily import into the lab (e.g. the winners' curse, see Chapter 6), or to phenomena that were first created in the lab and then exported to the field under similar conditions (e.g. the allocations of the Federal Communication Commission, FCC, auction, to be presented in Chapter 10). In fact, both examples refer to auctions that can be imported from and exported to the real world. This is so because auctions are fairly rigid institutions that can constrain the actions of individual players in such a way as to ensure a fairly stable operation and robust results (recall Smith's double-auction). This suggests not only that external validity claims are inferences from experimental systems to similar targets, but also that they are inferences of a particular kind: they are circumscribed to highly controlled microeconomic systems, the institutions of which constrain the actions of participants in such a way that they succeed in reproducing the same results in and outside the laboratory.

To conclude, the generalization of results from the lab to the real world is a complex engineering endeavour. It requires intervening in the target or in the experimental system, or in both, to make them resemble each other. The external validity of experimental results is thus a rather local and context-specific achievement.

A pervasive topic in discussions about the generalization of experimental results has been the so-called trade-off between internal and external validity. Guala explicitly states that '[t]he stronger an experimental design is with respect to one validity issue, the weaker it is likely to be with respect to the other' (2005a: 144). But this way of presenting external validity is misleading since internal validity is a precondition of external validity. If experimenters fail to obtain valid inferences inside the laboratory, they are left with no results to apply in the first place. To put it another way, it only makes sense to export from the lab results that are valid therein.

Guala attributes the trade-off to experiments' artificiality, of which he highlights two critical elements: the 'preparation' of experimental subjects in the instruction phase of the experiment and the abstract tasks that subjects carry out in the course of experiment (Guala 2005a: 144–145). As we have seen, these two factors are part of the standard procedures of experimental economics used for obtaining internally valid inferences. They do this by ensuring that the experimental context is understood by subjects as intended by experimenters, and thus that the behaviour observed can be interpreted by reference to the design of the experiment. The elimination of some of these artificial elements (e.g. by omitting the purpose of the experiment or evoking concrete real-world contexts) may introduce 'noise' in the experimental system, which makes inferences from observed behaviour more difficult. Experimenters would, then, be in a more difficult position to attribute the behaviour observed to the structure of the social situation rather than to some uncontrolled factor (e.g. subjects' speculation about the purpose of experiment or subjects' preconceptions about the context created in the laboratory). That is, the experiment would hardly produce an internally valid, exportable result.

Economics experiments are necessarily artificial and simple systems. The simplicity of experimental systems is deliberately and purposefully engineered by experimenters to make inferences from them. Of course, there may be some (though not much) room for manoeuvre. Within a given experiment, it might be possible to eliminate some level of artificiality and still produce internally valid inferences. Nonetheless, internal validity is a precondition of externally valid inferences.

The point I would like to make, though, is that control over individual actions is the critical factor of external validity. It is the control experimenters exercise over experimental systems that makes both internal and external validity inferences possible. This is implicit in Guala's account. Exporting the lab into the real world, or importing a real world system into the lab, requires a huge amount of control both in the experimental and in the target systems. This control may have already been exercised in the real-world system that the experimenter wants to import to the lab, or must accompany the exportation of the experimental system to the real world. An experiment where control is weakly exercised is likely to be unintelligible and to produce results with both weak internal and external validity.

In the next chapter, we will see that, even in the case of auctions, the demonstration of externally valid claims is far from being a trivial endeavour. This should not be surprising. The achievement of control in real world circumstances is an incredibly difficult task, even when designing and implementing auctions from scratch, as is the case of the FCC auctions.

The generic inferences of experimental economics

Guala distinguishes between two modes of experimental inference. Internally valid inferences are inferences within a specific experimental system that apply to it and to it only (e.g. '*this* double-auction experimental market converges to equilibrium'). Externally valid inferences are inferences from a specific experimental system to a specific target in the real world (e.g. 'the efficient outcomes observed in the experimental auction were also obtained in the FCC auction'). The fact that externally valid inferences are thus far rare in experimental economics could, then, lead one to conclude that economics experimenters are merely devoted to the production of results that are only valid in the laboratory. I will argue instead that the analysis is incomplete.

The discussion around internal and external validity is informed by Guala's overall conception of economics as a 'non-laboratory science' and his view of experiment as a mediating device between theory and some real-world target. Following Hacking's (1992) characterization of laboratory sciences, Guala endorses the view that economics is a non-laboratory science 'whose claims to truth do not answer primarily to work done in the laboratory' (Guala 1998: 901). Laboratory experiments in the non-laboratory sciences, as is the case of economics, 'demonstrate with experimental systems that "stand for" the target systems of interest' (2005a: 211, emphasis omitted). Following Margaret Morrison's and Mary Morgan's (1999) conception of theoretical models as mediators, Guala ascribes to experiment the same function of mediating entity between theory and reality. They are '"intermediate" steps in the long path leading from the formulation of ideas or hypotheses about the real world to their final application' (2005a: 203).

This conception possibly conveys the goal to which experimental economists should aspire. The problem is that it leaves unaccounted a significant bulk of experimental practice that falls short of that final and ultimate goal. As the present book testifies, most economics experiments are inspired by theory or by previous experimental results. Only a small fraction of experiments have attempted to explain naturally occurring phenomena. That is, the majority of experimental economics (and theoretical work inspired by it) revolves around the phenomena created in the laboratory.

One could conclude that experimental economists are lagging far behind the goals non-laboratory sciences should be pursuing and that they should redirect their research efforts to do work that has a higher chance of providing understanding about particular targets in the real world. This is the conclusion Guala draws: 'If economic research does not end in the lab, it follows quite naturally that economists should invest more time and effort in showing that their experimental results can be generalized to real-world contexts' (2005a: 222).

The conception of experiment as an epistemic mediator of non-laboratory sciences renders the justification of experiment too dependent on some predefined target system and places excessive emphasis on external validity issues. The generic kind of inference to be presented obviates the need of having the epistemic justification of experiments dependent on some predefined and concrete real-world reference. The internal and external inferences do not exhaust the kinds of inference one can make from experiments. A generic mode of inference is also available. Whereas internal validity refers to a specific experimental system and external validity refers to a specific experimental system and its target, generic validity inferences are inferences from series of experiments that apply generically to a specified class of situations in the real world.

The inferential operation involved in generic inferences is similar to that involved in modelling in economics. Much of modelling in economics aims to generate generic inferences from models to the real world. Indeed, the derivation of results that were only applicable to the model world would be a very unsatisfactory justification for model-building (both epistemic and social). Economists aim instead to derive generic hypotheses that apply to the economy. Allan F. Gibbard and Hal R. Varian (1978), for instance, argue that economic models provide understanding of the world. As they put it,

> [o]ften when a model is presented, only the briefest suggestive remarks are made about its bearing in the world, and yet it seems clear that, when an economist investigates a model, it is often because he thinks the model will help to explain something about the world.
>
> (Gibbard and Varian 1978: 676)

The relation between the model and its domain of application is a relation between the model and a class of circumstances with which it shares common features. In Gibbard's and Varian's account, this relation consists of 'casual' application of the model's conclusions, which provides understanding of 'aspects of the world that can be noticed or conjectured without explicit techniques of measurement' (p. 672).

Along the same lines, Robert Sugden (2002) claims that the possibility of inferring from a model to the real world does not require that the former be built upon a concrete real-world situation. What justifies inference is instead the extent to which the model is a 'credible counterfactual world' that describes how the world could be. The upshot is that the potential 'reality' of the entities, properties and relations described in the model worlds bestows credibility to the generalizations obtained from them, so that they can legitimately be assumed to be applicable to the real world were it to be arranged in the same way. For instance, in Akerlof's lemons model the world of the used-car market model is more uniform and regular than the real world, but '[t]he "cars" and "traders" of his model are not just primitives in a formal deductive system'. They are 'cars which are like real cars, and traders which are like real traders, inhabiting a world which Akerlof has imagined, but which is sufficiently close to the real world that we can imagine its being real' (Sugden 2002: 131).

In theoretical modelling, as Guala also acknowledges, '[i]nstead of focusing on one specific real-world economy, the modeller may examine a set of factors or features that are likely to be relevant *generically* to a nonempty but not necessarily well-specified set of economies'. These models, however, 'can rarely be applied directly to the functioning of a specific economic system' (2005a: 225, emphasis in original).

Similarly to the inferences derived from theoretical models, the generic inferences from economics experiments do not aim to apply to a concrete situation in the real world. They apply to a class of situations that are taken to be relevant to economic analysis. The generic inferences from economics experiments are epistemically superior, however. Their epistemic superiority stems from their ontological similarity to a class of real-world situations. It is this similarity that explains experimenters' ease in constructing experimental worlds, irrespective of whether a specific real-world reference exists. It is this ontological similarity that allows for extending experimental conclusions beyond the laboratorial world. This similarity also makes the distinction between non-laboratory sciences and laboratory sciences of difficult applicability in economics. Experimental economists always experiment on objects that are to some degree similar to real-world targets. Economics experimental systems are themselves socioeconomic systems, though of a very special kind.

The epistemic superiority of experimental generic inferences

The participation of the 'material world' in the natural sciences and the 'human world' in the human sciences is the main factor that accounts for the epistemic superiority of laboratory experiments relative to models or simulations. This superiority has been noted by students of experiments (e.g. Mäki 2005; Morgan 2002, 2003, 2005; Guala 2002, 2005a).

Both models and experiments are simple systems that are used to study the more complex and intractable real-world systems. The inferential power of experiments is higher because of the deeper ontological resemblance between experimental systems and real-world systems, whether these are well-specified targets or more generically defined in terms of classes of particular circumstances. This ontological resemblance, however, may vary, as the materials used and the way they are assembled in the laboratory may differ from real-world materials and systems. The inferential strength of experimental results therefore declines as the media and the composition of the elements of experimental systems deviate from real-world systems. The use of model organisms in biology, to give an example, allows scientists to make valid inferences from them to other organisms of the same population (e.g. from mice to mice). But in order to infer from experimental organisms to other organisms (e.g. from mice to humans), the former must somehow be typical of the latter (Morgan 2003: 227–28).

Mary Morgan uses the terms 'sameness' and 'similarity' to distinguish two kinds of ontological resemblance between experimental objects and their references in the real world. The degree of artificiality of model organisms that their natural counterparts lack (insofar as lab mice are prepared for research purposes) is not problematic, because 'they are of the same type and the same stuff'. They are 'representatives of' their population and this is an attribute that validates a range of relatively unproblematic inferences beyond the particular strain but within the species. The extrapolation of these inferences to organisms from other species requires extra care. In this case, a similarity relation must be demonstrated between the experimental subject and its real-world reference. In Morgan's view, it must be demonstrated that the former is an adequate 'representative for' the latter. That is, experiments 'allow inference to the *same* kinds of things in the world if they can be considered *representative of* them and to *similar* things if they are *representative for* them' (2003: 230–31, emphasis added). In both cases, ontological proximity between the experimental object and the reference object is the source of the epistemic superiority of laboratory experiments relative to other methods of inquiry.

Mathematical models, in contrast, can only aspire to be 'representations of' processes, objects or relations existing in the world. This ontological difference 'creates an immediate and deeper inferential gap between the object of experiment and the object of reference … for the experimental and reference object are no longer made of the same stuff' (2003: 230). Moreover, evaluating the adequacy of representation is a more complicated matter, given that there is less agreement on criteria for deciding when a representation is a good one (2003: 231). In sum, whereas the extrapolation of results from the world of models to the real world involves 'representation of' other kinds of thing in the world, the extrapolation of results from the experimental world involves relations of 'sameness' or 'similarity' between the object of scrutiny and the object of reference.

Morgan expresses this difference in yet another way. Whereas laboratory experiments involve 'replication', model experiments involve 'representation':

> In the case of laboratory science, successful experiments depend on accurate *replication* in the laboratory of the elements, changes and outcomes in that part of the world relevant to the question. Only then can inferences be made from the results of experiment to teach us something about the world. In the case of modelling science, successful experiments depend on accurate *representation* in the model of the parts of the world relevant to our questions. Otherwise, we can only learn about the world in the model, which may be rewarding for theory development but not for learning about the world.
>
> (Morgan 2002: 57, emphasis added)

Thus, whereas experimenters can reproduce the phenomenon of interest in the laboratory (which involves same or similar inputs, processes and outcomes), modellers can only represent them by having recourse to different media. In economics, the issue is cast in the following terms:

> In experimental economics, the [internal] validity of experimental results is defended by referring to the design of experiment. Control is dependent on the choice of experimental set-up, circumstances and procedures … These choices are guided by the experimenter's need to design the experiment in such a way that economic behavior is made manifest in the experiment. Although there are arguments as to whether experimental subjects … really do behave "naturally" in the artificial situation like, for example, managers in industries, nevertheless, *they share the quality of being humans*, and so that part of the inference gap is surely less than for

> mathematical model experiments. *These design features are then adduced by experimentalists as reasons why the results they find in their controlled situations carry over to the uncontrolled world.* This may make it possible to infer to the same type of situations (in terms of the objects, structure and circumstances) in the world, but that very same tightness of controls and high levels of specificity involved in the laboratory experimental set-up makes inferences to related or similar situations in the world more problematic.
> (Morgan 2002: 54–55, emphasis added)

Morgan stresses the importance of analyzing the materiality of experiments. In economics, one has to pay attention to the fact that experimental subjects are not quite made of the same 'stuff' of economic agents in the real world (recall the simplicity and the artificiality criticisms discussed in the previous chapter). The tightness of controls and the high level of specificity of the experimental systems alter the 'material quality' of experiments in such a way that inferences from the experimental world to related situations in the world may be problematic. In Morgan's view, similarly to Guala's account, these inferences are specific in character and of limited applicability. Mathematical models, in contrast, allow inferences to a class of situations with which they share common circumstances; they allow 'general' inferences that have little import for specific cases (2002: 53–57). The view defended in this chapter is, however, that economics experiments also allow generic inferences to classes of situations with which they share similar conditions.

Guala also stresses the epistemic superiority of experiments as 'epistemic mediators' that 'help in bridging the gap between a theory and its target domain of application' (2002: 66–67). Experiments are superior epistemic mediators because the relationship between the experimental and the target system 'holds at a "deep", "material" level' as 'the same material causes as those in the target system are at work'. This contrasts with other mediating devices, such as simulations where the similarity between the simulating model and the target system is 'abstract' and 'formal' (Guala 2005a: 214–15).

Experimental economies are made of the same 'stuff' as their targets. External validity requires, as we have seen, that experimenters use materials that resemble as closely as possible those of which the parts of the target are made, and that they assemble these materials as they are put together in the target, while ensuring that nothing else is interfering. But Guala does not consider the possibility that, when the same 'materials' are arranged in a different manner, they can produce relevant knowledge of the real world. They only produce, according to Guala, 'a library of phenomena', the relevance of which has still to be demonstrated in concrete applications (Guala 2005a: 229–30).

The view endorsed here is that the generic mode of inference makes relevant claims about the phenomena created in the lab prior to their demonstration in concrete applications. Similarly to the inferences made from models, generic inferences from economics experiments do not aim to apply to concrete real-world situations. They nonetheless provide knowledge about the real world. This possibility is afforded by the ontological similarity between experimental systems and real-world systems. Generic inferences make claims that apply generically to a given class of real-world situations. These claims describe phenomena and, more or less explicitly, the circumstances in which they are likely to be observed in the real world. Economics experiments or, better put, series of experiments provide knowledge about the human and the social worlds prior to establishing a correspondence between the experimental world and a concrete real-world situation.

To sum up, whereas internal validity refers to the derivation of valid conclusions that apply to the laboratory world, and external validity refers to the generalization of these conclusions to a concrete real-world situation, generic valid inferences extend knowledge claims from the laboratory world to a class of situations in the real world. Generic inferences do not require appraising the similarity between a given experimental system and a specific target system. The validity of generic inferences is conferred by the ontological similarity between experimental systems and real-world systems. Experimental systems are special socioeconomic contexts from which knowledge can be acquired about individual preferences, motivations and behaviour, as well as about socioeconomic institutions. Whether or not a parallel context exists in the real world is a relevant question that can be answered subsequently.

Generic inferences: the case of reciprocity

The generic kind of inference has been widely used in constructing models of human behaviour that attempt to account for behaviour observed in the laboratory. This has been, in fact, the proclaimed goal of the field of behavioural economics, which grew in tandem with the accumulation of experimental results, namely in the fields of individual decision-making and game theory (Camerer and Loewenstein 2004).

Ernst Fehr's and Simon Gächter's (2000) 'economics of reciprocity' provides a good illustration of the generic mode of inference. Reciprocity is a behavioural pattern that has been observed and scrutinized in various experiments (e.g. ultimatum game, gift exchange game, public good game) and has inspired the construction of models that attempt to account for pro-social behaviour (e.g. Rabin 1993; Fehr and Schmidt 1999; Bicchieri 2006). This is how Fehr and Gächter describe it:

> People repay gifts and take revenge even in interactions with complete strangers and even if it is costly for them and *yields neither present nor future material rewards.* Our notion of reciprocity is thus very different from kind or hostile responses in repeated interactions that are solely motivated by future material gains.
>
> We term the cooperative reciprocal tendencies "positive reciprocity" while the retaliatory aspects are called "negative reciprocity".
>
> (Fehr and Gächter 2000: 159–60, emphasis in original)

According to Fehr and Gächter the manifestation of reciprocity depends on the interplay between the context of interaction and the composition of the population, which is divided between reciprocal and self-interested types:

> [i]n competitive markets with incomplete contracts, the reciprocal types dominate the aggregate results. Similarly, when people face strong material incentives to free ride, the self-interest model predicts no cooperation at all. However, if there are individual opportunities to punish others, then the reciprocal types vigorously punish free riders even when the punishment is costly for the punisher. As a consequence of the punishing behaviour of the reciprocal types, a very big level of cooperation can in fact be achieved. Indeed, the power to enhance collective actions and to enforce social norms is probably one of the most important consequences of reciprocity.
>
> (Fehr and Gächter 2000: 160)

Even though Fehr and Gächter refer to laboratory behaviour, reciprocity is a pattern of human behaviour that is deemed pervasive in the real world. They explicitly state that this behavioural pattern is more likely to be observed in competitive markets with incomplete contracts and in collective action problem-situations where there is the opportunity to punish those who deviate from shared social norms. And they claim that this behaviour is relevant to enhance collective action and to enforce social norms.

Reciprocity has been studied, for instance, in public goods experiments that have shown the role of social norms in promoting cooperative behaviour. Their relevance lies in 'the analytical structure of the public good problem [which] is a good approximation to the question of how social norms are established and maintained' (Fehr and Gächter 2000: 166).[1] Public goods experiments have shown, in particular, how cooperative behaviour depends on the shared belief that one ought to cooperate, which enforces the prescribed behaviour by informal mechanisms of rewarding and punishment, i.e. by positive or negative reciprocation. The classes of situations in the real world to which these results apply are varied, of which Fehr and Gächter list work relations, consumption and savings decisions, human capital decisions, the use of common pool resources, tax evasion and the abuse of welfare payments, the functioning of markets, and so forth (p. 167).

Gift-exchange experiments, to give another example, study reciprocal behaviour which is deemed typical of social interactions under incomplete contracts. These experiments do not aim to explain a specific situation in the real world. But the 'analytical structure' of gift-exchange experiments has been taken as adequate to study the employer–employee relationship typical of labour markets.[2] Experimental evidence has suggested that in response to generous job offers, employees are on average willing to put in extra effort above what is implied by purely pecuniary considerations. This result is deemed to apply, generically, to labour markets and it has been used to explain employers' resistance to reduce wages, even in periods of recession, in fear of retaliation (i.e. negative reciprocity) by their workers.

Because economics experiments are deliberately designed to study particular problems of economic interest, they allow aspects of real-world situations to be investigated by experimental means that are not as easily studied by other means. Even though experimental systems are artificial and simple contexts of social interaction, their ontological similarity to real-world situations allows experimenters to derive generic inferences from them. The generic applicability of experimental results stems from the possibility of reproducing in the lab the structure of real-world situations and from the direct participation of experimental subjects in these social interactions. It is this ontological similarity that gives experimenters confidence that the same or similar patterns of behaviour and their underlying causes are in operation in circumstances that share the same structure.

Fehr and Gächter show that economics experiments can generate knowledge of individual motives and of the impact of socioeconomic institutions on individual behaviour and on collective outcomes prior to the demonstration of a strict correspondence between the experimental system and a concrete target in the real world. Generic claims may in fact bring understanding to real-world phenomena, the underlying causes of which cannot be easily ascertained in the field.

Generic inferences are constructed through series of experiments that explore a given phenomenal domain and simultaneously define the classes of situations in which the phenomenon is likely to be observed, in the lab and in the real world. Experimental research on reciprocity has produced generic inferences about reciprocal patterns of human behaviour, the motivational factors that lie behind them, and the circumstances in which they are likely to be observed. It has also made claims about the interaction between social contexts and reciprocal behaviour. This research programme has thus made generic claims about individual motives, behaviour and institutions without a particular real-world target as a reference model.

It should also be pointed out that generic claims are made in the latter stages of knowledge production, when the phenomenon studied has been fully understood and explanatory hypotheses tested. Like other genres of inference, however, assessing the validity of generic inferences is an empirical matter. In fact, Fehr's and Gächter's 'economics of reciprocity' is one among alternative explanations of cooperative and retaliatory behaviour observed in the lab. Various explanations have in fact been proposed and tested (see, for example Camerer 2003 and Woodward 2009). The view endorsed here is that this assessment requires the analysis of the 'materiality' and 'sociality' of series of economics experiments.[3]

All kinds of inference, however, rely on the control experimenters exercise in experimental systems and/or the presence of constrained environments in the real world. As we have seen, internally valid inferences rely on the control exercised over a given experimental system, which allows experimenters to demonstrate that the phenomenon is 'real' rather than an 'artefact' of the material procedure. Externally valid inferences rely on the possibility of creating, both in the lab and in the field, highly structured environments that severely constrain human behaviour in predetermined ways. Generic valid inferences rely on the control exercised in series of experiments through which various groups of experimenters, with various theoretical commitments and beliefs, test each others' interpretations of experimental results. The generalization of generic claims from the lab to the class of situations where generic inferences apply also requires that the situations in the real world be somehow structured and relatively isolated. The classes of situations to which experimental results apply must share the same 'analytical' structure so that the same behavioural patterns may be observed in both situations and be accountable by the same causal factors. Because what is exported from the lab is a generic claim, it is not necessary as a high level of experimenters' intervention as it is involved in external validity. Generic inferences are generic claims that apply to a category of situations (e.g. reciprocal patterns of behaviour are likely to be observed in social interactions under incomplete contracts) rather than specific assertions about the actual causes of a given phenomenon (e.g. the winners' curse) or the actual outcomes of a given socioeconomic arrangement (e.g. the allocations of the FCC auction).

To conclude, internal validity inferences make claims that apply to a specific experimental system. External validity inferences make specific claims that apply to similar and specific systems. Generic validity inferences make generic claims that apply to a class of social situations that share a similar structure. Generic inferences provide reasons for belief that the same phenomenon or causal relations observed in the lab may be in operation in the same class of situations. The reasons for belief in generic inferences rely on the structural aspects of the classes of situation these inferences are meant to apply. Generic inferences can be brought to bear on real-world situations in which it is not possible to disentangle by other means the actual causal factors in operation.

The artificiality of economics experiments, revisited

In the previous chapter we saw that experimenters dismissed the criticism that experimental systems are artificial (i.e. the artificiality criticism) by repeatedly asserting that experimental systems are *real* systems where *real* people motivated by *real* money make *real* decisions and suffer, or enjoy, the *real* consequences of their decisions. We have also seen that the reaction of experimenters to the charge that experiments cannot capture important aspects of the real world (i.e. the simplicity criticism) introduced an asymmetry between the purposes of experiments: theory testing v. understanding behaviour outside the laboratory.

The relative confidence that experimenters revealed in economics experiments as testing tools, for which the simplicity, or even the artificiality, of the situation is not so great a problem, contrasts with their lack of confidence in the prospects of learning about real-world situations from experiments, for which criticisms were deemed relevant. This tension is still evident among experimenters. Chris Starmer says:

> As experimentalists, for the most part we simply do not know whether the results of laboratory experiments apply more generally in everyday contexts of economic significance. The official theory-testing rhetoric of experimentalists attempts to insulate us from this fact. As experimentalists, then, let us admit this limit to our present knowledge and pursue a broader exploration of the extent to which laboratory findings generalize outside the laboratory.
>
> (Starmer 1999a: 25)

And Arthur Schram says the following, when referring to bargaining experiments:

> [i]t appears to me that the artificiality of these experiments is very high. Therefore, it is not clear what the value is of this documentation of empirical regularities. If the aim is to make any claims about other regarding preferences in the world at large, the high artificiality appears to render the experimental results useless. If, in contrast, the aim is to document robust, causal laboratory effects to confront theorists with ... artificiality is less of a problem. This does have the danger of theorists and experimentalists creating their own world, however. ... For gathering empirical regularities that aim at telling ... something about behavior outside of the laboratory, it is important that the artificiality of the situation is considered. Much more than in the case of testing theories, the data must be relevant for the situation one is interested in.
>
> (Schram 2005: 233)

The ease with which experimenters accept and use experimental results for theoretically related purposes and their discomfort at making more general claims from them leaves unexplained the epistemic relevance of experiments as auxiliary tools of theories. One could thus be led to conclude that experimentation in economics is the extension of theoretical work by other means. For if experiments had empirical value for theory testing and development, this value should remain when experiments are used for other purposes.

No doubt experimental control, and how it is implemented in the laboratory, limits the kind and the content of knowledge that can be produced by experimental means. We have seen that economics experiments are suitable for the study of socioeconomic phenomena that can be framed (with minor or major adjustments) within the conceptual framework of the experimental microeconomic systems as defined by Smith (this topic is extensively developed in the next chapter). But not only are economics experiments limited in their scope, they also introduce an artificial element that is epistemically relevant.

Economics experiments elicit behaviour in particularly artificial circumstances, the most significant of which is that in the lab subjects are conscious that they are taking part in an experiment. This means that the establishment of a strict identity between the laboratory and some real-world situation is always disturbed by the fact that subjects are conscious that they are participating in an experiment (recall that deceiving subjects is banned in economics). This artificial element excludes many interesting phenomena from being studied by experimental means. Nicholas Bardsley (2005) provides, in this regard, an eloquent illustration of what is at stake.

Bardsley excludes 'relational' phenomena, i.e. phenomena that depend on particular kinds of relationship between people and on people's perceptions that the relational criteria are satisfied in a given instance. The laboratory cannot elicit this kind of behaviour because subjects will be aware of the fact that they are taking part in an experiment. In the tax evasion experiment, for example, subjects are asked to report the amount of money received by the experimenter, on the basis of which they pay an experimental tax. Bardsley argues that this experiment cannot provide information about tax evasion as it occurs outside the laboratory. This is so because none of the subjects' decisions can be interpreted as instances of tax evasion. As a tax is revenue collected by a government, which has an authority relationship over a group of citizens, for an action to be taken as an instance of tax evasion, it must be seen by the individual as an attempt to evade paying this revenue to the government. Bardsley concludes that the results of these experiments are more adequately taken as 'discoveries about how people behave in laboratory public good games with a probability of being punished for non-contribution' because '[p]eople might recognise a civic or legal duty to pay taxes whilst not recognising a duty to be honest to experimenters in labs, or indeed vice versa' (p. 242).

From this it does not follow that experiments cannot provide understanding of human behaviour outside the laboratory. It means, though, that special care should be taken when analyzing the results of experiments. The analysis of experimental phenomena must never lose sight of the fact that laboratory phenomena are the outcome of the anonymous decisions of experimental subjects in fairly neutral and aseptic environments, in which students know they are taking part in an experiment. The behaviour observed in these conditions may nonetheless teach us something relevant about human behaviour and institutions, which might help us understand real-world behaviour and the functioning of real-world institutions.

By focusing on the two main sources of epistemic value of experiments – participation of human subjects and the social validation of experimental results – the social epistemology of experiment (SEE) supplies an account of experimental practice that does not need to refer to a theoretical or a real-world reference model. It therefore dissolves the tensions created by the epistemic division between the two goals of experiments – theory testing and production of knowledge about the real world. Its main assertion is that economic experiments are instruments that produce knowledge by observing how individuals behave in the artificial and simple environments of the laboratory.

Conclusion

This chapter reviewed Guala's valuable contribution to the examination of the relation between experiment and the real world. It brought to the fore the work required when applying experimental results to concrete real-world situations. It made evident the extent to which an economics experiment is a complex social arrangement in which experimental participants interact with one another or solve problems of individual and collective decision-making. The knowledge experimenters gain by assembling these complex arrangements in their labs is at times valuable for explaining real-world phenomena (winners' curse) and for implementing market institutions in the real-world economy (FCC auction). But these applications of experimental knowledge are as yet extremely rare. Guala's account therefore left unexplained an important part of experimental work in economics.

Even though Guala abstained from accusing experimenters 'of pursuing futile research', his account nonetheless conveys the idea that experimental economists are not doing what they should, which is to do applied research. If external validity, as Guala defines it, should be the goal of experimental economics, then a complete reconfiguration of the field would be required, one that would move in the direction of field experiments (cf. Harrison and List 2004). Given the characteristics of the experimental method of economics, as fully documented here, experimental economics is not expected to become a more applied field of research.

The social epistemology of experiment presents an overall conception of experimental economics that is more supportive of fundamental research, a conception that is entailed by the notion of generic inference. Economics experiments can be used to study human behaviour by observing how individuals behave in particularly interesting situations. Nonetheless, it is a legitimate and justified concern that experimenters may lose sight of the world outside the laboratory and that the laboratory may become the only world in which economists are interested. How far and the extent to which this knowledge applies to some concrete real-world situation is, no doubt, a relevant question that students of experimental economics should continue to raise. The fact that the experimental context departs in significant ways from real-world situations does not in itself undermine the epistemic value of economics experiments. It has, however, important implications for the kind of knowledge that can be obtained by experimental means. These implications are the topic of the next chapter.

10 Human agency (or lack thereof) in economics experiments

The social epistemology of experiment (SEE) identifies as the main sources of the epistemic value of any experiment the direct participation of its subject matter and the social nature of knowledge production. These two factors create possibilities for the manifestation of both 'material' and 'social' resistances that force experimenters to conceive and answer relevant questions and thereby produce more reliable and robust experimental results. In economics, the sources of epistemic value are the participation of human subjects and the interactive way in which experimental knowledge is produced by series of experiments.

In the previous chapters I argued that the key epistemic issue of experimental economics is not the simplicity, nor is it the artificiality of the experimental contexts. An economics experiment is irremediably an artificial and simple system. The relevant epistemic issue is instead the trade-off between experimenters' control and the potential for independent action on the part of the participants in experiments. This is the topic this chapter addresses. It brings to the fore an epistemic distinction between two kinds of experiment – technological experiments and behavioural experiments.

The technological experiments of economics

The participation of the 'material world' in knowledge production is the distinguishing feature of experiment, as compared to other modes of scientific inquiry. This participation is epistemically relevant because the actual properties of the aspect of the world under scrutiny play an active role in the production of knowledge about them. This participation is, however, constrained by experimenters' interventions. Experimenters materially interfere with their objects to learn about them. In so doing, they risk obtaining results that are determined by their actions rather than by the agency of the material word. The trade-off between the actions of the experimenters and the agency of the material world is thus a key epistemic issue of experimentation. In economics, the experimental trade-off concerns the actions of experimental economists and those of the participants in economics experiments.

In the previous chapters, examination of the experimental method and of the market experiments showed that economics experiments possess a low level of 'human agency'. The standard procedures constrain the agency of experimental subjects by inducing the motives presupposed by economic theory – self-interest and income-maximization – and by restricting the available range of choices to a few admissible options. The control of subjects' motives and actions is intended to warrant the intelligibility of the experimental systems, namely, the relation among individual behaviour, institutions and aggregate outcomes. This chapter introduces a distinction between two categories of experiment according to the participation of human subjects and the kind of knowledge that can be generated by experimental means: the technological and the behavioural experiments of economics. To put it bluntly, technological experiments produce knowledge claims about microeconomic institutions and behavioural experiments produce knowledge claims about human behaviour.

Technological experiments focus on the relation between the microeconomic institutions (*I*) and the performance of the microeconomic systems (*X*) (depicted in Figure 10.1 by the elliptic involving the relation between *I* and *X*). The ultimate goal of technological experiments is to learn how to design market institutions that accomplish particular goals. Specifically, the aim is to design incentive-compatible rules of communication and exchange that achieve the best alignment between individuals' actions and desirable aggregate outcomes at the market level. Experimenters investigate the incentive-compatibility of these rules (*I*) by observing their impact on the messages (m^i) individuals send and the effect of these on individual (x^i) and aggregate outcomes (*X*) (see Figure 10.1). The performance of different rules can then be compared and appraised according to relevant criteria for the problem at hand.[1] This means that technological experiments generate knowledge claims that establish mappings from microeconomic institutions to the aggregate outcomes they bring about.[2] The crucial 'material' of technological experiments is thus the institution that organizes the actions of the experimental participants and ensures that the market outcomes are stable.

Technological experiments are the experiments of economics that can be used to design and test market institutions before they are implemented in real-world economies. It is this potential applicability of technological experiments that explains the label attributed to them.

Technological experiments can be what Charles Plott calls 'testbed' experiments, i.e. tests of 'a working prototype of a process that is going to be employed in a complex environment' (1997: 605), or devices for building 'economic machines', as Guala puts it, which 'are supposed to work for several years, in different contexts and without constant supervision of their manufacturer' (2001: 464). To this end, experimenters must design market rules that exercise a high level of control over individual actions to guarantee a stable relationship among the market institution (*I*), individual messages (m^i),

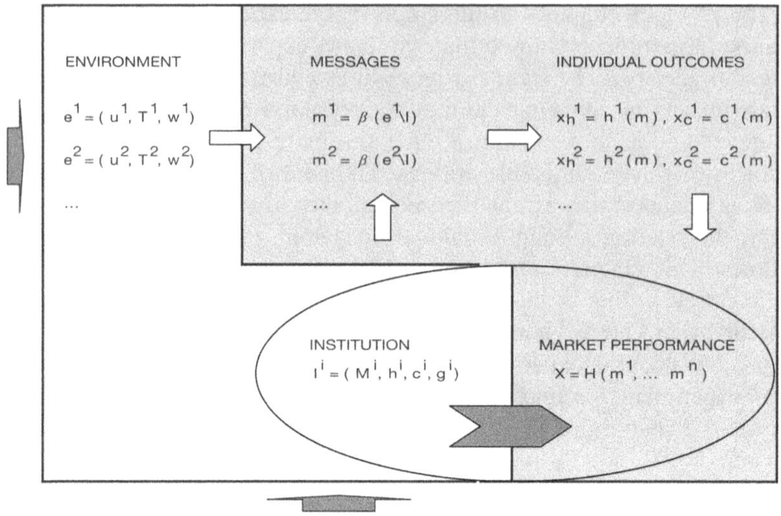

Figure 10.1 The technological experiments of economics

individual (x^i) and aggregate outcomes (X). It is the possibility of exercising a high level of control over individual actions, both in the lab and in the economy, that explains technological experiments' potential to work as tools for market engineering.

The potential use of technological experiments as tools for institutional engineering is afforded by the possibility of designing and implementing in the lab market institutions that effectively control human agency. In these experiments, the exercise of a high level of control over human motivations is fairly straightforward, given that these experiments concern the transaction of fictional goods where experimenters can easily implement the standard procedures of experimental economics (depicted in Figure 10.1 by the dark arrows pointing to the environment and the institution). These procedures can effectively induce self-interested and income-maximizing motivations via an incentive structure that rewards economically successful decisions undertaken in a context of relative anonymity that is substantially shielded from the wider socio-economic context. The market institution additionally reduces the range of admissible actions to those that more effectively help reach the desirable aggregate outcomes.

Not only is control easily exercised, but also the goal of technological experiments is in fact to learn how to design market institutions that effectively control human agency in attaining particular goals. Their aim is to learn how to design institutions that best align individual goals with individual actions (e^i and m^i), and individual actions with some desirable social goal (m^i and X). This, in turn, requires the design of an incentive structure that induces individuals to take the actions that achieve particular results at the aggregate level.

Because control of human behaviour is at its highest in technological experiments, their potential to generate knowledge of human motivations and behaviour is modest, except of course for the knowledge of how to control individual actions for particular goals. In these experiments, subjects are merely instrumental to test the informational, communicational and exchange attributes of particular sets of market rules, which are evaluated on the basis of the aggregate outcomes resulting from the actions individuals take under these rules.

Within this category fall most market experiments in the subfields of industrial organization, asset markets and auctions (cf. Kagel and Roth 1995) that investigate the institutional characteristics of particular industries, special markets, or the transaction of commodities with singular properties. In the next section, I look into the Federal Communication Commission (FCC) auctions that have been presented as the most successful technological exemplar of game theory and economics experiments. We will see that the design and implementation of market institutions in real-world economies is far from trivial.

The FCC auctions

The FCC auctions have been announced as the biggest engineering success of economics, particularly of game theory and experimental economics. These auctions were designed from scratch to organize the trade of licences for wireless personal communication systems and were tested in the laboratory before being implemented in the field. This was a 'testbed' experiment that involved the work of prominent game theorists and experimenters, such as Robert Wilson, Paul Milgrom, Charles Plott and Preston McAfee.

In 1993 the US congress charged the FCC with the design of an auction mechanism that would allocate licences to use electromagnetic spectra for personal communication systems. In 1994 the FCC implemented what was to be known as the 'simultaneous – multiple-round – independent' auction, which would soon be praised as 'the greatest auction in history' (McAfee and McMillan 1996: 159).

The auction launched a market for thousands of spectrum licences in which most US telecommunication firms in the telephone and cable-television business participated. Its success in raising billions of dollars for the public treasury has been taken as a measure of success of the market and evidence for the practical usefulness of game theory. The FCC auction is deemed to have supplied 'a case study in the use of economic theory in public policy' (McMillan *et al.* 1997: 429), which constituted 'a triumph, not only for the FCC and the taxpayers, but also for game theory (and game theorists)' (*Fortune* in McAfee and McMillan 1996: 159).

According to the official version, as recounted by the game theorists themselves, the auctions aimed at creating a transparent and efficient market that would allocate the airwave spectrum rights to highest value users – those who most valued and made best use of them.[3] Until 1982, the spectrum licences were assigned by an administrative hearing process (recognizably slow and non-transparent), which allocated licences for free. After 1982, the licences were sold and allocated via a lottery system that significantly improved the speed and transparency of the allocation mechanism. But it did not prevent opportunistic behaviour. Licences could be bought and resold by individuals who did not want to use them, and thus undeservedly appropriated revenue raised with the commercial use of the public spectrum.

The auction mechanism seemed to offer a tremendous advantage over previous allocation mechanisms. It offered the possibility of identifying the firms with the highest use-values for the spectrum, which would be in the position of paying the highest prices for using it and, as a result, maximize the FCC revenue. This required the design of an auction mechanism that encouraged bidders to reveal their true valuations while preventing opportunistic behaviour on their part. This was thus the key alignment between individual motives and individual actions that the auction had to accomplish.

Auction design raised important practical questions for which theory had no answers. The reason for this was that existing theory did not address a crucial feature of the spectrum auction: the fact that licences complemented and substituted for each other (McAfee and McMillan 1996: 171–72). Because game theory did not provide a clear-cut recommendation for the auction form, the design of the auction proceeded in a piecemeal manner. The building of the FCC auctions was a complex endeavour, best depicted as a patchwork of various partial solutions to the particular issues that arise when building a new market. Auction design therefore resembled 'a kind of engineering activity', which resorted to all sorts of resources, from 'practical judgments, guided by theory and all available evidence' to '*ad hoc* methods to resolve issues about which theory is silent' (Milgrom 2000: 271).

The auction design had to address three key issues. First, to ensure that highest-value users bought and paid for the licences at their valuations; second, to allow for the composition of favoured combinations of licences, taking into account licences' complementarities and substitutability; and third, to prevent opportunistic behaviour on the part of the bidders that would jeopardize the competitive gains obtained from instituting the market. Theory would then help look at the strategic aspects of the decision problem and anticipate

> how bidders choose their bids, not knowing the value of the item for sale and not knowing what their rivals know; and what the seller can do to stimulate the bidding competition, not knowing how much any of the bidders is willing to pay.
>
> (McMillan 1994: 146)

Based on game theorists' recommendations, the FCC opted for the 'simultaneous – multiple round – independent' auction that gave bidders the possibility of operating in several markets at the same time, so that they could have the chance of composing desirable aggregations of items or of adjusting their aggregation to a last-resort composition if their first-choice aggregations became unattainable. The licences would be allocated to the highest bidders that paid their bid prices.

Many detailed rules were also devised to avoid the opportunistic exploiting of any gap. For instance, an activity rule required the payment of deposits on the total number of desired licences at the beginning of the auction to ensure that market participants actually intended to own and use the licences. Given the high stakes involved, the government was also concerned with simplifying tasks in order to reduce the incidence of mistakes. To avoid the 'winners' curse' or to avoid cautionary behaviour of risk-averse bidders, the bids were announced at every round so that traders could make better estimates of the values of the licences.[4] The incidence of unpredictable mistakes was further taken into account by allowing bid withdrawal, though with a penalty.

The next step of market building was to glue together these partial solutions and evaluate whether they could be implemented in an operational environment. To this end, experiments were used 'to test whether people bid as theory predicts, and to look for hidden gaps in the rules that might leave the auction open to manipulation by the bidders' (McMillan 1994: 151).

Game theorists suggest that laboratory experiments were used to test the relative magnitude of conflicting effects and work out the gaps left by theory. But experimental economists did more than that. They were crucial to actually putting the various pieces together into a workable mechanism and solving the complications that emerged while trying to do so (Guala 2001, 2005a; Nik-Khah 2008). The building of the FCC auctions therefore followed a division of labour, in which game theorists proposed the auction form and the rules that would organize the functioning of the market, and experimental economists implemented these rules in an electronic market.[5]

After stabilizing the auction rules, the experimenters subsequently tested the auction under conditions that closely resembled the market to be implemented. Only then were experimenters able to assess the combined effect of the auction's rules, which could not possibly be predicted by non-experimental means. Because the data collected from the laboratory and from the first FCC auctions were deemed similar in many relevant respects (e.g. bidding patterns, price trajectory, licence aggregations, etc.), the experimenters concluded that the same goals had also been achieved in the FCC auctions. Experimenters' confidence relied on the 'exportation of the lab' into the economy. As Guala puts it:

> The strength of Plott's argument [that justifies the efficiency of the FCC auction] lies in the work he and other consultants did to ensure that the same processes took place in reality as those they had observed in their laboratory. The same causes are supposed to operate because experimenters built the two systems so as to be structurally similar to one

> another. The transportation of the mechanism outside the laboratory was as smooth, gradual and careful as possible.
>
> (Guala 2001: 473)

Even though the accounts of the economists involved in the auction design make us believe otherwise, the success story of the FCC auctions has been contested. In an evaluation of the results, Crampton (1998: 735) recognizes that 'any auction would look good relative to the FCC's past experience with comparative hearings and lotteries', and that 'it is impossible to say exactly how efficient the auctions were', retreating to the more vague claim that the auctions were successful for the government and for the bidders (1998: 728). Granted that the auction raised billions of dollars, Nik-Khah, based on the archives of the FCC, tells a rather different story:

> It is demonstrably false that the spectrum auctions satisfied the congressional goals. Many businesses buying licenses defaulted on their down payments (Murray, 2002: 274–75), leading to considerable 'administrative delay' in re-awarding licenses. The lion's share of licenses won by 'small' and 'entrepreneurial' businesses went to entities bankrolled by large telecoms, representing a failure to get licenses into the hands of a 'wide variety of applicants'. The auctions have not lived up to their promise to promote 'rapid deployment [in] rural areas', as both large telecoms and smaller firms have tended to concentrate their effort on large metropolitan areas (Copps, 2004; Meister, 1999: 76–77). Overall, the allocation of licenses produced by the auctions proved to be unstable, as the industry has gone through a spate of mergers, acquisitions, and bankruptcies, ultimately leading to a high degree of license concentration (Murray, 2002: 289–91). Commenting on some of these events, one anonymous FCC official candidly observed, 'this certainly does make us look like a bunch of idiots' (Labaton and Romero, 2001). True, the auctions did capture a tidy sum for the government coffers – more, anyhow, than 'beauty contests' or lotteries would – but perhaps they did so at the expense of any solid foundations for the economic health of the industry over the medium term.
>
> (Nik-Khah 2008: 90, footnotes omitted)

The FCC auctions, nonetheless, show that the success of 'market engineering' depends on the possibility of controlling the actions of market participants. It depends on the feasibility of designing in the laboratory market mechanisms which, when implemented in the economy, continue to tame human agency as intended by the market engineers. The FCC auctions aimed to organize the decisions of economic agents in particular ways (i.e. by eliciting bidders' true valuations) while controlling anticipated and undesirable actions on their part (i.e. opportunistic behaviour). The failures identified indicate, not so surprisingly, that control was not complete. They indicate the incapacity of the regulator to control the influence of big companies during the design of the auction and after it was implemented. As a result, the market became more concentrated in the hands of a few large corporations.

The behavioural experiments of economics

The behavioural experiments of economics also study how institutions shape human behaviour. But rather than focusing on the relation between institutions and market outcomes, behavioural experiments focus on the relation between institutions and individual behaviour. In so doing, they bring to the fore the psychological and the social make-up of experimental participants (this difference is depicted in Figure 10.2 by the grey arrows connecting the institution (*I*) with the environment (*e*), and the environment with the messages sent (*m*), which are the focus of behavioural experiments). Behavioural experiments therefore study the impact of institutions on the principles guiding human action by varying the elements of the institution (*I*) and by observing the effects on individual messages (*m*). The ultimate goal is to arrive at the behavioural models (β) that account for the way individual values (*e*) and institutions (*I*) interact and together determine human behaviour.

The research domains of behavioural and technological experiments differ. As we have seen, technological experiments concern the allocation of special items in markets where the behaviour of participants is predominantly guided by self-interested and income-maximizing motivations. Behavioural experiments, instead, concern themselves with the study of decision problems in contexts where other motivational forces may also be in operation. Within this category of experiments falls individual decision-making and game theory experiments.

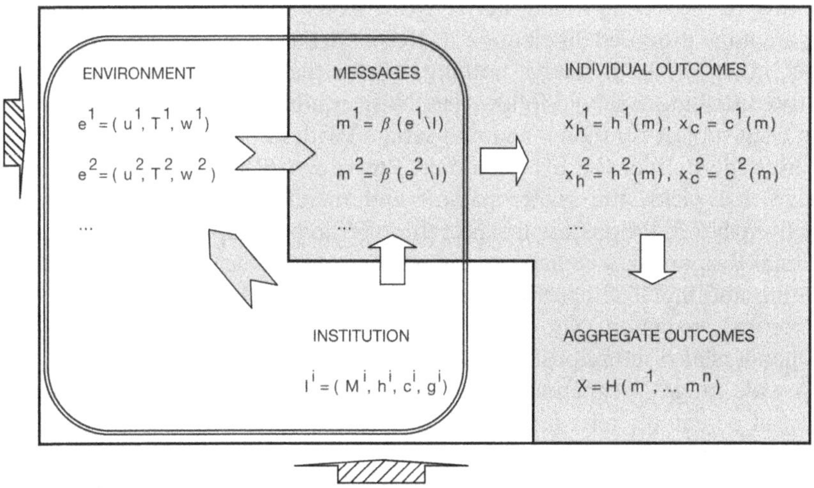

Figure 10.2 The behavioural experiments of economics

The former study individual preferences and individuals' decisions in contexts of uncertainty or risk – they focus on the relation between the environment (*e*) and the messages sent (*m*). The latter investigates how individuals solve particular strategic or cooperation problems and how these solutions depend on the particulars of the context of social interaction, i.e. they focus on the relation between the institution (*I*) and the environment (*e*). Behavioural experiments therefore produce knowledge of individuals' preferences and of the processes by which people select and apply heuristics, strategies or social norms for dealing with particular individual and collective decision problems.

The level of control exercised over human motivations and actions is lower in behavioural experiments than in technological experiments (represented in Figure 10.2 by the striped arrows depicting the intervention of the experimenters over the environment and the institution), which allows experimenters to derive behavioural claims from them. Given that experimental control is exercised by inducing self-interested and reward-maximizing motives, the reduced level of control means that these experiments carry a higher potential for producing knowledge of the factors that trigger other-regarding considerations and the pursuit of social goals. How this is achieved in actual experimental practice is now illustrated with the ultimatum game experiment.

The ultimatum game

The ultimatum game experiment, first conducted by Werner Güth, Rolf Schmittberger and Bernd Schwarz (1982) to test the Nash equilibrium prediction, consists of the partition of a fixed amount of money between two subjects who engage, anonymously, in a two-round game with one another. In the first round, Player 1 (the Proposer) divides the amount of money between the two. In the second round, Player 2 (the Responder) decides whether or not to accept the proposed distribution. If Responder accepts, each receives accordingly, otherwise both receive nothing. Under these conditions a very asymmetric distribution should follow. The Nash equilibrium prediction (assuming that each subject is rational and non-satiated with money) is that the Proposer receives the bulk of the fixed amount. Proposer will always prefer the alternative that yields the higher pay-off and therefore will offer the smallest positive pay-off. Proposer will expect this offer to be accepted by a non-satiated rational Responder, who accepts any positive offer rather than rejecting it and earning nothing. The experimental results, however, have diverged from this theoretical prediction. Not only do Proposers make more generous offers, but Responders also refuse positive pay-offs by opting for no rewards.

A wide range of experiments has since been carried out to investigate the effect of potentially relevant factors. The results, however, proved to be robust to varying conditions (e.g. subjects' experience, stakes, etc.).[6] The results of the ultimatum game experiment are now well-accepted stylized facts: (1) there are almost no offers below 10% or above 50% of the amount to be distributed; (2) the modal and median offers are in the interval between 40%-50%; (3) the means are around 30–40%; (4) offers of 40–50% are rarely rejected; (5) offers below 20% are rejected about half the time; (6) the rejection rate increases with the decrease of offers.

These results have been explained by reference to individuals' perceptions of the social context and the suitable courses of action therein. Güth *et al.* (1982) suggest that the ultimatum creates a situation in which the exploitation of the position of advantage by the Proposer is unacceptable. This is the case because the bargaining situation consists of a game between two opponents who would stand on an equal footing were it not for the arbitrary allocation of the different roles to them. Under these circumstances, the 50:50 split is the salient distribution. Proposers offer generous partitions and Responders reject low offers to punish what is perceived as the exploitation of an undeserved position of advantage. According to the authors, an asymmetric relation would be more acceptable in a market context such as the consumer markets of industrialized countries where 'buyers … might be used to have less strategic power' (1982: 369).[7]

The distinctive features of behavioural experiments can be easily identified by comparing the auction experiments with the ultimatum game experiments. As we have seen, the goal of the auction experiments is to study the performance of alternative auction mechanisms for the sale of a particular commodity. In these experiments, the experimental subjects are merely instrumental to test alternative mechanisms, the goal of which is to allocate particular items to the buyers who are willing to pay the higher prices for them. The data of these experiments consist of the licences' prices and their allocations to the bidders. Analysis of the auctions therefore focuses on aggregate results (e.g. whether or not they produce efficient allocations) and it is the basis for deriving generic inferences about the properties of microeconomic institutions. In contrast, the aim of the ultimatum game is to observe how individuals divide a sum of money between themselves and another individual. The relevant data of these experiments consist of the proposed partitions and the rates of acceptance or rejection. Analysis of ultimatum games thus focuses on individual decisions, which are the basis for deriving generic inferences about individual attitudes, perceptions of the social context and suitable courses of action therein (e.g. degree of acceptability of exploiting an asymmetric situation).

In the ultimatum game experiments, the participants' decisions are more effective in determining the experiment outcomes. This is the case because in these experiments different motives may give rise to different courses of action that are effective in determining the final outcomes.[8] In the auction experiments, in contrast, subjects are explicitly told they should try to make the highest profit by buying the licences at the lowest price and they have no reason to do otherwise. Moreover, in these experiments it is clear that, to accomplish that goal, subjects must raise their bids incrementally so that they raise their chances of buying the item at the lowest price. In the ultimatum game, Proposers are asked to divide a fixed amount of money. Even though it is in the self-interest of non-satiated Proposers to offer the lowest amount of money, the ultimatum game triggers other considerations because Proposers' decisions directly affect Responders. Moreover, various distributions are viable, from very unequal to equal partition. Thus, whereas auction experiments encourage self-interested motives and thus a single course of action that is common to all subjects, ultimatum games trigger various motives and actions that can determine the final outcome. The partition of income depends in particular on Proposers' views of what an adequate proposal is under those circumstances and of what might be Responders' views, and on Responders' views of the adequacy of the offer made. Thus, a variety of courses of action are equally likely. Different proposals can be made, which can either be accepted or rejected.

Behaviour in the ultimatum game is strictly related to the impossibility of satisfying the precept of 'privacy' (see Chapter 3). Privacy is not guaranteed, due to the nature of the game. As the pay-offs of the players are the very object of the decision problem, each player knows the pay-off of the player with whom they are interacting. Thus, despite the fact that the experimental subjects do not know with whom they are interacting, intersubjective considerations cannot be avoided. These considerations may be further stimulated by the fact that the ultimatum game consists of a bilateral interaction, in contrast with auctions, where subjects address a group of traders. Thus, whereas in the auction experiments subjects only know their own pay-offs, which depend on their own decisions as well as those of the group as a whole, in the ultimatum experiments the pay-offs are known and depend on the details of the interactive process with another (unknown) individual. As a result, in auctions subjects may be led to believe that they stand in a fairly symmetric relation to each other, i.e. that they enjoy equal opportunities to maximize the experimental pay-offs. Eventual asymmetries may be unperceived by the subjects, and if perceived they may be evaluated as more acceptable and dependent on their own decisions. Consequently, a preference for a more balanced distribution, or resistance towards inequality, cannot act as a countervailing motive to self-interest and income-maximizing behaviour.

Behavioural variety in the ultimatum game has been explained by subjects' perceptions regarding the context of interaction. Follow-up experiments have subsequently identified factors that may affect these perceptions, namely, the perception that one should conform to the norm that prescribes a fair division. These experiments have shown that deviations from the 50:50 split are observed when: Proposers earn the right to make the offer (e.g. by answering a quiz), which seems to justify keeping much more than the equal share (Hoffman *et al.* 1994); 'social distance' between subjects is high (Bohnet and Frey 1999) or the problem-situations are framed as market exchanges (Hoffman *et al.* 1994), which tend to generate less generous proposals that are more easily accepted; and offers are generated by a random device or determined by a third party who does not benefit from them, which are also more easily accepted (Blount 1995; Falk *et al.* 2003). The ultimatum game carried out in 15 small-scale societies in Papua New Guinea, in the Amazon and in Africa also revealed significant cross-cultural differences (Henrich *et al.* 2001, 2004), suggesting that sharing norms closer to equal divisions is correlated with cultures more familiar with cooperative patterns of social interaction. Taken together, this series of experiments has shown that other-regarding considerations are more easily triggered in contexts where social proximity is high and cooperative modes of interaction are pervasive in real-world contexts.

Based on these findings, Cristina Bicchieri (2006) develops a theory of social norms that applies to contexts where human agency is high and evident inter-subjective considerations are present. In these circumstances, she argues, individuals must search for cues to help them interpret the social situation and select the appropriate norm of conduct. Selecting a social norm involves: identifying the adequate norm for the social situation in question; the expectation that others will conform to it; and the belief that one is expected to conform to it as well. In this view, behavioural experiments are tools for identifying social norms, that is, they allow us to establish mappings from social contexts to social norms, which are the generic inferences that can be derived from the ultimatum games.

The extent to which the ultimatum game experiment constitutes a behavioural experiment, as defined here, should by now be clear. Ultimatum game experiments focus on the study of the effect of the institution (*I*) on individuals' perceptions (*e*) of the social context which determines their behaviour (*m*). This, of course, does not preclude the fact that more general models can also be developed that articulate the relation between the institution (*I*), the environment (*e*) and aggregate outcomes (*X*). The point is that behavioural experiments promote scrutiny of the motives and the decision-processes underlying human action.

The knowledge claims of behavioural experiments

Behavioural experiments produce knowledge of other-regarding preferences and motives. The data generated by these experiments have, in recent years, been extensively used to construct new models and theories of human behaviour. This has been, in fact, the proclaimed goal of the field of behavioural economics, which grew in tandem with the accumulation of results from behavioural experiments (Camerer and Loewenstein 2004).

Based on the results of the ultimatum game and other experimental games, economists set out to develop theories incorporating motives other than self-interest and income-maximization. The theory of fairness by Ernst Fehr and Klaus M. Schmidt (1999) represents an attempt to organize within a 'coherent framework' competitive and cooperative behaviours both of which can be explained by 'self-centred' inequity aversion, i.e. an aversion towards inequitable distributions of pay-offs that is stronger when these distributions are unfavourable to the individual. This theory then predicts the prevailing behaviour in equilibrium via the interplay between the microeconomic institution and the distribution of inequity aversion in the population. If the majority of the individuals within the population is selfish, then the prediction will approximate conventional theory, but if individuals in the population care a great deal about equity, then the theory tends to predict egalitarian outcomes.

But this requires a social context in which inequality-averse individuals are capable of inflicting a cost on selfish individuals to enforce equitable outcomes. This was the case in the ultimatum games, as Responders could compromise Proposers' earnings by rejecting their proposals. Similarly, Gary E. Bolton and Axel Ockenfels (2000) explain experimental behaviour in terms of a preference for equity, defined in terms of both the absolute amount of the pay-off and its relative share to the average pay-off within the population. Both the Bolton–Ockenfels model and the Fehr–Schmidt model interpret experimental results in terms of a preference for given social states, neglecting the possibility that individual behaviour may also be explained by individual attitudes towards the processes that generated those states.

A second strand of models fills this gap. Matthew Rabin (1993) interprets experimental results in terms of 'reciprocal altruism'. The main intuition is that, rather than revealing their underlying preferences, in the ultimatum game individuals are reacting to the actions of others. 'If somebody is being nice to you, fairness dictates that you be nice to him. If somebody is being mean to you, fairness allows – and vindictiveness dictates – that you be mean to him' (p. 1281, emphasis omitted). This model thus explains behaviour in terms of players' beliefs about the intentions of other players. In the ultimatum game, Responders reject unfair offers because they believe Proposers intend to be unfair to them, which triggers the desire to retaliate. The wish to punish the Proposers is thus what justifies their willingness to undertake the cost of retaliating. It also explains why Responders more easily accept uneven but non-intended offers generated by random procedures. Along the same lines, Colin Camerer and Richard H. Thaler (1995) interpret the experimental results in terms of general rules of conduct, 'manners', that apply to any situation. They argue that fair behaviour is not explained by a concern for others' welfare, it is instead explained by the desire for some kind of equity in particular interactions. Because in these games subjects are on a relative equal footing, the advantageous position of the Proposer should not be exploited by him/her. If it is, rudeness is followed by punishment.

Alvin E. Roth and Ido Erev (1995) propose an evolutionary interpretation of pro-social behaviour. In their view, subjects have no concern for each other's pay-offs; they are merely using strategies that have been successful in the past. This is so because 'strategies which have been played and have met with success tend over time to be played with greater frequency than those which have met with less success' (p. 172). In the ultimatum game, Proposers learn to make fair offers because they learn at a cost that Responders reject low offers. As Proposers increase their offers, Responders have a better incentive to accept them. The incentive-structure of the interactive context, i.e. Responders' low cost of rejection and Proposers' high cost of rejection, is effective in inducing fairness. Other evolutionary models have explained pro-social behaviour in terms of the predisposition some individuals have 'to punish those who violate group-beneficial norms, even when this reduces their fitness relative to other group members' (Bowles and Gintis 2004: 17). This is a natural predisposition that cannot be cancelled out even in unnatural one-shot games with strangers.

To conclude, behavioural experiments generate data on human behaviour, which have been used to develop new models and theories of human behaviour. Because human agency is high in behavioural experiments, they have produced data on pro-social behaviour. The theories inspired by the results of behavioural experiments have explained social behaviour in terms of social preferences, social norms, genetic or cultural propensities, as well as strategic thinking that takes these factors into account. Even though these models and theories have been built upon the results of behavioural experiments, they aim at providing explanations of social behaviour that can apply to a class of real-world social situations. That is, these models and theories rely on generic kinds of inference from series of experiments to a class of real-world situations.

These theories have indeed brought understanding to real world situations. As we have seen in Chapter 9, Fehr and Gächter (2000) take the reciprocal behaviour observed in the ultimatum game (and in other experiments) as relevant to providing understanding of the employer–employee relationship in labour markets, such as the resistance of employers to reduce wages in periods of recession in fear of retaliation by their workers.

Establishing internal and external validity is more difficult in behavioural experiments, however. On the one hand, the higher level of 'human agency' requires a more extensive series of experiments to interpret their results. The higher level of 'human agency' of potentially parallel situations in the real world, on the other hand, makes it difficult to ascertain whether or not external validity holds. This means that behavioural experiments are not suitable for performing the role of 'test-beds'. Nonetheless, the results of behavioural experiments may be relevant for policy-making. To give an example, behavioural experiments have produced evidence showing that the introduction of monetary incentives can generate counterproductive effects in areas of human conduct that were previously guided by socially established norms. Rather than promoting the intended behaviour, pecuniary rewards and penalties may instead cause an overall reduction in the behaviour to be promoted (Gneezy and Rustichini 2000; Frohlich and Oppenheimer 2003). Monetary incentives are thought to 'crowd out' intrinsic motivations, i.e. the motives that come 'from within the person' and that guide human action without any reward in view, other than performing the activity itself (Frey 1997; Frey and Jegen 2001). They deprive individuals of the possibility of expressing their involvement and in so doing reduce behaviour led by intrinsic motivations. These insights are particularly relevant when considering that the removal of the incentive mechanism does not necessarily re-introduce the previously prevalent intrinsic motivations. The inhibition of ethical reasoning produces irreversible damage to individuals' 'ethical muscles':

> With the ICD [incentive compatible device], individuals confront a situation in which their self-interest and the interests of all others coincide exactly. What is best for them is, by explicit design, best for the group as a whole. There is no tension whatsoever between the best strategy from a rational self-interested point of view and the ethically best strategy. Thus,

> subjects need not take into account the effects of their choices on others *as distinct* from their own calculated self-interest. They can make the calculations solely on a self-interested basis without conflict with other-oriented values. That is, after all, the essence of incentive compatibility. Thus, the implementation of an incentive compatible device actually obviates the need for ethical reasoning. As Steve Turnbull commented: 'They don't have to flex their ethical muscles'.
>
> (Frohlich and Oppenheimer 2003: 290, emphasis in original)

By the same token, when individuals perceive external interventions as supportive of intrinsic motivations, self-esteem is fostered and individuals acquire a stronger sense of self-determination. Socially desirable outcomes are thereby promoted. It is thus in this way that behavioural experiments produce relevant information for policy-making. But rather than designing institutions that align individual self-interest with the collective good, behavioural experiments generate knowledge of the factors that affect the successful implementation of incentive-compatible mechanisms or the factors that render salient and effective desirable norms of conduct.

Before concluding this chapter, I should also mention individual decision-making experiments, which also fall within the behavioural kind of economics experiments. In these experiments, subjects are asked to solve problems the outcomes of which depend only on their own decisions and the resulting states of the world after the decisions are made. The goal of these experiments is to study individuals' preferences and the processes by which people select and apply rules or strategies for dealing with particular decision problems. Individual decision-making experiments therefore focus on the relation between the environment (*e*) and the messages individuals send (*m*). These experiments are behavioural experiments because a high level of agency on the part of the experimental subjects must be allowed in order to examine how individuals select and apply particular decisional rules to solve specific decision problems. This is explicitly stated by Graham Loomes, who urges the adoption of the behavioural kind of experiment, as defined here. He says: '[w]e should switch our attention and our efforts to understanding more about the processes by which people select and apply rules/strategies for dealing with particular forms of decision problems' (1998: 486). The implication of this for experimental economics is:

> to devise experiments which allow for the heterogeneity of human behaviour, and to develop techniques which give greater insights into the interactions between people's imprecise basic values and the environments in which they have to operate, tracing how they construct their responses and/or modify them in the light of experience.
>
> (Loomes 1999a: F44)

Similarly to game theory experiments, individual decision-making experiments have shown that human behaviour departs in significant ways from the predictions of conventional economic theory. They have identified a host of systematic errors in decision-making, the so-called 'anomalies' (Thaler 1992). To give an example, experiments have shown that people have a taste for immediate gratification, being averse to delaying present consumption. This bias towards present-preferences accounts for a wide range of behavioural patterns such as insufficient saving, credit-card debt, procrastination at work and at home, among other risky activities.

The results produced by these experiments have also generated new models of human behaviour (e.g. Laibson 1997), and have been used to inform policy-making. They have been used to guide 'debiasing' policies that induce people to behave more in accordance with some desirable model of decision-making, for instance, to deal with self-control problems (Thaler and Sunstein 2003, 2008). The characteristics of technological and behavioural experiments and their policy implications are now synthesized in Table 10.1 overleaf.

Conclusion

This chapter presented two categories of experiment, using as a criterion the epistemic role of the 'materials' of economics, namely that of the experimental participants. This classification not only highlights the content of knowledge generated by each kind of experiment, and its significance for policy-making, but it also revises our understanding of the trade-off between the control economists exercise over experimental systems and the agency of experimental participants.

The potential for independent action is not equally relevant in technological and behavioural experiments. Technological experiments produce knowledge of market institutions. Their ultimate goal is to establish stable mappings from market institutions to their performances. Specifically, technological experiments investigate whether the actions of self-interested and income-maximizing individuals, mediated by a particular market institution, bring about the best outcome at the aggregate level. The potential for independent action is not very relevant. Rather, a high level of control is an indication of experimental success. This is achieved when the performance of the market institution is stable and independent of the traits and attributes of economic agents. By contrast, the potential for independent action is crucial in behavioural experiments. Only then do the experimental results convey information about the cognitive, psychological and social make-up of human agents.

The taxonomy of economics experiments presented here shows that self-interested and other-regarding considerations coexist in every context. The relevance of each set of motives, however, depends upon the particulars of the social interaction. Human action is sometimes guided by self-interest and at other times by other motives. Behavioural experiments identify the contexts in which other motives are more likely to guide human behaviour. Technological experiments, in turn, make clear that self-interested motivations and rational behaviour are mainly to be found in highly structured and constrained markets.

Table 10.1 Technological and behavioural experiments compared

	Technological Experiments	*Behavioural Experiments*
Epistemic Goal	**Institutional engineering** Learn how to create incentive-compatible mechanisms.	**Measure preferences, social norms and values** Study processes of individual decision-making and how individual perceptions and behaviours are shaped by the wider social context.
Experimental Procedure	**Institution**: Manipulate the institutional rules and investigate the impact on aggregate outcomes. **Environment**: Induce self-interested income-maximizing behaviour; create simple decision-problems; and help subjects avoiding error.	**Institution**: Manipulate the institutional rules and investigate how they interact with individual perceptions and behaviours. **Environment**: Induce self-interested income-maximizing behaviour while allowing for human agency.
Epistemic Factor	The **institution** produces stable patterns of human behaviour and stable outcomes at the aggregate level.	The **experiment participants** bring into the laboratory their cognitive, psychological and social make-up that accounts for the observed behaviour.
Policy Implications	Induce changes in human behaviour via the design of incentive-compatible mechanisms.	Induce changes in human behaviour by creating contexts that render salient shared norms of social conduct, and frame decision-making problems in such a way to help individuals to avoid error.

11 Behavioural experiments

How economists learn about human behaviour

In the previous chapter I introduced the classification of behavioural experiments, the economics experiments that allow us to derive inferences about human behaviour. I argued that the potential for independent action is crucial in these experiments. Behavioural experiments must thus achieve a difficult balance. They must elicit intelligible behaviour while avoiding the result that the actions of experimental subjects are solely determined by the design set-up. Only then do experimental results convey information about the cognitive, psychological and social make-up of individual agents. In this chapter, I put forward criteria for the analysis of the level of human agency in behavioural experiments. The criteria aim at evaluating the extent to which the behavioural patterns observed in the laboratory are to be attributed to participants' traits or instead to economists' actions.

The experimental trade-off, again

The trade-off between control and human agency has been noted by other students of experiments (Starmer 1999a; Mäki 2005; Morgan 2005; Guala 2005a). Mary Morgan, as we have seen, in a comparative assessment of models and experiments, has explicitly remarked on the importance of assessing the potential for independent action in experiments. The reason is that the exercise of control may jeopardize the relative epistemic superiority of experiments that stems from the direct participation of human subjects. These controls 'raise the danger of over-taming the participants in the particular way so that participants are no longer domesticated, but agents whose behaviour is directed by models of the world, models dictated by the economist' (Morgan 2005: 325).

We have also seen that the high level of control imposed by the procedures of experimental economics has been taken as a reason for dismissing the relevance of the entire experimental enterprise or, at least, reducing its scope. Nikos Siakantaris, when discussing the generalizability of experimental results to non-laboratory situations notes that the 'better experimental economists do their job in controlling variables, the more they are threatened by a lack of parallelism and hence of the usefulness of their project'. This is so because 'situations of relative isolation', such as those obtained by experimental means, 'are the exception rather than the rule in economic life' (2000: 273–74).[1]

In an extensive discussion of the experimental practices in economics and psychology held in the journal *Behavioral and Brain Sciences*, Ralph Hertwig and Andreas Ortmann (2001) classified the procedures of experimental economics as 'regulatory' practices which contrast with those of psychology, deemed comparatively 'laissez-faire'. The mandatory practices of economics are perceived by the psychologist critic as illegitimate procedures that extricate rational behaviour by '"beating subjects over the head" through constant repetition, feedback, complete and detailed information, and anonymity'. Thus, it cannot come as a surprise that 'the subjects act in accordance with standard "economic" (i.e., Nash) theory when the experimental situation is arranged in this manner' (cf. Dawes 1999: 23).

The trade-off between control and human agency has also been debated among experimental economists in methodological discussions, as well as in actual practice. Experimental economists discuss control issues in their regular practice when they argue for the validity of their results or assess the results of others. Carrying out experiments and appraising experimental work consists first and foremost of making sure that the effects of crucial variables have been adequately controlled. This is particularly evident, as we will see below and in more detail in the next chapter, when economists obtain unexpected or surprising results. New experiments are then designed and conducted to investigate the effect of potentially uncontrolled or insufficiently controlled variables.

We have seen that control is a methodological requirement aiming to ensure that the behaviour of the participants can be interpreted by reference to the design of the experiment. Economists exercise control via the design of the microeconomic institution, which defines the admissible rules of communication and exchange that subjects are allowed to use in the course of the experiment, and via the design of a reward structure, meant to ensure that the experimental problem is relevant to the participants and that they have the right incentives to make an effort in trying to solve it. Economists thereby induce self-interested motives in a carefully sterilized and constrained environment where subjects face simple problems and have the opportunity to learn the incentive structure of the problem at hand.

Strict adherence to the methodological prescriptions of experimental economics does not ensure that individuals behave in a self-interested manner or that they succeed in taking the course of action that best suits their interests. Subjects' motives are multiple and their cognitive limitations may prevent them from perceiving and pursuing the 'best' course of action. This is, in fact, where the interest of economics experiments lies. But the manifestation of these motives or cognitive limitations requires that subjects must be able to reveal other-regarding considerations and/or take other courses of action. To put it in another way, the experiment must have a potential to generate 'anomalies', i.e. facts unexplained in the light of theory.[2] Of course, the relevance of providing conditions for human agency varies with the purpose of the experiment. Whereas some experiments might aim at extricating rational behaviour, others may explore heterogeneous motives and individual and collective processes of decision-making. This is eloquently explained by experimental economist John Ledyard in the case of the public goods experiments:

> It is possible to provide an environment in which at least 90% of subjects will become selfish Nash Players. Heterogeneous pay-offs and resources, complete and detailed information, particularly about the heterogeneity, anonymity from others and the experimenter, repetition and experience, and low marginal pay-offs will all cause a reduction in rates of contribution, especially with small numbers. Add unanimity to the mechanism and rates will go to zero. It is possible to extinguish any trace of "altruism" in the lab. [But] [i]t is [equally] possible to provide an environment in which almost all of the subjects contribute toward the group interest. Homogeneous interest, little or rough information, face-to-face discussions in small groups, no experience, small numbers and high marginal pay-offs from contributing will all cause an increase in contributions.
>
> (Ledyard quoted in Dawes 1999: 23)

The implication of this is that when inferring motivational factors from observed behaviour, special care should be given to the trade-off between control and human agency. Not infrequently, the results of experiments have been misleadingly used to convey the idea that economic agents are like rational economic man, and 'anomalies' have been dismissed because they are assumed not to be found in contexts where economic theory purportedly applies. Such a view is widespread and also endorsed by experimental economists themselves, as we will see below and in the next chapter.

Whether or not economic theory applies in the laboratory or in real-world markets is no doubt an empirical matter. Yet the belief that under the 'right' conditions individuals behave rationally has led to an overly excessive concentration of resources devoted to eliminating the anomalies of economic theory (Loomes 1991; Loewenstein 1999; Starmer 1999a). By improving the incentive structure of the experimental task and by providing participants enough time to learn it, economists have been able, on some occasions, to reduce the magnitude of the anomalous behaviour.[3] But along the way they seem to have neglected the effort undertaken to ensure participants behave like rational economic man.

The fact that economists are equally able to generate behaviour that conforms to and conflicts with the model of rational economic man does not undermine the experimental enterprise. But when experiments are used to study the motivational factors underlying human behaviour, the behavioural patterns observed in the lab must be attributed to participants' values, beliefs, expectations, and preferences or attitudes rather than to the design and rules of the experiment. The experimental set-up must thus allow room for participants' agency or, to put it another way, the experiment must be a *behavioural experiment*.

In contrast to technological experiments, where economists aim at learning how to control the actions of participants to neutralize the impact of individual idiosyncrasies on the performance of market institutions, in behavioural experiments participants must have a crucial role in determining the experimental results. What 'human agency' amounts to in a given experiment of course depends on the inferential exercise at hand. For instance, claims about trust and trustworthiness can only be made from experiments that create problem-situations in which trust is a key variable in the decision-making process, say by increasing the risk involved in trusting others, as well as the sacrifice involved in being trustworthy, and by allowing their expression via individuals' actions. The making of claims about individuals' willingness to reciprocate, to give another example, can only be made from experiments that allow the expression of generosity/meanness and the possibility of rewarding/sanctioning these actions. In the remainder of the chapter, other meanings of 'human agency' will be provided and their relevance demonstrated. But before that the three criteria for assessing human agency needs to be spelled out.

Evaluating 'human agency' in economics experiments

The analysis of human agency to be carried out focuses on behavioural experiments that aim to study the motivational factors underlying human behaviour. It is argued that this study requires carefully designed experiments so that the choices subjects make can be made to bear on the motivational attributes under scrutiny. The reason is that there is no univocal relation between a given choice and a corresponding motivational factor, as the same choice may be caused by various and divergent motives. For instance, in the ultimatum game (described in the previous chapter) the equal division of a fixed amount of money between two subjects may be explained by reasons other than a regard for the well-being of the other individual. It can be explained by the expectation that the pecuniary gain can only be obtained if a fair proposal is made. It can be motivated by the desire to please others by doing what one is expected to do. It can be explained by the desire simply to do the right thing under the circumstances or by the fear of experiencing feelings of guilt for not having done so, and so forth. This is why interpreting behavioural experiments often suggests follow-up experiments to evaluate the relative contribution of the various motivational factors in question. Within a given experiment, then, the analysis of the motivational factors underlying human behaviour requires close scrutiny of: (1) the range of motives elicited on participants; (2) the menu of options available to them; and (3) the individual and aggregate outcomes of the actions taken.

First, the experimenter must elicit the relevant set of motives, so that these can be manifested in the laboratory [(1) in Figure 11.1]. To give an example, an experiment in which dominance and privacy prevail cannot purportedly trigger concerns about the impact of one's actions on the well-being of others. The participants will simply be ignorant of the circumstances of others and the impact of their actions on them. Second, insofar as subjects' motives are manifested via the choices made, the range of options available (m) to experimental subjects must allow their expression [(2) in Figure 11.1]. To continue with the same example, other-regarding concerns can only be manifested in the laboratory if the range of options available includes choices that can improve the well-being of others, say the possibility of dividing the gains in the experiment with others. Finally, an investigation should be undertaken into whether the available actions can bring about the intended outcomes, i.e. those that would be obtained from the relevant motives under scrutiny. Otherwise, the experiment may not elicit these motives to their full extent [(3) in Figure 11.1]. If the proposal of an equal division of the experimental earnings cannot produce an egalitarian distribution, then subjects may make a different offer and concern for others may not be manifested in the laboratory. The three criteria together thus require that the design set-up be capable of eliciting the relevant set of motives, allow these motives to be manifested in the choices of the participants, and allow the choices made to be effective in producing intended outcomes.

Analysis of human agency therefore calls for the assessment of the relationship between motives (e), choices (m) and outcomes (X). A tight alignment between motives, the choices made and the resulting outcomes is critical to making inferences in experimental economics, because the latter are based on the observed choices and outcomes. This is, in effect, presented as a strength of the experimental method as compared to other methods. Experiments

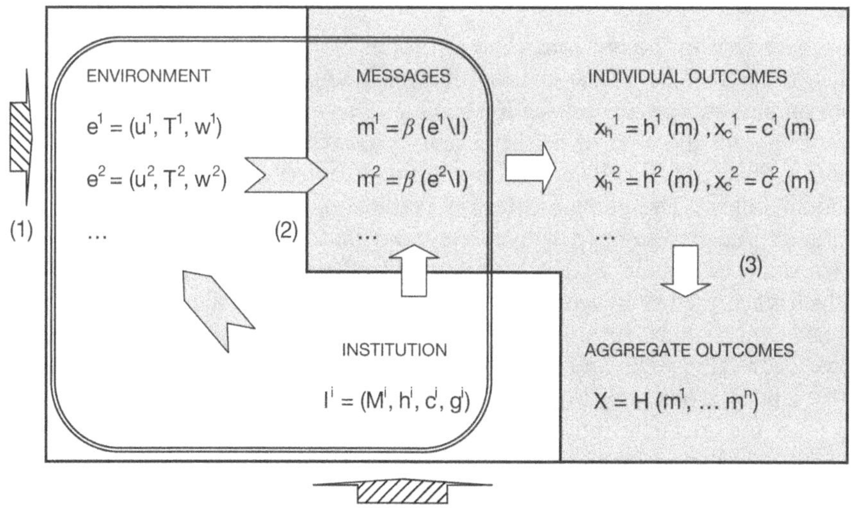

Figure 11.1 Assessing Behavioural Experiments

allow us to observe how people behave when confronted with choices that matter, i.e. that have pecuniary consequences, as opposed to assessing what they say they would do in hypothetical circumstances (Camerer and Hogarth 1999).

The alignment 'motives – choices – outcomes' is most easily achieved in individual decision-making problems where choices only affect the decision-maker. In situations where choices affect and are also affected by others, the one-to-one relationship between choice and underlying motivation is not as straightforward. In these cases, subjects' choices also depend on expectations about others' beliefs and actions. Under these more complex circumstances, choices reveal underlying motives only if individuals succeed in fulfilling their expectations. This is thus what the criteria purport to do: to evaluate whether choices individuals make in complex situations reveal individual motives.

More formally, and following the eliminative inductive approach synthesized by Francesco Guala (2005a), analysis of the relation 'motives – choices – outcomes' aims at assessing the strength of inductive inferences from experimental evidence to hypothesized conjectures about the motivational factors that account for the observed patterns. It assesses whether an inference from evidence to hypothesis comes from an experimental set-up such that 'the observation of *e* [evidence] would be probable if *H* [hypothesis] were true, but unlikely if it were false' (p. 136). The next sections analyse two follow-up experiments to the ultimatum game – the best-shot and the market game experiments – which were expressly designed to test hypotheses (*H*) about the motives underlying the fair partitions (*e*) observed in the ultimatum game. I show that by failing to achieve a close alignment among motives, choices and outcomes, the inductive inferences from evidence to hypothesis are weak.

Analysing the ultimatum game

We have seen in the previous chapter that in the ultimatum game experiment the Proposer proposes the division of a fixed amount of money between him/herself and another player, the Responder. Responder then decides whether or not to accept the offer. If he/she accepts, each receives accordingly, otherwise both receive nothing. Under these conditions a very asymmetric distribution should follow. The game-theoretical prediction, assuming that subjects are rational and non-satiated with money and that they gain utility from their own share of income, is that Proposer will offer the smallest positive pay-off which is accepted by Responder, who accepts any positive offer rather than reject it and earn nothing. Experimental results, however, have refuted the theoretical prediction. They were 'anomalous'. Not only did Proposers make more generous offers, but Responders also refused positive pay-offs by opting for no rewards.

From the brief description given above, it is easy to see that this experiment is a behavioural experiment that satisfies the three criteria identified above: (1) the range of motives are varied; (2) various partitions are feasible, from very asymmetric to the equal division of the fixed amount of money; and (3) participants' decisions are consequential, i.e. they determine the final outcomes.

The ultimatum game set-up does not influence in a particularly relevant way the motivations of the participants. Self-interest and other-regarding motives may be equally present. The decision-problem consists of the anonymous division of a sum of money that is described in fairly neutral terms. Under these circumstances, participants may well want to get the highest share possible. Proposers could then offer a low amount of money which could be accepted by Responders, who would then prefer to accept any positive amount rather than earn nothing. But as the more Proposer keeps for him/herself, the less remains for the other player, other-regarding considerations might interfere as well. If Proposers care about the amount received by the other player, they can make generous offers, which are accepted by the Responders.

As noted in the previous chapter the presence of other-regarding motives is strictly related to the impossibility of satisfying the precept of 'privacy'. Privacy is not guaranteed in this experiment because the pay-offs of both players are the object of the decision-making problem. Because each player knows the pay-off of the player with whom they are interacting, other-regarding considerations cannot be avoided. Subjects are aware that their decisions have an impact on others, and that the decisions of others affect them. These considerations are further magnified by the fact that the ultimatum game consists of a bilateral interaction. In sum, in the ultimatum game other-regarding motives may be present because the pay-offs are known and dependent upon the details of the interactive process with another individual.

Rather than being determined by the experimental set-up and rules, selection of a given partition depends on how subjects perceive the particular context of interaction and the suitable courses of action in it. Specifically, the experimental results express Proposers' views about what an adequate proposal is under the circumstances, as well as Responders' views about the adequacy of the offer made and which determines their decisions to accept or reject it. As we have seen in the previous chapter, the ultimatum game creates a situation in which the 50:50 split is the salient distribution. Proposers thus offer generous partitions, and Responders reject low offers to punish what is perceived as the exploitation of an undeserved position of advantage.

It could be argued that the experimental context is what determines subjects' motivations and actions even in behavioural experiments. But the behavioural diversity observed in these experiments does not support this. The patterns observed in behavioural experiments are the outcome of both subjects' attributes and the social context created in the laboratory. Moreover, a different range of motives may explain the generous partitions of income in the ultimatum game. On first impression, generous offers seem to be the expression of subjects' caring about others' well-being. But they could also express Proposers' strategic thinking based on a correct anticipation of the high probability of refusal of extremely low offers. That is, generous proposals could be strategic in the sense that they entail a higher chance of positive gains.

Further experiments have thus been carried out to find out whether ultimatum game results constituted evidence for strategic reasoning or were instead an indication of fairness motives, i.e. the desire to treat others fairly and punish those who do not behave like that. In the next two sections, I will show that discriminating strategic from fairness motives requires the design of an experiment that satisfies the three criteria identified above.[4]

The sequential best-shot game

The view that individual behaviour conforms to the rational choice model if individuals have time to learn from experience suggested new experiments to test whether considerations of fairness could be displaced by strategic considerations, as experience and understanding were acquired. To this end, Vesna Prasnikar and Alvin E. Roth (1992) ran a ten-period ultimatum game experiment (UG) and a best-shot (BS) experiment. The UG is a ten-period experiment that follows the standard two-round game. The BS is a ten-period public good experiment in which Player 1 first states the quantity q_1 he/she wants to supply of a public good, after which Player 2, knowing q_1, states the quantity q_2 he/she is willing to supply. The amount of the public good is then given by the maximum of these two quantities (q_1 or q_2, the best-shot). The incentive structure of the BS experiment dictates that Player 1 chooses $q_1 = 0$ and Player 2 chooses $q_2 = 4$, which yields the maximum pay-off of \$3.70 to Player 1 and \$0.42 to Player 2 (the best he/she can get, given the other's choice), resulting in an extreme distribution in the order of 8.8/1. As expected, fair shares were proposed in the UG, while extreme distributions were observed in the BS game.

These results were interpreted as providing evidence for strategic behaviour, in that the proposed partitions of income conformed to the incentive structure of both games. While in the UG Proposers did better (i.e. their pay-offs increased) by deviating from the equilibrium (i.e. by increasing their offers), in the BS Player 1 did better (i.e. their pay-offs increased) by converging towards the equilibrium (i.e. by decreasing their contributions).

Having shown that subjects' choices accord well with the incentive structure of the experiments, the authors concluded that subjects' decisions in the UG are primarily strategic. Specifically, fairness considerations of Responders matter because they have strategic value to Proposers, which is learned from the losses they incur when they make low offers. Of course, this interpretation only succeeds in explaining the behaviour of Proposers. Because subjects changed game partners between periods (while keeping the same roles), no strategic interpretation based on increased experience can explain the rejection of positive offers by Responders. Rejections cannot be part of building a ruthless reputation, which can eventually pay off in subsequent rounds.

On closer inspection, one can easily demonstrate that the claim that strategic considerations override fairness is not supported by the experimental results. The BS game is not a proper behavioural experiment. The BS game tips the scales in favour of strategic behaviour by constraining the attainment of the equal split and thence the manifestation of fairness. In this experiment, the equal contribution to the public good was inconsequential because subjects could not share the cost of public provision. To any positive offer by Player 1, the equal provision by Player 2 would worsen his/her pay-off, while it would not improve the pay-off of the other player. Under these circumstances, the best response of Player 2 is always to provide a zero quantity of the public good. Player 1, who had the first-mover advantage, chooses not to contribute and thereby benefit from the unequal distribution.[5] Because the cost of the public good could not be shared between the two players, the central issue the BS game raised concerned the selection of the beneficiary of the unequal distribution. The unequal distribution of income observed in the BS is thus attributed to a feature of the experimental design rather than to subjects' behavioural attributes.

In the BS experiment, subjects could have had fairness concerns and therefore they could have chosen to share the burden of providing the public good if it improved both their situations. But the structure of the game inflicted an unnecessary cost on one of the players. Nonetheless, there is some evidence for fairness concerns, given that some Player 2s did resist unequal distributions by opting for a zero provision of the public good when Player 1s did not contribute. But the structure of the game ultimately led Player 2s to accept the unequal outcome by being the sole providers of the public good. This means that this experiment does not satisfy the third criterion of a behavioural experiment. In the BS game, subjects could have had fairness concerns and they could have chosen the equal distribution of income. The problem is that attaining equal distribution is too demanding in that it requires on the part of one subject a willingness to support an unnecessary cost for the provision of the public good. The claim that strategic considerations overrode fairness considerations is therefore not warranted. The BS experiment is not an adequate behavioural experiment.

The sequential market game

The inefficiency of the BS experiment was identified by Werner Güth and Richard Tietz, who explicitly noted that '[i]f sharing the burden of providing the public good is impossible, fairness considerations cannot be applied' (1990: 428). In response, Prasnikar and Roth designed a ten-period market game experiment (MG) with extreme equilibrium predictions but in which equality is compatible with efficiency (i.e. the total pay-off is always distributed between the two players). In this market nine buyers compete to acquire one unit of a good provided by a single seller. Buyers tender bids up to \$10 (the redemption value of the good), and the seller either accepts or rejects the highest bid (if several, one of them is selected at random with equal probability). If the seller accepts it, he or she receives the corresponding amount, and the successful buyer receives the difference between the \$10 and the bid price. The other buyers do not earn anything. If the seller rejects it, all players receive zero earnings. The theoretical prediction is that buyers bid approximately the maximum amount, which is accepted by the seller. This is the case because buyers do not have the chance to get the market commodity at lower bids, and the seller never rejects the highest bid. The theoretical prediction is thus extreme distribution, also an efficient outcome (as defined above).

The results of the MG experiment converged to the equilibrium prediction and were also consistent with the incentive structure of the experiment. That is, buyers improved their earnings by converging to the equilibrium, and so the experimenters concluded:

> Taken together, these results suggest that although equilibrium predictions may need to be modified to take into account nonmonetary aspects of players' preferences (e.g., in the ultimatum games), nevertheless, even when equilibrium yields very unequal pay-offs, strategic considerations are not *displaced* by considerations of equity. On the contrary, the best-shot and market games show that whether equilibrium will be observed depends on the off-the-equilibrium-path behavior, which responds to the off-equilibrium-path incentives.
>
> (Prasnikar and Roth 1992: 886, emphasis in original)

But again the results are not as self-evident as Prasnikar and Roth suggest. It is not the case that in the face of conflicting motives individuals opt for self-interest. Even though the equal split is an efficient outcome, the design of the MG experiment simply prevented it. This means that the MG experiment did not satisfy the third criterion for 'human agency'. In the MG, buyers could have had fairness motives that could result in the choice of a more balanced distribution of income. However, the $5 bid (or one close to it) could not succeed in the market. Thus, this is not an adequate behavioural experiment from which inferences about motivational factors can be derived.

The problem is that sellers could only choose between accepting the highest proposal or rejecting it. They could not select fair partitions even if they were proposed. Implementing equal distribution would require that all buyers prefer equal division or that they could coordinate and agree not to tender bids above $5. But this was excluded at the outset by the design of the experiment because subjects could not communicate with one another. In fact, they did not even know with whom they were interacting. In the absence of communication, attaining equal partition would require that *all* subjects prefer equal partition and that they *all* expect others to share this preference too. Only then could they be confident that the $5 bid would be the winning bid and thus determine the equal split of the pay-offs. But this is not a credible expectation. As a wide range of experiments have shown (including the UG) individuals' expectations, beliefs and preferences are not homogenous.

Implementing the equal distribution of income between the winning buyer and the seller would require coordination among the buyers because none of them in isolation had sufficient bargaining power to impose it. In contrast to the UG, where Proposer could define income distribution, in the MG experiment the winning bid was determined by the interaction of nine players who competed among themselves. In the face of competition, buyers were compelled to tender attractive bids to raise their chance of winning. The implication of this is that the bids do not reflect buyers' views on what an adequate partition of income is between two individuals. It is more plausibly affected by the competition among them and their desire to be the winning bidder or their wish to prevent others from being so. Thus, the competition between subjects might have triggered other motivational factors not present in other experiments. Rather than raising the chance of being the winning bidder and earning an incredibly small amount of money, the escalation of bids can be explained by feelings of resentment and retaliation towards other players. The fact that buyers were willing to bid the maximum amount, and earn nothing by so doing, suggests just that.

Finally, the framing of the game as a market may also have changed the perceptions of the experimental setting rendering inequality between buyers and sellers more acceptable, especially so when individuals compete for a scarce good (cf. Güth *et al.* 1982, as mentioned in the previous chapter). In contrast, the UG and the BS experiments consist of resolving a distributive problem where obvious other-regarding considerations emerge. To conclude, not only does the MG render the attainment of equal pay-offs unfeasible, the outcomes actually arrived at might be explained by a different range of motives than fairness or strategic considerations. Quite perplexingly, this is recognized by the experimenters:

> Consider a hypothetical buyer whose preference for equality is such that his very first choice outcome would be to have all buyers submit identical bids of \$5 (or \$1), and who bids accordingly in the first two rounds. When he sees how high the actual transaction price is, he becomes annoyed with the other buyers, and (with the same motivation that would have caused him to express his displeasure by rejecting too small an offer if he were a seller in the ultimatum game) he decides to become the high bidder in round 3, in order to deprive other buyers of the benefits of what he sees as their unreasonable behavior. The point in considering such a hypothetical buyer is to observe that in *this* game his nonmonetary preferences cause him to behave in a manner indistinguishable from an income maximizer, while in the ultimatum game his preferences lead away from the equilibrium predicted for income maximizers.
>
> (Prasnikar and Roth 1992: 885, emphasis in original)

The experimenters overlook the fact that the extreme distributions of income are to be explained by experimental design that renders the equal split simply unattainable. Therefore, the assertion that strategic motives displace fairness considerations in the market game experiment is not warranted. The 50:50 split was simply inconsequential. Nonetheless, and similarly to the BS experiment, there is some evidence that these motives were also present in this experiment. The $5 bid was the modal bid in four out of 20 market rounds (including rounds 7 and 10, in which players had already acquired enough experience to understand that these could not be winning bids). This indicates that at times individuals like to express their preferences even when this is inconsequential. In the MG, they could do that because conditions 1 and 2 for 'human agency' were satisfied. Because criterion 3 was not, it is plausible that the manifestation of fairness motives via the choice of the equal split was severely constrained.

To conclude, neither the BS nor the MG experiments are adequate designs to confront fairness with strategic motives. In these experiments, unequal income distributions should be attributed to the microeconomic institutions that rendered the equal partition an inefficient or unattainable outcome.

Motivations, choices, outcomes and theories

Applying the three criteria to the UG and other follow-up experiments demonstrates the importance of assessing the level of 'human agency' when deriving inferences about the motives underlying human behaviour. Eliminating other-regarding behaviour by taming subjects' motives and by limiting the range of available options and outcomes is not very compelling. It only shows how a particular pattern of behaviour can be eradicated in particular circumstances.

The fact that economics experiments involve the participation of human subjects does not by itself warrant the conclusion that the observed behaviour is the result of subjects' attributes. This has to be carefully scrutinized, and this scrutiny requires assessing the range of motives present, whether subjects are given the opportunity to express them, and whether the actual consequences of subjects' actions adequately convey subjects' motives. This is particularly relevant now that the results of experiments are increasingly becoming the raw material for constructing new theories of human behaviour, and there is the risk that these results will be taken at face value and as presented by the experimenters themselves.

The theory of fairness developed by Ernst Fehr and Klaus M. Schmidt (1999) is based on the experiments reviewed above (and others), and it represents an attempt to organize within a 'coherent framework' competitive and cooperative behaviours, both of which can be explained by 'self-centred' inequity aversion, i.e. an aversion towards inequitable distributions of pay-offs that is stronger when these distributions are unfavourable to the individual. This theory, then, predicts the prevailing behaviour in equilibrium via the interplay between the microeconomic institution and the distribution of inequity aversion in the population. If the majority of individuals within the population are selfish, then the prediction will approximate conventional theory, but if individuals in the population care a great deal about equity, then the theory tends to predict egalitarian outcomes. When applying the model to the MG (with both Proposer and Responder competition), the authors conclude:

> The crucial observation in this game is that no single player can enforce an equitable outcome. Given that there will be inequality anyway, each proposer has a strong incentive to outbid his competitors in order to turn part of the inequality to his advantage and to increase his own monetary payoff. A similar force is at work in the market game with responder competition. As long as there is at least one responder who accepts everything, no other responder can prevent an inequitable outcome. Therefore, even very inequity-averse responders try to turn part of the unavoidable inequality into inequality to their advantage by accepting low offers. *It is, thus, the impossibility of preventing inequitable outcomes by individual players that renders inequity aversion unimportant in equilibrium.*
>
> (Fehr and Schmidt 1999: 834, emphasis added)

In Fehr and Schmidt's view, fairness is relevant when inequity-averse individuals have sufficient bargaining power to inflict costs on selfish individuals. Fair behaviour is enforced on selfish individuals because it is in their self-interest to behave fairly. In the ultimatum game Responders had such power because they could impose a cost on Proposers by rejecting extremely low offers, which the latter could avoid by making more generous offers. In the MG, this possibility is simply not available.[6]

Fehr and Schmidt thus use experimental results, from both behavioural and non-behavioural experiments, to develop a general theory that attempts to account for both competitive and cooperative behaviour. That fairness is relevant in social contexts where inequity-averse individuals can inflict costs on selfish individuals is a generic inference that Fehr and Schmidt derive from the experimental results. This inference is deemed to apply to real-world contexts. They in fact use it to draw a crucial distinction between goods markets and labour markets as 'fairness plays a smaller role in most markets for goods than in labor markets' (p. 835). While in labour markets, where workers have some discretion over their work level, '[b]y varying their effort … [they] can exert a direct impact on the relative material payoff of the employer', '[c]onsumers, in contrast, have no similar option available' (p. 835).

But from this it does not follow that markets are ruled solely by strategic considerations. The fact that fairness considerations were ineffective in experimental settings, in which fair actions were not available or were inconsequential, cannot be overlooked. Whether in the lab or in the real world, claims about motivational factors require assessing the relation between motives, choices and outcomes.

The analysis of economics experiments carried out in this book shows that laboratory markets tend to trigger and legitimize self-interest. Non-market contexts, where social proximity is high, tend instead to trigger other-regarding concerns. It also shows that laboratory markets are contexts that induce self-interest and income-maximizing behaviour by constraining the eliciting of heterogeneous motives and their expression in social outcomes. Market experiments are particularly successful in doing this by:

1 Framing the experimental situation as a social context in which self-interest and income-maximization are the salient norms of conduct.
2 Reducing social proximity between subjects, thereby inhibiting other-regarding considerations.
3 Reducing the range of options available to experimental subjects.
4 Rendering individual preferences, motivations and actions irrelevant to the resulting outcomes.

The analysis of experimental economics therefore suggests caution when using experimental markets to draw generic inferences about the motives underlying human behaviour. The extreme experimental conditions in which behaviour solely guided by self-interest is observed recommends this. In real-world environments the variety of human motives and the range of options available to individuals is much wider. This is also the case of real-world markets in which individuals may wish and may be capable of acting fairly.

Conclusion

Deriving inferences about individual motives from behaviour observed in economics experiments requires caution. Inferences about the motivational factors underlying human behaviour can only be made from experiments that allow the expression of individual motives by suitable actions that bring about intended outcomes. A tight correspondence among motives, choices and outcomes must be established for behavioural inferences to be made. When any of these partial relations does not hold, the inferences made may be attributed to factors other than individual values, beliefs, expectations, preferences or attitudes.

It may seem that the exercise carried out endorses the view that human beings are instrumentally rational, in the sense that their actions are always targeted at particular intended outcomes, whichever these may be. Such presupposition may be problematic when applied to behavioural experiments that aim at uncovering heterogeneous motivational factors, which may bring about actions that possess an intrinsic value in themselves because doing them is the envisaged reward.

Though the exercise is built on the analysis of the alignment 'motives – choices – outcomes', the instrumentalist reading is not implied by it. This is, instead, a feature of the experimental method of economics. Inferences from economics experiments are based on the choices participants make and resulting outcomes. And this is presented as a strength of the experimental method, as compared to other methods. Experiments allow us to observe how people behave when confronted with a concrete situation of interest, expressly prepared to that end, as opposed to assessing what they say they would do in hypothetical circumstances. Indeed, there is hardly any action more expressive of other-regarding concerns than the anonymous choice of a costly action that benefits others. In any case, experiments can also be designed to assess the importance of procedural issues. The follow-ups to the ultimatum game have, as we have seen in the previous chapter, tested the importance of various procedural matters, such as the mode of selecting the Proposer or the evaluation of Proposer's intentions. Analysis of the experiments reviewed here, in addition, showed that at points individuals like to express their values, beliefs and preferences, even when it is inconsequential to do so. The point is: when deriving inferences about human behaviour from the choices individuals make in experiments, attention must be paid to the range of choices available, as well as their social consequences.

To conclude, the framework presented provides a very general grid for the analysis of human agency that purports to evaluate the motives underlying human behaviour in complex social interactions. This, of course, does not exhaust the purposes of behavioural experiments. Behavioural experiments may have other goals that do not require the strict alignment between motives–choices–outcomes. But the making of inferences about motives from the choices individuals make demands it.

12 Preference reversals and critical practice in economics

The preference reversals research programme is one of the most well-studied episodes of experimental practice. It has been used to show the inconclusiveness of economics experiments or economists' dogmatism when confronted with evidence that contradicts their most ingrained beliefs. In this chapter, I use the preference reversals (PR) programme to illustrate the epistemic role of the collective dimension of experimental practice in economics, including the role of the dogmatic attitude of experimental economists. I show how experimental knowledge is produced in an incremental way by series of experiments that critically examine previous results; and how the disparity of the views in confrontation is crucial to the design of experiments that together resolve the points of contention and promote the identification and revision of scientists' beliefs. Because the PR programme has already been extensively studied, I shall keep the description of experiments to a minimum and focus instead on the various stages of the debate and on what they have accomplished.[1]

The preference reversal phenomenon

Preference reversal experiments differ from the experiments reviewed thus far as they aim to elicit and measure subjects' preferences rather than to induce them. Two basic principles underlie this category of experiment: first, the idea that the behaviour of economic agents is solely determined by their individual preferences, which are deemed to be stable across economically relevant situations; second, the principle of *procedure invariance* that posits the neutrality of elicitation procedures, which allows economists to infer individual preferences from individual behaviour in various economic contexts and by different means.

Psychologists do not share these basic principles. Preference reversal experiments, first reported by the psychologists Sarah Lichtenstein and Paul Slovic (1971, 1973), were in fact designed to show that preferences are contingent. Having noted in a previous experiment that choices between bets are primarily influenced by the probabilities of winning or losing and that pricing is primarily determined by the bets' pay-offs (Slovic and Lichtenstein 1968), the psychologists conjectured that if people process information differently when making choices and setting prices, then it should be possible to construct pairs of bets for which the same individual would choose the high probability and low pay-off bet, but set a higher price for the low probability and high pay-off bet. The preference reversal experiment was thus expressly designed to test this conjecture, that is, to test whether or not individuals choose the bet for which they set the lower price.

The experiment consists of two tasks. In the choice task, subjects are asked to choose between two lotteries, the probability bet (P-bet) with a high probability of winning a modest amount of money and a low probability of losing a small amount, and the money bet ($-bet) with a low probability of winning a larger amount of money and a high probability of losing a small amount. In the pricing task, subjects are asked to assign prices to these lotteries. The prediction that subjects tend to choose the P-bet while placing higher prices for the $-bet was confirmed. A large proportion of subjects chose the P-bet in the choice task and assigned a higher price for the $-bet in the pricing task (approximately 70 per cent). The unpredicted opposite reversal was also observed. Some subjects chose the $-bet and priced the P-bet higher, though this was less common (approximately 15 per cent). The psychologists concluded that preferences are unstable and dependent on the features of the decision-problem. The implication of this is that preferences are not the sole basis from which economic behaviour emerges, as presupposed in standard economic theory and in this category of economics experiment.

If it is assumed, as economists do, that individual decisions are solely determined by individual preferences, and that pricing and choice tasks are neutral mechanisms to elicit preferences, then subjects' decisions in this experiment reveal preference reversals. The reversal of preferences revealed in these two tasks is thus the preference reversal (PR) phenomenon. To use the terminology employed in the first part of this book, the PR phenomenon represents a 'material resistance' to economists' expectations, based on the well-established Expected Utility Theory (EUT) that predicts that rational agents place higher reservation prices on the objects of their choice.[2] But this resistance was generated in other fields of research and by scientists trained in a different scientific culture. Economists' immediate reaction was to undermine the significance of the PR phenomenon for economics.

David Grether and Charles Plott (1979), the first economists to take the PR phenomenon seriously, were confident that the phenomenon would not be reproduced in economics' experimental systems. They were proved wrong, however. The PR phenomenon continued to occur in experiments purposefully designed to make it go away.

Not surprisingly, a single experiment was not sufficient to persuade the profession of the significance of this phenomenon. Quite the contrary, economists were still confident that they were able to disprove it. Various strategies were pursued. Economists tried to undermine the relevance of the phenomenon by pointing to methodological differences between experimental economics and experimental psychology (Reilly 1982; Pommerehne *et al.* 1982). When the standard procedures of economics proved unsuccessful in eradicating it, economists then argued that the PR phenomenon was an artefact caused by the elicitation procedures (e.g. Holt 1986; Karni and Safra 1987; Segal 1988). As economists began to acknowledge the relevance of the phenomenon to economics, they started to propose explanations that attempted to amend less crucial parts of EUT, while leaving its fundamentals intact (e.g. Loomes and Sugden 1982, 1983). In recent years, the earlier debate re-opened (Harrison 1994; Bohm 1994, Cox and Grether 1996). But it too failed to disprove the relevance of the PR phenomenon.

The fact that after three decades of research experimenters were still discussing the relevance of the PR phenomenon was interpreted as a shortcoming of the experimental method. Experiments were deemed inconclusive and thus incapable of putting an end to this debate. Economists continued to question experimental results. And they had a great many to pick: the instructions given to subjects, the incentive structure, the procedures used to elicit preferences, the subject pool, and so forth. Some participants in the controversy took the PR phenomenon as a robust phenomenon (Camerer 1995), while at the same time others argued that the PR experiments did not conform to the standard procedures of experimental economics (Harrison 1994). All things considered, Chris Starmer concluded, '[t]he data will not speak for itself, and, ultimately, conclusions on these matters will turn on some degree of judgment leaving room for inter-subjective disagreement' (Starmer 1999a: 19).

That the PR research programme did not bring about a unanimous resolution does not necessarily condemn the experimental method to inconclusiveness. It does not even imply that the research has been infertile. It is, however, a sign of economists' resistance when confronted with evidence that challenges their most ingrained beliefs. But this resistance also kept the research programme going. That some economists disagree after three decades of research does not necessarily mean that all views are equally supported. In fact, they are not. It is now well established in the economics community that the PR phenomenon is robust. The robustness of the PR phenomenon stems precisely from its recalcitrance after an enormous effort to make it go away. As a result, economists began to raise new questions and put their most ingrained beliefs to the test.

Experimental economics versus experimental psychology

The PR research programme was brought to economics by the experimenters David Grether and Charles Plott (1979), who immediately recognized the challenge the phenomenon represented to economics. Here is how the economists perceived its implications:

> A body of data and theory has been developed within psychology which should be of interest to economists. Taken at face value the data are simply inconsistent with preference theory and have broad implications about research priorities within economics. The inconsistency is deeper

> than the mere lack of transitivity or even stochastic transitivity. It suggests that no optimization principles of any sort lie behind even the simplest of human choices and that the uniformities in human choice behavior which lie behind market behavior may result of principles which are of a completely different sort from those generally accepted.
>
> (Grether and Plott 1979: 623)

Even though economists found the phenomenon interesting in its own terms, it could not be taken at face value. The recognition that 'psychologists have uncovered a systematic and interesting aspect of human choice behavior' begged the question of 'whether this behavior should be of interest to economists' (p. 624). The answer to this question was to be found by experimental means. The expectation was that the phenomenon would not be reproduced in economics experiments, and thus it would not pertain to the domain to which economic theory generally applies. The experimental method of psychology rendered the 'material procedures' of the PR experiments inadequate to generate phenomena of interest to economics. Experimental economists then set out to design a new experiment that employed procedures recognizable by the economics profession. This was a natural step to take. On the one hand, the principles and practices of experimental economics were considered to be substantially different from those of experimental psychology. On the other hand, the PR phenomenon challenged fundamental principles of preference theory, which would not be easily questioned by a result produced in another field of research.

Experimental psychology relies on what are considered to be fundamentally different principles. The major methodological differences between experimental economics and experimental psychology have been recently presented by Ralph Hertwig and Andreas Ortmann (2001) in a paper published in *Behavioral and Brain Sciences*, which was discussed, in the same issue, by psychologists, economists and social scientists. Here is how Hertwig and Ortmann synthesize these differences:

> Whereas economists bring a precisely defined "script" to experiments and have participants enact it, psychologists often do not provide such a script. Economists often repeat experimental trials; psychologists typically do not. Economists almost always pay participants according to clearly defined performance criteria; psychologists usually pay a flat fee or grant a fixed amount of course credit. Economists do not deceive participants; psychologists, particularly in social psychology, often do.
>
> (Hertwig and Ortmann 2001: 384)

A major distinction between experimental economics and experimental psychology concerns the widespread use of monetary incentives in economics and its exceptional use in psychology. From the viewpoint of economists, this difference casts serious doubts on the ability of psychologists adequately to motivate subjects in experiments.[3] Even though pecuniary media has never been presented as the exclusive means to motivate subjects in experiments, for Grether and Plott monetary rewards are critical to create economically relevant situations. They write:

> Almost all economic theory is applied to situations where the agent choosing is seriously concerned or is at least choosing from among options that in some sense matter. No attempt is made to expand the theory to cover choices from options which yield consequences of no importance. Theories about decision-making costs do suggest that unmotivated choice behavior may be very different from highly motivated choice behavior, but the differences remain essentially unexplored. Thus, the results of experiments where subjects may be bored, playing games, or otherwise not motivated, present no immediate challenges to theory.
>
> (Grether and Plott 1979: 624)

Grether and Plott then added to the 'material apparatus' a pecuniary incentive structure in order to create a context of economic significance, though some psychology experiments did use money to motivate subjects. A second modification attempted to deal with so-called experimenter's effects, associated with the use of deception in experimental psychology. A major concern was that the practice of deceiving subjects could have created among the student population the idea that experimenters conceal the objectives of the experiment or mislead participants. As a result, rather than focusing on the actual experimental task, subjects' could have instead solved whatever experimental task they thought was being examined in the experiment.[4] In order to overcome these effects, economists avoided recruiting psychology students, who were deemed to belong to a 'very special population'. They instead recruited students from economics and political science classes, who were explicitly told they were to take part in an economics experiment.

Similarly to psychologists' PR experiments, subjects performed two decision tasks. In the choice task, they chose between the P-bet and the $-bet or expressed indifference between them (this was another innovation introduced in the 'material apparatus' that aimed to avoid counting as preference reversals indifference between bets). In the pricing task, subjects indicated the lowest price at which they would be willing to sell each bet. At the end of the experiment, a *random lottery selection* (RLS) procedure would randomly select one of these bets to determine subjects' pay-off. Rather than being paid on the basis of all the decisions made, subjects would receive the outcome of the selected bet. This procedure aimed to control income effects, i.e. the effect of wealth changes in the course of experiments on subjects' preferences.

If RLS procedure selected a bet that belonged to the choice task, subjects would receive the result of playing that bet. If the selected bet belonged to the pricing task, subjects would receive a randomly generated offer price, if this price was higher than the selling price set by the individual. Subjects would instead receive the result of playing the bet, if the offer price was lower than their selling price. This procedure is called the *Becker–DeGroot–Marschak* (BDM) mechanism, which aims to elicit bets' true certainty equivalents, i.e. the prices at which subjects are indifferent between selling the lotteries or playing them out.[5] The mechanism's underlying principle is that subjects have no incentive to place a higher price on a bet that is less preferred, for they risk keeping it, nor have they an incentive to place a low price on a preferred bet for they risk losing it for a price inferior to their subjective value. This procedure was carefully explained to subjects in the instruction stage of the experiment, when subjects were explicitly told that it was in their best interest to reveal their true reservation prices. Terms evocative of market behaviour were eliminated in order to avoid strategic responses from subjects (e.g. setting extremely high selling prices), and thus further to ensure the disclosure of subjects' true valuations. In addition, subjects were allowed to acquire experience with the experimental tasks in trials where they could clarify remaining doubts.

It is clear that Grether and Plott attempted 'materially' to shield the 'material apparatus' from the interference of 'background factors' that could be the causes of inconsistent behaviour. These included standard background factors well known to experimental economists: inadequate incentives, misconceptions about the purpose of the experiment, subjects' mistakes, income effects, and so forth. The new apparatus was considered a superior apparatus. It would give experimenters confidence that the behaviour generated would be attributed to subjects' preferences, rather than to some uncontrolled background factor.

Implementation of the new 'material apparatus' reproduced the standard pattern of the phenomenon. Approximately 70 per cent of the choices of P-bets were inconsistent with their announced selling prices. The opposite reversal occurred for just 13 per cent of the $-bets. And to experimenters' surprise, the inclusion of monetary incentives had a stronger effect on the rate of reversals. No significant effect of market terminology was found, nor did experimenters find an important effect associated with the ordering of the tasks (i.e. pricing after choosing and vice versa). The economists concluded that the PR phenomenon had been reproduced in economically significant circumstances.

It is worth noting that experimenters immediately accepted the result that was in conflict with their expectations. Instead of recommending further research to check the robustness of the phenomenon under more severe conditions (e.g. where choices could have been made more 'significant' to subjects), Grether and Plott concluded, without hesitating, that economic theory fails to account for the controversial phenomenon.

This suggests that experimenters had a great deal of confidence in the standard procedures of experimental economics, and thus in the capacity of the material apparatus to bring about economically relevant behaviour. Even though experimenters expected to make the phenomenon go away, the use of what was considered an adequate design and what were considered superior procedures sufficed for Grether and Plott to accept it. In other words, recognition that the PR phenomenon occurs in economically significant situations was supported by the consensual understanding, within the profession, of what an adequate experiment in economics is, and the belief that their practice had conformed to it. Of course, the results obtained were also consistent with the results produced by the psychologists. But this did not seem to have played a role here.

Naturally, acceptance of the PR phenomenon did not warrant the rejection of preference theory or any other related theory. As we have seen, practising scientists do not reject theories in the face of disconfirming results. They do even less so, when fundamental principles of standard economic theory are at stake.

> The fact that preference theory and related theories of optimization are subject to exception does not mean that they should be discarded. No alternative theory currently available appears to be capable of covering the same extremely broad range of phenomena. In a sense the exception is an important discovery, as it stands as an answer to those who would charge that preference theory is circular and/or without empirical content. It also stands as a challenge to theorists who may attempt to modify the theory to account for this exception without simultaneously making the theory vacuous.
>
> (Grether and Plott 1979: 634)

Rather than modifying theory to account for the exception, economists insisted on undermining the significance of the phenomenon by experimental means.

Incentives and the PR experiments: round two

Not surprisingly, the view that the PR phenomenon is significant to economics did not gain immediate collective assent. Standard economic theories were too well established to be undermined by an insufficiently understood phenomenon. Doubts about the significance of the PR phenomenon continued to revolve around the effectiveness of the PR experiments to motivate 'economic behaviour'.

Robert Reilly (1982) doubted that Grether's and Plott's incentive structure was adequate. The main problem, in Reilly's view, was that subjects might have perceived the decision-problem as one that involved the experimenters' income, rather than their own. Moreover, he suspected that the experimental tasks could have been too complex to be understood. Reilly then designed a new experimental set-up intended to raise subjects' motivation and their understanding of the experimental tasks. To this end, subjects were instructed in the meaning of expected value and were explicitly told that it was irrational to record selling prices in excess of the possible win of the lottery and to record a payout price higher than the amount that could be lost on that gamble (in this experiment subjects could both buy and sell lotteries). Understanding of the experiment was also improved by reducing the number of participants and by giving more time to the clarification of doubts in the instruction phase. Finally, the running time of the experiment was increased to allow for careful response. To induce the idea that it was their own money that was at stake, subjects received a fixed amount of money at the beginning of the experiment, a part of which would be immediately kept while the remainder would be used in the experiment. Further modifications were introduced to make decisions more relevant to subjects (e.g. increase the amount of losses).

Implementation of the new design produced the predicted pattern of reversals, though a lower rate was observed (34 per cent). Reilly concluded that the results 'provide further confirmation of preference reversal as a persistent behavioral phenomenon in situations where economic theory is generally applied' (p. 582). The reduced rate of reversals, however, raised the question of whether higher monetary incentives, together with additional information, would continue to reduce the rate of preference reversals. If so, it could be argued that 'individuals *are* likely to be consistent in making decisions on alternatives that *matter* to them when the principle characteristics of the alternatives are sufficiently comprehended' (p. 582, emphasis in original). Reilly thus produced a result that was somehow coherent with his expectations. Insofar as the net effect of the corrections he introduced to the 'material apparatus' moved in the predicted direction, he could venture that the phenomenon could be significantly reduced.

Werner Pommerehne, Friedrich Schneider and Peter Zweifel (1982) conducted an experiment along the same lines and with the same objectives. The Swiss team regarded the amounts that could be won or lost too small to motivate rational behaviour. To this end, they decided to increase the face value of the stakes by a factor of 100. The conversion rate of Swiss Francs to real cash pay-off would be unknown until the end of the experiment. Further amendments were introduced to improve subjects' decision-making (e.g. possibility of keeping track of past experience). But again, they continued to reproduce the PR phenomenon, this time obtaining 45 per cent of the predicted pattern of reversals. They concluded that '[e]ven when the subjects are exposed to strong incentives for making motivated, rational decisions, the phenomenon does not vanish' (p. 573).

Because these experiments introduced various modifications to Grether's and Plott's design, it is not possible to infer the effect of stronger economic incentives on the PR phenomenon. As Grether and Plott (1982) note, in a commented reply to Pommerehne *et al.* (1982), '[t]he subjects pools differed. The experiments differed. The language differed, so naturally the questions were "framed" differently. Substantially different motivation conditions were imposed' (p. 575). Grether and Plott argue that the lower rate of reversals cannot support the conclusion that this reduction is due to a stronger incentive structure. In fact, Grether and Plott doubted that the incentive structure had been improved. Its effect was ambiguous because it raised the face value of bets by using a monetary unit, the conversion rate of which was unknown to subjects.

In any case, they all agreed that the PR phenomenon resisted attempts at eliminating it. Grether's and Plott's experiment showed that the introduction of monetary rewards does not eradicate the phenomenon. Reilly's experiment showed that increased motivation and a more transparent experimental design can reduce but not eliminate the reversals. The experiment by Pommerehne and colleagues provided evidence that reversals are robust to pay-off differentials between bets, learning and registered track of past experience.

The three experiments taken together reproduced the PR phenomenon. Three different experimental systems involving three different material apparatuses did generate behaviour consistent with the reversal of preferences. More importantly, the PR phenomenon persisted despite substantial efforts to eliminate it. In the context of the PR experiment, this meant that experimenters' insistently tried to assist subjects in consistent decision-making, but alas, subjects continued to behave inconsistently. Economists' readiness to eradicate PR phenomenon conveys epistemic value to their failed attempts to do so. The PR phenomenon is a recalcitrant phenomenon that resists even when scientists' social, psychological or cognitive biases pull in the opposite direction. And it is this recalcitrance that in the end succeeds in convincing experimenters that the phenomenon is real rather than an artefact of the material apparatus. In the next section I look at the opposite situation. I argue that the later success in reducing the PR phenomenon is not epistemically significant.

Incentives and the PR experiments: round three

A decade later new experiments were designed that aimed further to improve the incentive structure of the PR experiment and make sure that the precepts of experimental economics were implemented. Glenn W. Harrison (1994), for example, argues that the conditions for a valid experiment in economics were not met in previous experiments because the incentive structure did not satisfactorily compensate for the subjective costs associated with the experimental tasks, that is, 'dominance' was not satisfied. Even though the critiques targeted all PR experiments, Harrison only focused on the experiments by Grether and Plott (1979), Reilly (1982) and Pommerehne *et al.* (1982), for which he estimated the opportunity cost of inconsistent reports (i.e. the expected income that the individual did not receive by making inconsistent decisions), which were deemed too low. In his view, preference reversals occurred because the opportunity cost of mistakes in the pricing task was negligible. His conjecture was that if subjects had had the opportunity to experience the consequences of their mistakes, inconsistent behaviour would have been corrected and the anomaly eliminated.

In order to overcome this deficiency, Harrison designed an experiment that attempted to increase the opportunity cost of errors, which indeed succeeded in reducing the rate of reversals, obtaining a minimum rate of reversals of about 10 per cent. He then concluded that inconsistent behaviour can be corrected if individuals suffer the consequences of their inconsistent decisions. Because various modifications were introduced to the 'material apparatus', the results were not unambiguous. For example, the introduction of a scale for selling prices could have hidden reversals that otherwise would have been revealed. That is, the design of the experiment might have inhibited the manifestation of the PR phenomenon (cf. Tammi 1999: 364–65 and references therein). Because the design of the experiment was substantially different from standard experiments, the decline in reversals could not be directly imputed to the increase in the opportunity costs.

Peter Bohm (1994) also obtained a substantial reduction of preference reversals (15 per cent) in an experiment with 'competent' decision-makers (i.e. third-year business school students specializing in finance) in the context of markets for claims of non-negligible magnitudes. James C. Cox and David M. Grether (1996) succeeded too in reducing the magnitude of the PR phenomenon in an experimental market with high monetary incentives, immediate feedback and repetition. They concluded, however, that market institutions with strong incentives and immediate feedback are not sufficient to make reversals disappear. The reduction of preference reversals only obtains when subjects also have the opportunity to learn from experience. It is thus the repetitive nature of the tasks in market experiments in conjunction with feedback that can eliminate the behavioural anomaly.[6]

To give a final example, the market experiment by Yun-Peng Chu and Ruey-Ling Chu (1990) introduced an arbitrager who could take advantage of subjects' inconsistent behaviour. In this experiment, subjects had to choose and state monetary values for each pair of bets. The arbitrager would then exploit subjects whenever they incurred in a preference reversal. In the case of the predicted reversal, the experimenter would sell the $-bet at the higher stated prices, exchange the P-bet for the $-bet, and then buy the P-bet at the lower stated price. Because the price of the $-bet is higher than the price of the P-bet, arbitrage would money-pump subjects. It is not extraordinary that preference reversals were eliminated in a market where subjects were exposed to repeated transactions that caused them monetary losses. But arbitrage alone did not suffice to reduce the PR phenomenon. Chu and Chu's experiment suggests that the main factor responsible for the eradication of the phenomenon is the continued exposure to arbitrage. This result is supported by the arbitrage experiment conducted by Joyce E. Berg, John W. Dickhaut and John R. O'Brien (1985) that failed to reduce the frequency of reversals when subjects were exposed to arbitrage over only one period.

These experiments have been used to argue that, in economic contexts, experimental subjects behave as predicted by economic theory. However, experimenters failed to take into account that the behaviour observed was substantially induced by experiments' 'material procedure'. In other words, the experiments were not behavioural experiments. Because subjects' actions were significantly constrained by experimenters' interventions, these experiments do not provide sound evidence for individual preferences. Under such circumstances, subjects could not have acted otherwise. These experiments, however, show how hard it is to 'correct' inconsistent behaviour. This requires the construction of market experiments that give subjects the opportunity to learn the incentive structure and act in conformity.

Explaining the PR phenomenon away

Rather then evoking the standards of good experimental practice in economics, a second strategy focused on specific features of the PR experiment, namely the procedures used to elicit and measure individual preferences. Subjects' inconsistent behaviour could still be attributed to the RLS procedure and the BDM mechanism used to elicit the selling prices of the bets.[7] But this strategy was pursued by conceptual means. Economists set out to present alternative explanations for the PR phenomenon, especially explanations that were the least damaging to EUT. This is explicitly recognized:

> Preference reversals could also be generated by intransitivities, but to abandon transitivity would be a drastic step that would make it difficult to construct a formal choice theory with empirical content. The transitivity assumption is needed for the existence of a utility functional that represents preferences over lotteries; independence is a strong assumption about the functional form of this utility functional (that pertains to the linearity with respect to the probabilities). There has been a considerable amount of recent work on preference theories that involve weaker versions of the independence axiom and that permit more general functional forms.
>
> (Holt 1986: 514)

Charles Holt (1986) conjectured that the PR phenomenon could be caused by the RLS procedure if the independence axiom was not satisfied.[8] He argued that if subjects perceived the experiment as a two-stage lottery (the first stage consisting of selecting the bet to be played out and the second stage of the actual playing of the bet of the pricing task) the choice between the P-bet and the $-bet would be a choice between two compound lotteries. If the independence axiom held, the choice between the two compound lotteries would be equivalent to the choice between the two bets. But if the independence axiom did not hold, then the choice between the two compound lotteries would be different from a direct choice between the two bets. That is, the compound lottery could not be used to reveal subjects' preferences over the bets. But this was a mere conjecture and one that was the most convenient because it was the least damaging to EUT. Moreover, there were already available theories that did not require a strong version of the independence axiom.

Edi Karni and Zvi Safra (1987) also considered that preference reversals could be caused by a violation of the independence axiom. But in their view the problem lay in the ability of the BDM procedure to elicit the certainty equivalents of the lotteries. Economists' attempted to demonstrate this by showing that within the context of theories of choice under risk there is a class of models that do not require the independence axiom but retain other axioms of EUT (completeness, transitivity, continuity and monotonicity), for which the maximization of the value of the compound lottery does not require the elicitation of the lottery's certainty equivalents.[9] For this class of theory, then, maximizing agents may reveal a preference ordering between two compound lotteries consistent with an inverted ranking of selling prices. However, these results are valid only under very strict specifications of the model (pertaining to the utility function and the probability transformation function, and to the restricted class of lotteries used in the demonstration). This means that Karni and Safra at best show that some of the reversals might be explained by a violation of the axiom least damaging to EUT.[10]

These were conjectures that hypothesized that observed behaviour might not have manifested preference reversals. But they could be experimentally tested, and so they were. James C. Cox and Seth Epstein (1989) conducted a new experiment that did not use the RLS procedure nor the BDM mechanism. In this experiment, subjects would state prices for both lotteries to decide which among the two they would keep. They could keep and play the lottery to which they had given the higher selling price and they would receive a fixed price in return of the lottery to which they had given the lower selling price. Subjects would reveal consistent preferences if they priced higher the lottery for which they had manifested their preference. Otherwise, they would exhibit a preference reversal or, better, a 'choice reversal' since the pricing task is, in effect, a choice task between two bets. This experiment produced a rate of reversals of about 35 per cent, but both the predicted and the unpredicted types of reversal were of the same magnitude. Subsequent experiments produced further evidence to the effect that the PR phenomenon could not be fully attributed to the RLS procedure (Beattie and Loomes 1997; Cubitt *et al.* 1998) nor the BDM mechanism (Starmer and Sugden 1991; Keller *et al.* 1993).

To conclude, faced with a well-established theory for which there were no competing alternatives, economists first tried to test the relevance of disconfirming evidence. When they finally acknowledged it, they then tried to put forward explanations that were the least damaging to theory. The PR phenomenon represented a serious challenge to EUT that experimenters were not ready to acknowledge. But in the course of practice, economists gradually started to concede that the PR phenomenon is robust and that it is significant to economics. Before moving to the stage of the revision of prior beliefs, first I look at the psychologists' take and the subsequent dialogue with economists.

Constructing preferences: the psychologists' take

Economists' theoretical work attempted to accommodate the occurrence of the PR phenomenon, while preserving two fundamental principles of standard preference theory: the principle that individuals have clear, well-specified and stable preferences that account for the decisions they make; and the principle that individual decisions are optimal in the light of their preferences. For this reason, Chris Starmer (2000) classified these recent, non-expected utility theories 'conventional' choice theories.

A more radical interpretation takes the results of PR experiments, not as evidence for a violation of some of the axioms of EUT but as evidence against a taken-for-granted assumption – the principle of procedural invariance – which takes elicitation procedures to be neutral mechanisms. Individual behaviour and underlying preferences are thus to be explained by the decision-problems themselves. In fact, as mentioned above, Lichtenstein's and Slovic's (1971) experiment was expressly designed to demonstrate this. Having confirmed this expectation, the natural next step for the psychologists was to try to interpret the relation between the decision-problems and the decisions individuals take. Various alternative interpretations were proposed.

Slovic and Lichtenstein (1983) put forward the 'anchoring and adjustment' hypothesis according to which individuals first 'anchor' on certain key features of the problem and then 'adjust' their decisions to take into account other elements of the problem. In the choice task of the PR experiments, subjects 'anchor' on the probabilities of winning and then revise their choice to take into account bets' pay-offs. When setting a price, individuals 'anchor' on the pay-offs of the attractive bets and then adjust the price downwards to take into account the probability of winning, and the amount that could be lost. Because the adjustment process is never complete, the 'anchor' substantially affects subjects' decisions and it is the cause of the different orderings of a given pair of bets. The 'anchoring and adjustment' hypothesis thus accounts for the choice of the P-bet for the pairs with a larger \$-bet loss relative to the P-bet loss, and the setting of higher prices for the \$-bets that have a larger win relative to the P-bet win.

Many other equivalent explanations were proposed. Briefly, the *prominence hypothesis* (Tversky *et al.* 1988) selects as key explanatorily variables the prominent dimensions associated with the choice and pricing tasks. Choice is deemed to evoke qualitative reasoning and ordinal considerations, whereas pricing is deemed to appeal to quantitative assessment and cardinal considerations. The *scale compatibility hypothesis* (Tversky *et al.* 1990) conjectures that the weight of a particular feature of a task is enhanced if it is compatible with the response mode. Incompatible attributes have a smaller impact on decision-making because they demand a mental conversion on the part of the subject, which increases error. The PR phenomenon is then explained by the over-weighing of the pay-offs in the pricing task, insofar as both the response and the pay-offs are expressed in monetary units. To give a final example, Daniel Kahneman's and Amos Tversky's (1979) *prospect theory* interprets preference reversals in terms of an editing phase prior to the decision in which individuals organize and reformulate the alternatives with the aim of simplifying the second phase of evaluation and choice. This makes decisions highly dependent on the editing of the problem.[11]

Because psychologists were trained in a different tradition, and were not as committed to Expected Utility Theory and its underlying presuppositions, they could more easily put the procedure invariance principle to the test. There were, however, a few exceptions among the economists. Richard Thaler, who had been working for a long time on so-called behavioural anomalies of economic theory and had carried out collaborative work with psychologists, also rejected the procedure invariance principle. Here is how Tversky and Thaler put it:

> First, people do not possess a set of pre-defined preferences for every contingency. Rather preferences are constructed in the process of making a choice or judgment. Second, the context and procedures involved in making choices or judgments influence the preferences that are implied by the elicited responses. In practical terms, this implies that behavior is likely to vary across situations that economists consider identical.
>
> (Tversky and Thaler 1990: 210)

Psychologists' research on individual-decision making ultimately gave rise to a more general hypothesis about the formation of individual preferences, the hypothesis that preferences are 'constructed' during the decision-making process and that this construction involves various mental operations.

> Construction strategies include anchoring and adjustment, relying on the prominent dimension, eliminating common elements, discarding non-essential differences, adding new attributes into the problem frame in order to bolster one alternative, or otherwise restructuring the decision problem to create dominance and thus reduce conflict and indecision. As a result of these mental gymnastics, decision making is a highly contingent form of information processing, sensitive to task complexity, time pressure, response mode, framing, reference points, and numerous other contextual factors.
>
> (Slovic 1995: 369)

Slovic (1995) also notes that preference contingency is present in economically relevant contexts. It is present in 'judgements and choices among options that are important, complex, and perhaps unfamiliar, such as gambles, jobs, careers, homes, automobiles, surgical treatment, and environments' (p. 369).

Procedure non-invariance, at last

Two different and plausible interpretations of the PR phenomenon remained. The PR phenomenon could be either explained as a violation of the transitivity axiom or as a violation of procedure invariance. As Holt (1986) states, to abandon the transitivity axiom is a far more drastic step than relaxing any other axiom of EUT.[12] But it could still be consistent with the basic presupposition that individuals have stable preferences and that they are rational and maximizing agents. Regret theory (Loomes and Sugden 1982, 1983) had indeed been proposed to account for various violations of EUT, which relaxed this axiom while preserving the fundamental principles.[13] The coexistence of two alternative interpretations, one proposed by psychologists and the other by economists, triggered a new phase of interdisciplinary dialogue intended to discriminate between them.

The experiments conducted by the economists and the psychologists produced preference reversals that could be accounted for by both non-transitivity and non-invariance. But whereas psychologists (Tversky *et al.* 1990) considered that non-invariance is the main cause of the reversals, economists (Loomes *et al.* 1989) concluded otherwise. Nonetheless, economists acknowledged the violation of procedure invariance as a cause of reversals. And they continued to affirm this in subsequent experiments (Loomes 1991; Loomes *et al.* 1991). In Graham Loomes's own wording:

> The overall conclusion appears to be that, although explanation 2 [violation of other axioms of EUT] can be rejected, failures of transitivity and failures of invariance both seem to be in evidence. These are not mutually exclusive, and their relative contribution to the preference reversal phenomenon has not yet been established beyond doubt (and, indeed, may never be precisely quantified, since the relative contributions may themselves vary with factors such as the parameters of the lotteries or the particular format in which the problems are presented).
>
> (Loomes 1991: 602)

What seemed to be incompatible results were, in fact, complementary and reinforcing results. Intransitivity and the failure of procedure invariance were considered the two main causes of preference reversals whose relative contribution depended on the 'material procedures' used to elicit preferences (cf. Starmer and Sugden 1998; Loomes 1998). Economists finally accepted the violation of a key principle in most experimental and theoretical practice in the field of individual decision-making.

Recognition that the violation of procedure invariance was a cause of the PR phenomenon had serious implications for economics. The stakes were further raised when economists started to take seriously the study of decision-making processes.

> By focusing attention on particular axioms such as independence and transitivity, we have overlooked an even more fundamental assumption, which most economists seem to take for granted, but which is almost certainly false: namely, that people come to problems armed with a clear and reasonably complete set of preferences, and process all decision tasks according to this given preference structure. But I believe that the reality is very different, and that most people's preferences are generally imprecise

> and in many respects incomplete, with the result that they are liable to process different decision tasks in rather different ways.
>
> (Loomes 1999a: F37)

The revision of the assumption of preference stability, in turn, suggested a new research agenda. In Loomes's view:

> Instead of continuing to try to devise some general theory of an essentially conventional (e.g. axiomatically based) form, perhaps we should switch our attention and our efforts to understanding more about the processes by which people select and apply rules/strategies for dealing with particular forms of decision problem. As part of *this* agenda, we would need to examine how robust such rules/strategies are, how they may evolve or be modified in response to feedback or experience, and in what ways the predictions (and, where relevant, the prescriptions) that follow from them may diverge from those derived from more conventional models.
>
> (Loomes 1998: 486, emphasis in original)

The implications tfor experimental economics were:

> The challenge is not to refashion existing experiments to incorporate even tighter controls until they succeed in generating results consistent with conventional theory by reducing participants to barely more than 'zero intelligence traders'. Rather, the real challenge for the future is to devise experiments which allow for the heterogeneity of human behaviour, and to develop techniques which give greater insights into the interactions between people's imprecise basic values and the environments in which they have to operate, tracing how they construct their responses and/or modify them in the light of experience.
>
> (Loomes 1999a, F44)

It is clear that Loomes is here advocating 'behavioural experiments' to study the processes of decision-making. A high level of 'human agency' is necessary in order to examine the interaction between subjects' basic values and the contexts wherein they operate. 'Technological experiments' are not suitable to this end, as the experiments designed by Bohm, Chu and Chu, and Harrison were not. Instead they provided knowledge of how to tame individual actions so as to make subjects behave as economic theory predicts they should and would do.

Revising prior beliefs … or not really

The profession at large still resisted abandoning the principle that preferences are consistent and stable and acknowledging the work required to extricate rational behaviour from experimental subjects. At the same time, they could no longer ignore the substantial amount of evidence for inconsistent behaviour, produced by both economists and psychologists.

Plott's (1995) 'discovered preference hypothesis' illustrates this tension well. This hypothesis can be here conceived of as a generic claim built upon experimental data but that is meant to apply to a class of situation that shares common properties, in the experimental setting and in the real world. The main claim of the discovery preference hypothesis is that preferences are stable but not always revealed in individual decisions. Preferences have to be 'discovered' during the process of decision-making as individuals come to learn what they want. As Plott presents it:

> The hypothesis suggests that attitudes like expectations, beliefs, risk-aversion and the like, are discovered, as are other elements of the environment. People acquire an understanding of what they want through a process of reflection and practice. In a sense, they do not know what they want and it may be costly, or even unpleasant, to go through the process of discovery. Attitude discovery is a process of evolution which has a direction, and in the final stage results in the 'discovery' of a consistent and stable preference.
>
> (Plott 1995: 227)

Plott identifies a gradation in 'attitude' discovery. In the most critical situation there is an absolute lack of experience and a very limited awareness of the immediate environment or the consequences of the decisions made. The individual is nevertheless purposeful and optimizing. He/she is simply unable to avoid inconsistent decisions when dealing with new tasks. In these cases, 'responses are "instantaneous" or "impulsive", reflecting whatever may have been perceived as in their self-interest at the instant' (p. 226). Even though 'systematic aspects of choices might exist, reflecting attention and perception, … they might not make sense when viewed from the perspective of a preference based model' (p. 227). As individuals acquire some experience, 'choices begin to reflect and incorporate an awareness of the environment, and can be recognised by an "outsider" as a stable form of "strategy" or "decision"' (p. 227). But it is only when choices comprehend expectations about the behaviour of others that individual behaviour may be regarded as rational. The upshot is that 'under conditions of substantial incentives, and with the accumulating information that is obtained from the process of choice, the attitudes stabilize in the sense of a consistent decision rule, reflecting the preferences that were "discovered" through the process' (p. 228).

It is now easy to see that the discovery preference hypothesis narrows down the scope of rational choice theory to very constrained environments in which it is questionable whether human behaviour reflect individuals' preferences. The effort required to extricate rational behaviour from subjects suggests that. Rational behaviour in economics experiments, which amounts to consistent actions with the experiments' incentive structure, requires: the motivational dominance of the monetary reward, the possibility of experiencing the financial consequences of individual actions, and the opportunity to learn and to adjust behaviour accordingly. To put it in another way, rational behaviour occurs when the 'material procedure' teaches subjects how to behave rationally by inflicting losses when they fail to do so. That the 'material procedure' succeeds in triggering consistent behaviour does not mean that it has also elicited subjects' preferences. Rather then being 'discovered' or 'constructed' by subjects, preferences seem instead to have been induced onto subjects.

Implicit in the discovery preference hypothesis is the idea that economic theory applies to structured environments where experienced and highly motivated subjects are capable of making rational choices. This view is endorsed by experimental economists who have explicitly argued that economic theory only applies to experimental contexts of this kind. Ken Binmore, for example, says:

> My own experimental papers therefore insist that economic theory should only be expected to predict in the laboratory if the following three criteria are satisfied:
>
> - The problem the subjects face is not only 'reasonably' simple in itself, but is framed so it seems simple to the subjects;
> - The incentives provided are 'adequate';
> - The time allowed for trial-and-error adjustment is 'sufficient'.
>
> (Binmore 1999: F17)

The fact that assessing the validity of disconfirming evidence to economic theory has revolved around the precepts of experimental economics, has produced the perplexing result of transforming the precepts into boundary conditions of economic theory. As we have seen, simplicity and the use of monetary incentives are requirements that are meant to achieve control over economic experimental systems. They ensure that subjects understand the experimental situation in the intended way and act accordingly. The inclusion of repetition, on the other hand, depends on the problem-situation. Robin P. Cubitt, Chris Starmer and Robert Sugden (2001), for instance, argue that single-task individual-choice designs may be effective in exercising control over experimental systems without the use of market institutions, feedback mechanisms and high incentives. Moreover, there are many economically interesting problems that do not require experience, such as decisions that are rare and/or irreversible (e.g. childbearing, marriage, job-taking, decisions relating to health, education, and so forth). Finally, and more importantly, the fact that experimental subjects behave in accordance with the incentive structure of economic experiments is not very informative, unless economists want to learn how to tame behaviour for the attainment of particular goals.

Conclusion

The research programme of preference reversals illustrates how the social dimension of knowledge production and the specificity of the experimental method of economics interact. In the early stages of a research programme, not much is known about the means and the results of experimental practice, and as a result, there is ample room for disagreement. At first, follow-up experiments investigate whether or not the experimental phenomenon is to be attributed to an artefact of the experimental procedure. This normally calls for the re-examination of the standard procedures of experimental economics, especially so if the phenomenon seems to disconfirm a well-established theory. Experimenters then check instructions for lack of clarity, subjects' inexperience, adequacy of the reward structure, and other familiar sources of 'error'. If the phenomenon remains recalcitrant, attention is directed at investigating its causal factors. Only at a later stage, when results are better understood, do experimenters try to put forward and test tentative explanatory hypotheses. Earlier results may then be reinterpreted, areas of disagreement narrowed down, and what were apparently conflicting results may eventually reinforce each other. The conditions under which the phenomenon occurs becomes more narrowly defined and better understood. In the case of the PR programme, we have seen that fundamental assumptions were also identified and revised.

The PR research programme is, moreover, a good illustration of the fruitfulness of the process of critical interaction, when it is carried out among scientists educated in different theoretical and experimental traditions. Not only was the PR phenomenon anticipated by psychologists, but psychologists were also more willing to derive its full implications to experimental and theoretical practice. Economists were, in turn, receptive to explore the implications of the phenomenon for economics, even though the first incursions were motivated by the expectation that they could make the PR phenomenon go away. Because the phenomenon was recalcitrant, economists tried even harder to eradicate it. Given the high stakes in presence, economists explored the sources of 'error' they could conceive of and tried to eliminate them. Because these attempts have failed, it is now consensual (though not unanimous) that the PR phenomenon is a robust phenomenon. It is also well established what the main causes of preference reversals are. Identification and scrutiny of a major assumption of experimental and theoretical economics – preference consistency and stability – would not have been possible without this interchange.

Social and individual willingness to accept results consistent with previous expectations, and to doubt results that conflict with them, convey epistemic value to the results that challenge established knowledge. While confirming evidence is too easily accepted, disconfirming evidence is accepted only after potential sources of error have been thoroughly explored and rejected as causes for the recalcitrant and unexpected phenomena.

The PR dispute has been interpreted as a demonstration of dogmatism on the part of economists. Experimental economists were accused of devoting too much time attempting to eradicate a phenomenon that was already well established in psychology. The analysis carried out, however, shows that the 'dogmatic' attitude of the experimental economists has epistemic value. Not only is it important to improve understanding of an 'anomalous' phenomenon, but it is also crucial for accepting it. The persistent and failed attempts at materially eliminating or explaining the phenomenon away ultimately convince economists of its significance. Belief revision is facilitated when experimenters themselves produce evidence that challenges their prior expectations. However, the epistemic value of 'dogmatism' requires an effective critical community in which scientists are compelled to investigate conflicting results generated in neighbouring fields of research.

The reluctance of economists to accept experimental evidence cannot be attributed to the experimental method of economics. Economics experiments are relatively transparent experimental systems that allow for discriminating experimenters' actions from subjects' actions, or in other words, it allows for assessing the 'materiality' and 'stringency' of the 'material procedure'. The fact that the PR phenomenon was eradicated only when subjects had the opportunity to learn that they suffered economic losses with inconsistent decisions indicates that these experiments cannot support claims about subjects' preferences. In these experiments, subjects' actions were tamed by the experimenter to behave rationally.

13 Conclusion

What about the social epistemology of experiment?

This book proposes a comprehensive framework – the social epistemology of experiment – that aims to account for and appraise the processes and practices by which knowledge is produced by experimental means.

The framework is built upon various studies of experimental practice in both the natural and social sciences. These studies support a reconstructed account of experimental practice as an activity that consists of forging relations of coherence among heterogeneous items of scientific culture until a three-way coherence is achieved among the components of the experimental system. The mutual support of the material procedure, the instrumental model and the phenomenal model is what gives experimenters confidence in their practice and in the outcome of that practice. Achieving a three-way coherence is epistemically relevant. It involves the direct participation of the material world and it is collectively constructed and validated by a process of critical interaction that helps scientists to avoid the partiality of beliefs framed in the context of a particular scientific practice.

Experimental coherence is worked out during knowledge production via conceptual and material manoeuvring of the experimental system until scientists succeed in making sense of the phenomenon produced. When coherence obtains, the material procedure interpreted through the instrumental model produces a phenomenon that is interpreted by the phenomenal model. Experimenters then believe they have made sense of their practices and respective outcomes. When coherence is attained, inquirers no longer have the inclination to revise the elements of their experimental system any further. The experiment ends.

The social epistemology of experiment (SEE) pays special attention to scientists' predisposition to obtain confirmation of prior beliefs and to the enforcement of group commitments by scientific communities. The conceptualization of experimental practice as an endeavour in which scientists strive for the attainment of coherent resolutions must thus take into account that scientists tend to produce results that fit their conceptual frameworks while overlooking conflicting results.

Two major sources of epistemic value were identified: direct participation of the material world and the social dimension of knowledge production, the value of which lies in the potential to promote the revision of scientists' prior beliefs. Participation of the material world and the social validation of experimental results force scientists to conceive questions they had not imagined and to provide answers they had not thought of, and consequently to revise and correct the partiality of their viewpoints.

Insofar as the participation of the material and the social worlds in knowledge production varies, the epistemic value of experimental results varies too. The implication of this is that the epistemic appraisal of the processes and products of experiment must take into account the participation of both the material and the social worlds. That is, the epistemic appraisal of experiments requires evaluating the extent to which the material and the social worlds participated in knowledge production.

The research carried out here, however, is not immune to the problems it identified in scientific experimentation. The study of experimentation and of economics experiments has itself been an exercise in forging coherent relations between the selected set of items of scientific culture. The results arrived at may thus be informed by the partiality of belief and biased by the particular resources mobilized in the endeavour. Moreover, the epistemological framework has been designed for the analysis of the processes and products of experiments. The strategy to tackle this problem, however, has been the same as that used by experimental scientists. The framework is supported by coherent relations with heterogeneous items of scientific culture and has been submitted to public scrutiny. That is, the research carried out attempted to conform to both the descriptions and the prescriptions of SEE. The demonstration of this claim is thus the natural topic of the concluding chapter of this book.

Appraising SEE

The study of experimental economics had recourse to an analytical framework that was purposefully constructed to that end. I will try to show that SEE is a coherent resolution that tries to avoid the epistemic problems that arise when both the means and the outcomes of knowledge production are at stake. To show this, enumerated below is the list of the coherence procedures followed and the results achieved. Naturally, conformity to SEE's prescriptions should be independently appraised by those who were not directly involved in its production. This test is still incomplete, however.

1 *The social epistemology of experiment is a robust and coherent analytical device.* The construction of SEE relied upon various and heterogeneous items of scientific culture of philosophy, history, sociology, economics and psychology, all of which seem to concur with the account of scientific experimentation put forward.
2 *The knowledge production process that generated SEE involved the participation of its object of scrutiny*, though indirectly via the recollection of various studies of experiment. The social epistemology of experiment

therefore attempted to accommodate the 'material agency' of its subject matter, i.e. actual experimental practice.

3 *The social epistemology of experiment is a stringent framework of analysis* insofar as it has been able to generate conclusive and unambiguous results.
4 *The social epistemology of experiment has a high level of technological applicability* insofar as it has been applied to various episodes of experimental practice, experiments, social processes, methods and results of experiments.
5 *The social epistemology of experiment has a potentially high level of social robustness* insofar as it is amenable to the scrutiny of a wide and heterogeneous audience.
6 The major contribution of SEE is, as argued, the reformulation of key methodological and epistemic issues pertaining to experimental economics. The focus on experimenting in the natural sciences has brought to the forefront the role of the 'materials' of experiments. This has contributed to build an account of economics experiments that emphasizes the role of human subjects and downplays the role of theory or some real-world reference model in justifying the function of experiments in economics.

Applying SEE to experimental economics

The application of SEE to experimental economics has been fruitful. A broad portrayal of experimental economics has been offered along with a more fine-grained analysis of particular episodes of experimental practice and results. These included the scrutiny of arguments intended to justify the relevance of the experimental method in economics, the analysis of research programmes, experiments, experimental procedures and social practices.

The social epistemology of experiment also identified common features of scientific enterprise, specificities of experimental practice and characteristic attributes of the experimental field of economics. It has brought new insights into ongoing methodological debates and controversies and identified topics that deserve more attention from students and practitioners of experimental economics. The appraisal of SEE thus supports the adequacy of the framework for both the descriptive and normative analysis of the processes and products of experiments. The main results are now synthesized below.

SEE on scientific practice

1 The establishment of a new field of research is the outcome of a long collective process of knowledge production. Scientists have first to become experts in the new field before they are able to justify it. They first need to stabilize the fields' aims, standards, conceptual and instrumental tools. They also have to wait for the opportunity to fill the space left open by some dominant theoretical or empirical research programme.
2 In contrast, work carried out in well-established fields of research does not have to be self-justificatory. Their relevance has been determined and they

already have a consolidated basis for knowledge production. Scientists know which problems are worth pursuing and which tools to use to solve them. This explains the rapid accumulation of knowledge therein.

3 New fields of research carry a higher potential to produce knowledge that promotes the revision of prior beliefs. In contrast, work in well-established fields consists first and foremost in furthering the articulation of already fairly established items of scientific culture.

4 The collective nature of knowledge production promotes the confrontation of subsets of scientific culture and beliefs. The realization of this potential, however, depends on the critical attitude of scientific communities. This attitude is facilitated in heterogeneous communities or in communities that more often communicate with others. The wider the disparity of the views in confrontation, the more interesting and unforeseen questions can be raised and given due attention.

5 The social organization of science must actively encourage the exercise of effective and transformative criticism because the social, psychological and the cognitive make-up of scientists do not naturally promote it.

SEE on experimentation

6 To experiment is actively to produce a phenomenon of interest under the favourable conditions of the laboratory to examine it. This requires a high level of control over the object of inquiry and the experimental conditions, so that experimenters can be confident that the data obtained by experimental means pertain to the object of study and to this object only.

7 Scientists' control over the conditions of knowledge production and the direct participation of the material world are thus two characteristic features of scientific experimentation.

8 The key epistemic question of scientific experimentation concerns the trade-off between experimenters' actions and the agency of the material world. Control is necessary to produce valid results, i.e. results that scientists believe are no artefacts of the experimental procedures. But the more control is exercised, the more the results are the outcome of scientists' actions rather than the agency of the material world.

9 This trade-off calls for the analysis of the extent to which the results of experiments are the outcome of scientists' material and conceptual manipulation rather than the agency of the material world.

10 The social dimensions of knowledge production can somehow overcome arbitrariness and the partiality of belief informing scientists' interventions in the material world. The collective way whereby experimental results are produced and socially validated is critical. It improves the replicability and robustness of experimental results by suggesting new experiments and by giving assent that the process of knowledge production was reliable.

11 There is no dividing line between the natural and human sciences as far as the epistemic value of experiments is concerned. The direct participation

of the subject matter renders experiments epistemically superior devices to other methods of knowledge production.

SEE on experimental economics

12 Economics experiments allow for the creation of manageable microeconomic systems in the laboratory to study how the attributes of economic agents, the institutional rules and the actions agents take under those rules interact and bring about individual and social outcomes.

13 Economists create and control microeconomic systems by designing and enforcing institutional rules that define the experimental task and how it is to be carried out, and by paying experimental subjects in accordance to the outcomes of the actions they take during the experiment. A controlled experiment in economics hence elicits behaviour that can be interpreted in the light of motives induced by the reward structure and the institution that organizes subjects' interactions. Experimenters can then understand how the subjects' attributes and the institution translate into individual behaviour and how this, in turn, affects individual and aggregate outcomes.

14 The direct participation of human subjects is the major source of epistemic value of economics experiments. Participants in economics experiments may 'resist' economists' expectations and thereby prevent experimental results from being exclusively determined economists' material and conceptual interventions on the experimental microeconomic systems.

15 Experimental microeconomies are highly artificial and simple systems. The control exercised in economic experiments, however, renders economic experiments fairly transparent and intelligible systems from which inferences can be made with a high degree of confidence.

16 Experimental practice in economics is conducted in a fundamentally interactive way by series of experiments through which economists build upon one another's results and thereby control the effect of experimenters' prior beliefs on experimental results.

17 Economics experiments are amenable to scrutiny by a wide audience because they are simple contexts that are fully described in the published reports of experiments. The exposure of experiments to critical scrutiny favours the identification of conscious and unconsciously held beliefs and the arbitrariness of decisions taken in the course of experiment. In so doing, it promotes the autonomy of the results from particular sets of beliefs and practices and thereby promotes the replicability and robustness of experimental results.

18 Insofar as experimenters control human behaviour by eliciting self-interest and income-maximizing behaviour, the participation of human subjects in economics experiments allows for the identification of the circumstances that affect the manifestation of this behaviour. Because control is the hallmark of experimentation, economics experiments also allow for learning how to control individual actions for the attainment of predefined goals.

19 Applying the results of economic experiments to concrete situations in the real world depends on the possibility of creating, both in the laboratory and in the real world, social contexts that constrain human behaviour in such a way that ensures that the same results obtain.

SEE's insights

The major contributions of SEE are the insights it has brought to the study of scientific experimentation in economics and the topics of research it identified.

The social epistemology of experiment selects the notions of 'materiality' and 'sociality' as the main attributes around which scientific experimentation should be accounted for and appraised. Analysis of the 'materiality' of economic experiments points to the importance of assessing the contribution of the 'material' components of the experimental systems, namely the participation of human subjects. Even though the participation of human subjects is the distinguishing feature of experimental economics, its role has not been explicitly addressed; nor has it been examined the differentiated role participants play in experiments. Experimental economists do not seem to be fully aware of the fact that the more control is exercised over subjects' motives and actions, the less support the experiment provides to the making of claims about human behaviour. The more control is exercised, the more the results are to be attributed to experimenters' actions.

The social dimension of knowledge production proved to be epistemically relevant to experimental economics, which attenuate the significance of the methodological and epistemic problems associated with the high degree of control exercised in the laboratory. The susceptibility of economics experiments to public scrutiny is critical to the interactive way through which knowledge is produced by series of experiments. This feature of experimental practice improves the reliability of the experimental process of knowledge production as well as the robustness of experimental results.

The study of experimental economics undertaken thus far has revolved around the comparative analysis of experiment with other scientific devices, and on the relation between experiment and theory or some concrete real-world target system. The social epistemology of experiment highlights instead the study of the sources of epistemic value of economic experiments – the actual participation of human subjects in experiments and the social dimension of knowledge production – and their role in overcoming the methodological difficulties associated with the effect of individual and collective biases in knowledge production.

These two factors ground a third kind of inference that has not yet been acknowledged and articulated in methodological analysis – the generic inferences of experimental economics. Besides internal inferences that pertain to single experiments, and external inferences that concern the transferability of experimental results from the lab to concrete real-world targets, experimental economists also derive generic inferences from series of experiments that apply generically to specified classes of situations in the real world. Generic inferences are supported by the ontological similarity between the social situations defined by series of experiments and a particular class of real world situations. It is this similarity that explains experimenters' ease in constructing experimental worlds without having a specific real world reference as a model. That is, experimental systems are themselves special socioeconomic contexts from which knowledge can be acquired about individual motives and behaviour, as well as about socioeconomic institutions.

The social epistemology of experiment identified and distinguished the technological and the behavioural experiments of economics; the epistemological functions of each have not been made explicit by the experimenters themselves. Economists do not seem to be fully aware that some experiments in economics – the technological experiments – can only provide knowledge about how best to control human behaviour for specific purposes. Inferences about human motives and behaviour can only be derived from experiments that provide room for human agency – the behavioural experiments of economics. In these experiments, the design set-up must be capable of eliciting the relevant set of motives, allow these motives to be manifested in the choices of the participants, and allow for the choices made to be effective in producing intended outcomes.

Experimenters and students of experiment have to date focused on the few success stories of the technological experiments of economics. These seem to accomplish the traditional aspirations of the discipline, which is to provide guidance for policy-making. They have, in fact, become tools of social engineering for the design of market institutions to be implemented in the economy. The behavioural experiments of economics are not suitable for this kind of application. The results they produce do not have a direct application to concrete real-world situations. Nonetheless, they can generate relevant knowledge about human behaviour, which is also relevant for policy-making.

The insights of behavioural experiments are now starting to feedback into economic theory with as yet unknown impact. The potential for generating knowledge that challenges the basic presuppositions of conventional economic theory suggests, however, that behavioural experiments may have a substantial impact on the discipline. The social epistemology of experiment therefore strongly supports the methodological and the epistemological study of behavioural experiments and their impact on economics.

The social epistemology of experiment identifies other fruitful areas for future research. Particularly promising investigations concern the study of experimental work at the cross-section of various experimental traditions. The emergence of the experimental method in economics is a result of the interdisciplinary research carried out in the USA right after the Second World War, which joined economists, psychologists, cognitive scientists, physicists and mathematicians, among other scientists. At present, the recent collaboration between economists, psychologists and neuroscientists suggests the emergence of another exciting field of research with a high potential to feedback upon the discipline of economics – neuroeconomics.

The social epistemology of experiment, in addition, highlights the relevance of the study of the organization of science institutions to further both the growth of knowledge and the values of good science. The social organization of science must create favourable conditions for multicultural dialogue and thus the exercise of effective criticism. This dialogue and criticism are required not only for raising pertinent but also socially responsible research agendas that can take account of those whose interests tend to be under-represented in scientific practice – the less privileged and the future generations. This is, in the end, the concern that guides, or at least should guide, the practice of scientists and that of students of science. The increasing complexity of science and its growing influence on human and non-human affairs make this study a pertinent research question for all sciences. The growing engineering prospects of economics, including experimental economics, stress the importance of studying the mechanisms through which economics participates and shapes social life.

Notes

1 Introduction: epistemology, experiments and economics

1 See Hacking (1983), Giere (1988) and Mayo (1996) for a more complete account of the neglect of scientific experimentation in the philosophy of science.
2 Volumes of collective papers have been edited by Achinstein and Hannaway (1985), Gooding, Pinch and Schaffer (1989), Pickering (1992a), Buchwald (1995), Heidelberger and Steinle (1998) and Radder (2003a). Surveys of this literature can be found in Ackermann (1989), Hacking (1989), Pickering (1992b), Mayo (1996), and Franklin (2007). Philosophical discussion of experiment include the volumes of the symposia of the Philosophy of Science Association (1988, 1990, 1996).
3 http://nobelprize.org/nobel_prizes/economics/laureates/2002/index.html

2 Creating phenomena in the lab

1 Replicability and robustness are the standard criteria for evaluating the validity of experimental results and they will be analysed in more detail in Chapter 6. For now it suffices to note that a replicated and robust result is a result that has been reproduced with different experimental systems and is supported by various three-way coherences.
2 This strategy has grown in importance with complexity in experimentation. The use of large-scale and expensive material apparatuses, such as those characteristic of high-energy physics, renders the construction of new devices or their adaptation to new problems unfeasible. Under these circumstances, much of the experimental work leading to an experimental conclusion relies on work done after operating with a relatively stable apparatus. It relies specifically on data-processing procedures that search through the mass of experimental data for the fraction that constitutes evidence for the phenomenon of interest. This means that data analysis has to deal with the backgrounds and errors that could not be controlled or eliminated by material means (Galison 1987: 263–66).

3 Creating microeconomic phenomena

1 Smith's account of experiment applies more directly to market experiments. It is nevertheless sufficiently general to provide a useful framework to organize experimentation and the various kinds of economics experiments. In every experiment economists manipulate environmental and instrumental variables in order to study human behaviour or microeconomic institutions. Three grand categories of experiment can nonetheless be distinguished: *market experiments* are particularly tailored to study the performance of market institutions, *game theory experiments* are devoted to study

problems of conflict, coordination and cooperation, and *individual decision-making experiments* address decision problems that only concern the decision-maker. Various examples of these kinds of experiment are provided throughout the book.

2 The relevance of these procedures may vary, however. For example, anonymity and privacy are not as important background factors in individual-decision making experiments because decisions affect only the decision-maker therein.

4 Intervening in the 'material world'

1 Pickering also recognizes that the conceptual items of scientific practice play 'an analogous role in conceptual practice to that of material agency in material practice' (1995a: 29). We will see below how they do this.

2 Galison does not explain how 'constraints' have come to perform this role and what their relative epistemic import is. According to the account provided here, constraints are rigid resources of practice, the epistemic value of which lies in a dense web of coherences forged in past practice (cf. section 2.3).

5 Intervening in the 'social world'

1 In a later study of instrumentation in twentieth century high-energy physics, Galison (1997) emphasizes the differences between experimental traditions. But Galison still conceives of the possibility of dialogue among different traditions with the help of what he calls 'creole interlanguage'.

2 This point had already been remarked on by Latour and Woolgar (1986 [1979]) as a necessary stage in the process of transforming experimental results into 'scientific facts'.

3 The machine analogy and the conception of scientific experimentation as engineering are two related ideas that have been explored by philosophers of science (e.g. Cartwright 1999).

6 The social epistemology of experiment

1 This classification follows Kagel and Roth's (1995).

2 In a First-Price Sealed Bid Auction, the commodity is awarded to the highest bidder after all bids have been collected; in an English Auction the commodity is awarded to the last bidder remaining in the auction after all other bidders have dropped out as the price of the commodity increases; in the Dutch Auction, the commodity is awarded to the bidder who accepts to buy the good at the auction price as the price decreases.

3 For a review of the winner's curse phenomenon see Thaler (1988a).

7 The foundation of experimental economics

1 http://nobelprize.org/nobel_prizes/economics/laureates/2002/index.html

2 Smith's major contribution was in the field of market experiments, but this does not mean that this was Smith's only experimental practice. Smith also made incursions in other topics of research such as public goods (1979a, 1979b, 1980a), bargaining theory (with Hoffman, McCabe and Shachat 1994, and with Hoffman and McCabe 1995, 1996a, 1996b), and individual decision-making (with Knez 1987), and more recently in neuroeconomics (with McCabe, Houser, Ryan and Trouard 2001).

3 The same strategy was followed by Charles Plott in the field of public choice theory. Plott argued that similarly to (New)^2 Welfare Economics, which aims at designing 'resource allocation mechanisms' according to pre-defined performance

criteria, public choice theory engages in 'institutional engineering' that aims at constructing '"new" or "synthetic" institutions which have prespecified performance characteristics' that 'may or may not resemble any existing institution' (1979: 139).

4 For a biography of Vernon Smith see www.gmu.edu/departments/economics/faculty bios/smith.html and http://nobelprize.org/economics/laureates/2002/smith-autobio.html, and other links therein.

5 The Allais paradox refers to choices among uncertain prospects that show that a significant majority of individuals order them in a way that is inconsistent with the independence axiom of expected utility theory. That is, these orderings reveal that choice is affected by factors other than the differences between the alternatives.

6 For a survey on this experimental work see Camerer (1995).

7 The RAND Corporation is a non-profit organization that resulted from the independence of Project RAND from Douglas Aircraft Company of Santa Monica, California, USA, in 1948.

8 The Cowles Commission for Research in Economics was founded in 1932 by Alfred Cowles at Colorado Springs, USA. It developed into the Cowles Foundation for Research in Economics in 1955, when it became an institute of the Department of Economics at Yale University. Similarly to the RAND Corporation, the major research goal in the 1950s was to foster the development of logical, mathematical and statistical methods of analysis and its application in economics and other social sciences (see Mirowski 2002, Ch. 5).

9 In his 1962 article, Smith quotes Siegel and Fouraker (1960). See Smith (1992) for other first-person accounts about the mutual influence pioneers exercised upon one another.

8 Early methodological debate in experimental economics

1 The permeability of econometric results to scientists' priors was at the centre of a huge crisis in econometrics in the 1980s (see Mayer 1980; Leamer 1983). This crisis has subsided due to the development of more sophisticated procedures and the promotion of a more methodologically self-conscious practice. At any rate, the comparative advantage of the experimental method to control and observe preferences remains.

2 Field data are also more vulnerable to non-scientific goals, given that they are often collected by non-scientific agencies for non-scientific purposes. Consequently, 'when things appear not to turn out as expected the quality of data is more likely to be questioned than the relevance and quality of abstract reasoning'. Experiments, in contrast, produce credible data because they 'brought to the economist direct responsibility for an important source of scientific data generated by controlled processes that can be replicated by other experimentalists' (Smith 1987: 242).

3 Falsificationism is, to date, the most influential methodological proposal in economics. Wade Hands interprets the appeal of falsificationism to economists in terms of its simplicity and adoptability insofar as it seemed to provide a 'set of easily implemented methodological rules for the proper conduct of scientific inquiry' (Hands 2001: 276). Hands also argues that Popper's interest in the social sciences, Popper's work in political philosophy, and Popper's personal and professional connections at the London School of Economics might also have contributed to importating falsificationist ideas to economics.

4 'Orthodox' economic theories are charged with being too abstract (rather than applied to concrete real world situations), with assuming narrow or false postulates about individual preferences and human cognitive capabilities (e.g. the assumption that individuals are solely guided by self-interest and that they possess unbounded rationality), and with neglecting the influence of the institutional and the social setting on individual and aggregate behaviour. This debate has obvious connections

with economists' diverging views on what are the purposes and the adequate level of realisticness of economic theories. For reasons of economy of space, this topic will be addressed only in passing below. For an overview of this debate in economics see, for example, Mäki (1996, 1998, 2002).

5 Smith is not clear on what a 'realistic' theory amounts to. However, he seems to endorse the view that the representations of economic theories can and should capture the relevant elements of the domains to which they purportedly apply (i.e. the 'fundamental structure of the economy' or the 'the way the world works', cf. Mäki, 1998: 312–13). If some of these are left out or false, they should be included or revised.

9 Economics experiments and the real world

1 In the public goods experiment, each member of a group of n subjects is given, say, 10 tokens. They must then decide simultaneously how many tokens to keep for themselves and how many tokens to invest in a common public good project. For each token that is privately kept by a subject, that subject earns exactly one token. For each token a subject invests in the project, all subjects, whether they have invested in the public good or not, earn a part of it, say 0.4. The private return for investing one additional token in the public good is 0.4 tokens, while the social return is $0.4n$ tokens. As the cost of investing one token is exactly one token while the private return is 0.4 tokens, it is always in the material self-interest of a subject to keep all the tokens. In a group of four members, if all group members keep all the tokens, each subject earns 10 tokens, but if they all invest their total endowment in the public good, each subject earns 16 tokens. In a public goods experiment with punishment, subjects are given the opportunity to observe the contributions of others, and to punish those who do not contribute by inflicting a penalty on them.

2 In a gift-exchange game with a labour market framing, firms offer a wage w and the worker who accepts it then chose an effort level e. Firms' earnings increase with effort and effort is costly to workers. Firms cannot contract with specific workers and do not know their identities, so workers cannot build up reputations. Once workers are hired, firms cannot control workers' effort and self-interested workers will choose the minimal effort. Anticipating this, firms should pay the minimum market-clearing wage.

3 Chapter 11 provides a partial illustration of the kind of assessment required, by assessing two competing explanations to the ultimatum game.

10 Human agency (or lack thereof) in economics experiments

1 For instance, a market institution may be deemed incentive-compatible if it yields a Nash equilibrium that is a Pareto Optimum, which means that the communication and exchange rules guide each individual in choosing messages that constitute the best response to the other messages, which then results in a market outcome that maximizes social welfare.

2 See Holt (1995, Section V) for a review of well-established mappings from trading institutions to market outcomes.

3 This account is based on game theorists' reports of the events after efficiency had been set the main goal of the auction to the detriment of other welfare goals defined by the congress, such as the expansion of public access to new technologies, products and services, and the decentralization of the licences awarded to include small businesses, rural telephone companies and minority groups. For a more complete account of the political process involving the FCC auctions see Nik-Khah (2008).

4 The 'winners' curse' is likely to occur in common value auctions where the values of the items transacted are unknown at the time of the sale. The curse is that the winning bidders are likely to be the traders who mostly overestimate the value of the items and therefore are prone to incur high losses.
5 This is a very brief account of FCC auctions. See Guala (2001, 2005a Ch. 8) for a more detailed and technical account of the role experiments played in the various stages of the engineering process leading to the final implementation of the FCC auctions.
6 See Camerer (2003, Ch. 2) for a review of the main results of the ultimatum games.
7 This conjecture is based on Fouraker's and Siegel's (1963) bilateral monopoly experiment in which the seller is successful in exploiting his or her monopoly position. It also points to the framing effects of market institutions that make salient and legitimize self-interest and income-maximizing motives.
8 See Leonard's (1994) account of bargaining games that highlights the relevance of the personal attributes of bargainers in the haggling process.

11 Behavioural experiments: how economists learn about human behaviour

1 Siakantaris's analysis takes parallelism as a requirement for the validity of economics experiments. The analysis undertaken here is less demanding. As argued in Chapter 9, economics experiments can provide understanding of human behaviour, before verifying whether experimental results apply to a concrete real-world situation.
2 The growing accumulation of empirical results that cannot be explained 'by assuming that agents have stable, well-defined preferences and make rational choices consistent with those preferences in markets that (eventually) clear' constituted the motivation for the column 'anomalies' in the *Journal of Economic Perspectives* (e.g. Thaler 1988b).
3 The extensive survey by Camerer and Hogarth (1999), for instance, is inconclusive regarding the capacity of financial incentives and learning opportunities to induce rational behaviour.
4 See Chapter 10 for other explanations.
5 When Player 1 chooses $q_1 = 4$ we will always get \$0.42, whether Player 2 chooses $q_2 = 0$ or $q_2 = 4$. Though $q_2 = 0$ yields an income of \$3.7 and $q_2 = 4$ yields an income of \$0.42 to Player 2. The equal contribution ($q_i = q_1 = q_2$) that yielded positive pay-offs ($w_i = w_1 = w_2$) were: (q_i; w_i) = (4, \$0.42) (5, \$0.4), (3, \$0.39), (6, \$0.33), (2, \$0.31); (7, \$0.21), (1, \$0.18), (8, \$0.04).
6 This result has been replicated in other experiments, such as the public goods experiments in which the possibility of punishing was effective in forcing cooperative behaviour on 'selfish rational' individuals (cf. Fehr and Gächter 2000).

12 Preference reversals and critical practice in economics

1 See (Guala 2005a, Ch. 5) for a technical account of the preference reversals experiments and references therein.
2 If preferences obey a particular set of axioms (completeness, transitivity, continuity, reduction, independence, monotonicity), Expected Utility Theory posits that rational agents choose the course of action that yields the highest expected utility, where expected utility is the sum of the utilities of each possible outcome of an action multiplied by the probability of the outcome's occurrence ($\sum u_i.p_i$). In the PR experiment, a rational agent should have chosen the bet that maximizes his/her utility and given the highest price to it.
3 The discussion on performance-based incentive structures points to different conceptions of subjects' behaviour. Whereas economists believe that subjects' efforts depend on the adequacy of the rewards to compensate subjects for carrying out the

experimental tasks, psychologists presuppose instead that subjects are intrinsically motivated to do their best. Psychologists therefore do not believe that effort improves with financial incentives. The study on the effect of financial incentives by Camerer and Hogarth (1999) is inclusive, however.

4 See McDaniel's and Starmer's (1998) discussion on the use of deception in economics.

5 The BDM procedure is named after the authors who proposed it: Gordon M. Becker, Morris H. DeGroot, and Jacob Marschak (1964).

6 This result had been already obtained in previous market experiments (e.g. Knez and Smith 1987).

7 See Guala (2000, 2005a Ch. 5) for a more detailed account of this discussion, which is framed as an instance of the 'theory ladenness of observation' in that 'the phenomenon at stake is inconsistent with expected utility theory, but the instruments used to observe the phenomenon are constructed on the hypothesis that expected utility is correct' (2000: 56).

8 The independence axiom asserts that only the outcomes that distinguish two lotteries are relevant to choosing between them. Thus, if lottery *A* is preferred to lottery *B*, then the compound lottery (*A*, *p*; *C*, 1-*p*) is preferred to (*B*, p; *C*, 1-*p*).

9 These include, for example, generalized expected utility (Machina 1982), weighted utility theory (Chew and MacCrimmon 1979; Fishburn 1983) and expected utility with rank-dependent probabilities – EURDP (Quiggin 1982; Yaari 1987).

10 It should be borne in mind, though, that economists continued to ignore psychology experiments, namely those that did not use the BDM mechanism and still obtained a high rate of reversals (e.g. Lichtenstein and Slovic 1971).

11 A more complete account of psychology explanations of the PR phenomenon can be found in Tversky and Thaler (1990) and Slovic (1995).

12 The transitivity axiom specifies that if an individual prefers object *a* to *b*, *b* to *c*, then he/she also prefers *a* to *c*.

13 The key idea of regret theory is that individuals compare their current situations with those they would have been in, had they made different choices in the past. 'If they realize that a different choice would have led to a better outcome, they may experience the painful sensation of regret; if the alternative would have led to a worse outcome, they may experience a pleasurable sensation we call "rejoicing"'(Loomes and Sugden 1983: 428). Regret theory, then, predicts that individuals choose the action that maximizes rejoicing and/or minimizes regret. This is consistent with the choice of the P-bet in the PR experiment because the choice of the low-probability $-bet is associated with large regrets that individuals wish to avoid, though they may prefer this bet.

Bibliography

Achinstein, P. and Hannaway, O. (eds) (1985) *Observation, Experiment and Hypothesis in Modern Physical Science*, Cambridge, Mass.: MIT Press.

Ackermann, R. (1985) *Data, Instruments and Theory*, Princeton, N.J.: Princeton University Press.

——(1989) 'The New Experimentalism', *British Journal for the Philosophy of Science*, 40: 185–90.

Allais, M. (1953) 'Le Comportement de l'Homme Rationnel devant le Risqué: Critique des Postulats et Axioms de l'École Americane', *Econometrica*, 21: 503–46.

Arrow, K.J., Karlin, S. and Suppes, P. (eds) (1960) *Mathematical Methods in the Social Sciences*, Stanford: Stanford University.

Arrow, K.J., Colombatto, E. Perlman, M. and Schmidt, C. (eds) (1995) *The Rational Foundations of Economic Behaviour*, IEA Conference, London: Macmillan Press.

Bacon, F. (1620; 1st printing 1994) *Novum Organum*, Chicago: Open Court.

Banks, J.S., Ledyard, J.O. and Porter, D. P. (1989) 'Allocating Uncertain and Unresponsive Resources: An Experimental Approach', *RAND Journal of Economics*, 20: 1–25.

Bardsley, N. (2005) 'Experimental Economics and the Artificiality of Alteration', *Journal of Economic Methodology*, 12: 239–51.

Barnes, B. (1974) *Scientific Knowledge and Sociological Theory*, London: Routledge & Kegan Paul.

——(1977) *Interests and the Growth of Knowledge*, London: Routledge and Kegan Paul.

——(1982) *T.S. Kuhn and Social Science*, London: Macmillan.

Batens, D. and van Bendegen, J.P. (eds) (1988) *Theory and Experiment: Recent Insights and New Perspectives on Their Relation*, Dordrecht: D. Reidl.

Beattie, J. and Loomes, G. (1997) 'The Impact of Incentives Upon Risky Choice Experiments', *Journal of Risk and Uncertainty*, 14: 155–68.

Becker, G.M., DeGroot, M.H. and Marschak, J. (1964) 'Measuring Utility by a Single Response Sequential Method', *Behavioral Science*, 9: 226–32.

Berg, J.E., Dickhaut, J.W. and O'Brien, J.R. (1985) 'Preference Reversal and Arbitrage', in V.L. Smith (ed.) *Research in Experimental Economics*, Vol. 3, Greenwich, CT: JAI Press. pp. 31–72.

Bicchieri, C. (2006) *The Grammar of Society*, Cambridge: Cambridge University Press.

Bijker, W., Hughes, T.P. and Pinch, T. (eds) (1987) *The Social Construction of Technical Systems: New Directions in the Sociology and History of Technology*, London: MIT Press.

Binmore, K. (1999) 'Why Experiment in Economics?', *The Economic Journal*, 109: F16–24.

Binmore, K., Shaked, A. and Sutton, J. (1985) 'Testing Noncooperative Bargaining Theory: A Preliminary Study', *The American Economic Review*, 75: 1178–80.

Blaug, M. (1992; 2nd edn 1980) *The Methodology of Economics: Or How Economists Explain*, Cambridge: Cambridge University Press.

Bloor, D. (1976) *Knowledge and Social Imagery*, London: Routledge.

——(1991; 2nd edn 1976) *Knowledge and Social Imagery*, Chicago: University of Chicago Press.

Blount, S. (1995) 'When Social Outcomes Aren't Fair: The Effect of Causal Attributions on Preferences', *Organizational Behavior and Human Decision Processes*, 63: 131–44.

Bohm, P. (1994) 'Time Preference and Preference Reversal among Experienced Subjects: the Effects of Real Payments', *Economic Journal*, 104: 1370–78.

Bohnet, I. and Frey, B.S. (1999) 'Social Distance and Other-Regarding Behavior in Dictator Games: Comment', *The American Economic Review*, 89: 335–39.

Bolton, G. E. and Ockenfels, A. (2000) 'ERC: A Theory of Equity, Reciprocity, and Competition', *The American Economic Review*, 90: 166–93.

Bolton, G.E. and Zwick, R. (1995) 'Anonymity versus Punishment in Ultimatum Bargaining', *Games and Economic Behavior*, 10: 95–121.

Bostic, R., Herrnstein, R.J. and Luce, R.D. (1990) 'The Effect on the Preference-Reversal Phenomenon of Using Choice Indifferences', *Journal of Economic Behavior and Organization*, 13: 193–212.

Bowles, S. (1998) 'Endogenous Preferences: The Cultural Consequences of Markets and Other Economic Institutions', *Journal of Economic Literature*, 39: 75–111.

Bowles, S. and Gintis, H. (2004) 'The Evolution of Strong Reciprocity: Cooperation in Heterogeneous Populations', *Theoretical Population Biology*, 65:17–28.

Buchwald, J.Z. (ed.) (1995) *Scientific Practice: Theories and Stories of Physics*. Chicago: Chicago University Press.

Camerer, C.F. (1995) 'Individual Decision Making', in J.H. Kagel and A.E. Roth (eds), *The Handbook of Experimental Economics*, Princeton: Princeton University Press, pp. 587–703.

——(2003) *Behavioral Game Theory: Experiments in Strategic Interaction*, Princeton, New Jersey: Princeton University Press.

Camerer, C.F. and Hogarth, R.M. (1999) 'The Effects of Financial Incentives in Experiments: A Review and Capital-Labor-Production Framework', *Journal of Risk and Uncertainty*, 19: 7–42.

Camerer, C.F. and Loewenstein, G. (2004) 'Behavioral Economics: Past, Present, Future', in C.F. Camerer, G. Loewenstein and M. Rabin (eds) *Advances in Behavioral Economics*, Princeton: Princeton University Press, pp. 3–51.

Camerer, C.F. and Thaler, R.H. (1995) 'Ultimatums, Dictators and Manners', *Journal of Economic Perspectives*, 9: 209–19.

Capen, E.C., Clapp, R.V. and Campbell, W.M. (1971) 'Competitive bidding in high-risk situations', *Journal of Petroleum Technology*, 23: 641–53.

Cartwright, N. (1999) *The Dappled World*, Cambridge: Cambridge University Press.

Chamberlin, E.H. (1948) 'An Experimental Imperfect Market', *Journal of Political Economy*, 56: 95–108.

Chew, S.H. and MacCrimmon, K. (1979) 'Alpha-Nu Choice Theory: a Generalisation of Expected Utility Theory', Working Paper no. 669, University of British Columbia.

Chu, Y.P. and Chu, R.L. (1990) 'The Subsidence of Preference Reversals in Simplified and Market Experimental Settings: A Note', *The American Economic Review*, 80: 902–11.

Collins, H.M. (1985) *Changing Order: Replication and Induction in Scientific Practice*, London: Sage Publications.

Coursey, D., Isaac, M.R. and Smith, V.L. (1984) 'Natural Monopoly and the Contested Markets: Some Experimental Results', *Journal of Law and Economics*, 27: 91–113.

Cox, J.C. and Epstein, S. (1989) 'Preference Reversals Without the Independence Axiom', *The American Economic Review*, 79: 408–26.

Cox, J.C. and Grether, D.M. (1996) 'The Preference Reversal Phenomenon: Response Mode, Markets and Incentives', *Economic Theory*, 7: 381–405.

Crampton, P. (1998) 'The Efficiency of the FCC Spectrum Auctions', *Journal of Law and Economics*, 41: 727–36.

Cross, J.G. (1980) 'Some Comments on the Papers by Kagel and Battalio and Smith', in J. Kmenta and J.B. Ramsey (eds), *Evaluation of Econometric Models*, Academic Press, pp. 403–6.

Cubitt, R.P. (2005) 'Experiments and the Domain of Economic Theory', *Journal of Economic Methodology*, 12: 197–210.

Cubitt, R.P., Starmer, C. and Sugden, R. (1998) 'On the Validity of the Random Lottery Incentive System', *Experimental Economics*, 1: 115–31.

——(2001) 'Discovered Preferences and the Experimental Evidence of Violations of Expected Utility Theory', *Journal of Economic Methodology*, 8: 385–414.

Davis, D.D. and Holt, C.A. (1993) *Experimental Economics*, Princeton, NJ: Princeton University Press.

Dawes, R.M. (1999) 'Experimental demand, clear incentives, both, or neither?', in D.V. Budescu, I. Erev and R. Zwick (eds) *Games and Human Behavior: Essays in Honor of Amnon Rapoport*, N.J.: Laurence Erlbaum Associates, pp. 21–28.

Dimand, R.W. (2005) 'Experimental Economic Games: The Early Years', in P. Fontaine and R. Leonard (eds) *The Experiment in the History of Economics*, London and New York: Routledge, pp. 5–24.

Eatwell, J., Milgate, M. and Newman, P. (eds) (1987) *The New Palgrave: A Dictionary of Economic Theory and Doctrine*, Macmillan Press.

Falk, A., Fehr, E. and Fischbacher, U. (2003) 'On the Nature of Fair Behavior', *Economic Inquiry*, 41: 20–26.

Fehr, E. and Gächter, S. (2000) 'Fairness and Retaliation: The Economics of Reciprocity', *Journal of Economic Perspectives*, 14: 159–81.

Fehr, E. and Schmidt, K.M. (1999) 'A Theory of Fairness, Competition, and Cooperation', *The Quarterly Journal of Economics*, 114: 817–68.

Fiorina, M.P. and Plott, C.R. (1978) 'Committee Decisions Under Majority Rule: An Experimental Study', *American Political Science Review*, 63: 561–604.

Fishburn, P.C. (1982) 'Nontransitive Measurable Utility', *Journal of Mathematical Psychology*, 26: 31–67.

——(1983) 'Transitive Measurable Utility', *Journal of Economic Theory*, 31: 293–317.

Flood, M.M. (1958) 'Some Experimental Games', *Management Science*, 5: 5–26.

Fontaine, P. and Leonard, R. (eds) (2005) *The Experiment in the History of Economics*, London: Routledge.

Forsythe, R., Horowitz, J., Savin, N.E. and Sefton, M. (1994) 'Fairness in Simple Bargaining Games', *Games and Economic Behavior*, 7: 347–69.

Fouraker, L.E. and Siegel, S. (1963) *Bargaining Behavior*. New York: McGraw-Hill.

Franklin, A. (1986) *The Neglect of Experiment*. Cambridge: Cambridge University Press.

——(1989) 'The Epistemology of Experiment', in D.C. Gooding, T. Pinch and S. Schaffer (eds) *The Uses of Experiment*, Cambridge: Cambridge University Press, pp. 437–60.

——(1990) *Experiment, Right or Wrong*, Cambridge: Cambridge University Press.

——(1991) 'Do Mutants Have to Be Slain, or Do They Die of Natural Causes?', in *PSA 1990, Volume 2*, A. Fine, M. Forbes, and L. Wessels (eds), East Lansing, MI: Philosophy of Science Association, 2: 487–94.

——(1999) *Can that be Right?*, Dordrecht: Kluwer Academic Publishers.

——(2007) 'Experiment in Physics', in E.N. Zalta (ed.) *The Stanford Encyclopaedia of Philosophy*, http://plato.stanford.edu/entries/physics-experiment.

Frey, B. (1997) *Not Just For The Money – An Economic Theory of Personal Motivation*, Aldershot: Edward Elgar.

Frey, B. and Jegen, R. (2001) 'Motivation Crowding Theory', *Journal of Economic Surveys*, 15: 589–611.

Friedman, D. and Cassar, A. (2004) *Economics Lab: An Intensive Course in Experimental Economics*, London: Routledge.

Friedman, D. and Sunder, S. (1994) *Experimental Methods: A Primer for Economists*, Cambridge: Cambridge University Press.

Friedman, M. (1953) 'The methodology of positive economics', in M. Friedman (ed.) *Essays in Positive Economics*, Chicago: The University of Chicago Press, pp. 3–43.

Frohlich, N. and Oppenheimer, J. (2003) 'Optimal Policies and Socially Oriented Behavior: Some Problematic Effects of an Incentive Compatible Device', *Public Choice*, 117: 273–93.

Galison, P. (1987) *How Experiments End*, Chicago: The University of Chicago Press.

——(1997) *Image and Logic*, Chicago: University of Chicago Press.

Gibbard, A.F. and Varian, H.R. (1978) 'Economic Models', *Journal of Philosophy*, 75: 664–77.

Giere, R.N. (1988) *Explaining Science: A Cognitive Approach*. Chicago: Chicago University Press.

Gintis, H. (2000) 'Strong Reciprocity and Human Sociality', *Journal of Theoretical Biology*, 206: 169–79.

Gintis, H., Bowles, S., Boyd, R. and Fehr, E. (2005) 'Moral Sentiments and Material Interests: Origins, Evidence, and Consequences' in H. Gintis, S. Bowles, R. Boyd and E. Fehr (eds) *Moral Sentiments and Material Interests: The Foundations of Cooperation in Economic Life*, Cambridge, Mass.: The MIT Press, pp. 3–39.

Gneezy, U. and Rustichini, A. (2000) 'Pay enough or don't pay at all', *Quarterly Journal of Economics*, 115: 791–810.

Gode, D.K. and Sunder, S. (1993) 'Allocative Efficiency of Markets with Zero-Intelligence Traders: Markets as a Partial Substitute for Individual Rationality', *Journal of Political Economy*, 101: 119–37.

Gooding, D.C. (1985) 'In Nature's School: Faraday as an Experimentalist', in D.C. Gooding (ed.) *Faraday Rediscovered: Essays on the Life and Work of Michael Faraday*. Badingstake: Macmillan, pp. 105–35.

——(ed.) (1985) *Faraday Rediscovered: Essays on the Life and Work of Michael Faraday*, Badingstake: Macmillan.

——(1986) 'How Do Scientists Reach Agreement about New Observations', in A.I. Fine and P.K. Machamer (eds) *Proceedings of the Biennial Meeting of the Philosophy of Science Association*, East Lansing, MI: Philosophy of Science Association, 1: 205–30.

——(1989) 'Magnetic Curves and the Magnetic Field: Experimentation and Representation in the History of a Theory', in D.C. Gooding, T. Pinch and S. Schaffer (eds) *The Uses of Experiment*, Cambridge: Cambridge University Press, pp. 183–223.

——(1990) *The Making of Meaning*, Dordrecht: Martinus Nijhoff.

——(1992) 'Putting Agency Back Into Experiment', in A. Pickering (ed.) *Science as Practice and Culture*, Chicago: University of Chicago Press, pp. 65–112.

——(1998) 'Picturing Experimental Practice', in M. Heidelberger and F. Steinle (eds) *Experimental Essays: Versuche zum Experiment*, Baden-Baden: Nomos Verlagsgesellshaft, pp. 298–322.

Gooding, D.C., Pinch, T. and Schaffer, S. (eds) (1989) *The Uses of Experiment*, Cambridge: Cambridge University Press.

Grether, D.M. and Plott, C.R. (1979) 'Economic Theory of Choice and the Preference Reversal Phenomenon', *The American Economic Review*, 69: 623–38.

——(1982) 'Economic Theory of Choice and the Preference Reversal Phenomenon: Reply', *The American Economic Review*, 72: 575.

Grether, D.M., Isaac, R.M. and Plott, C.R. (1989) *The Allocation of Scarce Resources – Experimental Economics and the Problem of Allocating Airport Slots*, Boulder, San Francisco, London: Westview Press.

Guala, F. (1998) 'Experiments as Mediators in the Non-laboratory Sciences', *Philosophica*, 62: 901–18.

——(1999) 'The Problem of External Validity (Or 'Parallelism') in Experimental Economics', *Social Science Information*, 38: 555–73.

——(2000) 'Artefacts in Experimental Economics: Preference Reversals and the Becker-DeGroot-Marschak Mechanism', *Economics and Philosophy*, 16: 47–75.

——(2001) 'Building Economic Machines: The FCC Auctions', *Studies in History and Philosophy of Science*, 32: 453–77.

——(2002) 'Models, Simulations, and Experiments', in L. Magnani and N.J. Nersessian (eds), *Model-Based Reasoning: Science, Technology, Values*, New York: Kluwer, pp. 59–74.

——(2003) 'Experimental Localism and External Validity', *Philosophy of Science*, 70: 1195–1205.

——(2005a) *The Methodology of Experimental Economics*, New York: Cambridge University Press.

——(2005b) 'Economics in the Lab: Completeness vs. Testability', *Journal of Economic Methodology*, 12: 185–96.

Güth, W., Schmittberger, R. and Schwarz, B. (1982) 'An Experimental Analysis of Ultimatum Bargaining', *Journal of Economic Behavior and Organization*, 3: 367–88.

Güth, W. and Tietz, R. (1990) 'Ultimatum Bargaining Behavior: A Survey and Comparison of Experimental Results', *Journal of Economic Psychology*, 11: 417–49.

Güth, W. and Yaari, M. (1992) 'Explaining Reciprocal Behavior in Simple Strategic Games: An Evolutionary Approach', in U. Witt (ed.) *Explaining Process and Change: Approaches to Evolutionary Economics*, Ann Arbor: University of Michigan Press, pp. 23–34.

Hacking, I. (1983) *Representing and Intervening*, Cambridge: Cambridge University Press.

——(1989) 'Philosophers of Experiment', in A. Fine and J. Leplin (eds), PSA 1988, Vol. 2, East Lansing, MI: Philosophy of Science Association, pp 147–56.

——(1992) 'The Self-Vindication of the Laboratory Sciences', in A. Pickering (ed.) *Science as Practice and Culture*, Chicago: University of Chicago Press, pp. 29–64.

——(1999) *The Social Construction of What?*, Cambridge, MA: Harvard University Press.

Hands, D.W. (2001) *Reflection without Rules: Economic Methodology and Contemporary Science Theory*, Cambridge: Cambridge University Press.

Harrison, G.W. (1994) 'Expected Utility Theory and the Experimentalists', *Empirical Economics*, 19: 223–53.

Harrison, G.W. and List, J.A. (2004) 'Field Experiments', *Journal of Economic Literature*, 42: 1009–55.

Hausman, D.M. (1992) *The Inexact and Separate Science of Economics*, Cambridge: Cambridge University Press.

Heidelberger, M. and Steinle, F. (eds) (1998) *Experimental Essays: Versuche zum Experiment*, Baden-Baden: Nomos Verlagsgesellshaft.

Henrich, J., Boyd, R., Bowles, S., Camerer, C.F., Fehr, E., Gintis H. and McElreath, R. (2001) 'In Search of Homo Economicus: Behavioral Experiments in 15 Small-Scale Societies', *American Economic Review*, 91: 73–78.

Henrich, J., Boyd, R., Bowles, S., Camerer, C.F., Fehr, E. and Gintis, H. (eds) (2004) *Foundations of Human Sociality: Economic Experiments and Ethnographic Evidence from Fifteen Small-Scale Societies*, Oxford: Oxford University Press.

Hertwig, R. and Ortmann, A. (2001) 'Experimental Practices in Economics: a Methodological Challenge for Psychologists?', *Behavioral and Brain Sciences*, 24: 383–451.

Hey, J.D. (1991) *Experiments in Economics*. Oxford: Basil Blackwell.

Hoffman, E., McCabe, K. and Smith, V.L. (1995) 'Ultimatum and Dictator Games', *Journal of Economic Perspectives*, 9: 236–39.

——(1996a) 'Social Distance and Other-Regarding Behavior in Dictator Games', *The American Economic Review*, 86: 653–60.

——(1996b) 'On Expectations and Monetary Stakes in Ultimatum Games', *International Journal of Game Theory*, 25: 289–301.

——(1999) 'Social Distance and Other-Regarding Behavior in Dictator Games: Reply', *The American Economic Review*, 89: 340–41.

Hoffman, E., McCabe, K., Shachat, K. and Smith, V.L. (1994) 'Preferences, Property Rights and Anonymity in Bargaining Games', *Games and Economic Behavior*, 7: 346–80.

Holt, C.A. (1986) 'Preference Reversals and the Independence Axiom', *The American Economic Review*, 76: 508–15.

——(1995) 'Industrial Organization: A Survey of Laboratory Research', in J.H. Kagel and A.E. Roth (eds) *The Handbook of Experimental Economics*, Princeton: Princeton University Press, pp 349–443.

Holt, C.A., Langan, L. and Villamil, A. (1986) 'Market Power in Oral Double Auction', *Economic Inquiry*, 24: 107–23.

Hon, G. (1989) 'Towards a Typology of Experimental Errors: An Epistemological View', *Studies in History and Philosophy of Science* 20: 469–504.

——(2003) 'The Idols of Experiment: Transcending the "Etc. List"', in H. Radder (ed.) *The Philosophy of Scientific Experimentation*, Pittsburgh: University of Pittsburgh Press, pp. 174–98.

Houser, D., McCabe, K., Ryan, L., Smith, V.L. and Trouard, T. (2001) 'A functional imaging study of cooperation in two-person reciprocal exchange', *Proceedings of the National Academy of Science*, September, Vol. 98 (20): 11832–35.

Hurwicz, L. (1960) 'Optimality and Informational Efficiency in Resource Allocation Processes', in K. Arrow et al. (eds) *Mathematical Methods in the Social Sciences*, Stanford: Stanford University, pp. 27–46.

Isaac, R.M. and Smith, V.L. (1985) 'In Search of Predatory Pricing', *Journal of Political Economy*, 93: 320–45.

Kagel, J.H. (1995) 'Auctions: A Survey of Experimental Research', in J.H. Kagel and A.E. Roth (eds) *The Handbook of Experimental Economics*, Princeton: Princeton University Press, pp. 501–85.

Kagel, J.H. and Roth, A.E. (eds) (1995) *The Handbook of Experimental Economics*, Princeton: Princeton University Press.

Kagel, J.H. and Levin, D. (1986) 'The Winner's Curse and Public Information in Common Value Auctions', *American Economic Review*, 76: 894–920.

Kahneman, D. and Tversky, A. (1979) 'Prospect Theory: An Analysis of Decision Under Risk', *Econometrica*, 47: 263–91.

Kahneman, D., Knetsch, J.L. and Thaler, R. (1986) 'Fairness as a Constraint on Profit Seeking: Entitlements in the Market', *The American Economic Review*, 76: 728–41.

Kalisch, G.K., Milnor, J.W., Nash, J.F. and Nering, E.D. (1954) 'Some experimental N-persons Games', in R.M. Thrall, C.H. Coombs, and R.L. Davis (eds) *Decision Processes*, New York: Wiley, pp. 301–27.

Karni, E. and Safra, Z. (1987) '"Preference Reversal" and the Observability of Preferences by Experimental Methods', *Econometrica*, 55: 675–85.

Keller, L.R., Segal, U. and Wang, T. (1993) 'The Becker-DeGroot-Marschak Mechanism and Generalized Utility Theories: Theoretical Predictions and Empirical Observations', *Theory and Decision*, 34: 83–97.

Kitcher, P. (1990) 'The Division of Cognitive Labor', *The Journal of Philosophy*, 87: 5–22.

——(1993) *The Advancement of Science*, Oxford: Oxford University Press.

——(1994) 'Contrasting Conceptions of Social Epistemology', in F. Schmitt (ed.) *Epistemology: The Social Dimensions of Knowledge*, Lanham, MD: Roman and Littlefield, pp: 111–34.

——(2001) *Science, Truth, and Democracy*, New York: Oxford University Press.

Kmenta, J. and Ramsey, J.B. (eds) (1980) *Evaluation of Econometric Models*, Academic Press.

Knez, M. and Smith, V.L. (1987) 'Hypothetical valuations and preference reversals in the context of asset trading', in A.E. Roth (ed.) *Laboratory Experimentation in Economics: Six Points of View*, Cambridge: Cambridge University Press, pp. 131–54.

Knorr-Cetina, K. (1981) *The Manufacture of Knowledge: An Essay on the Constructivist and Contextual Nature of Science*, New York: Pergamon.

Krohn, W., Layton, E.T. and Weingart, P. (eds) (1978) *The Dynamics of Science and Technology*, Dordrecht, Boston: D. Reidel Publishing Company.

Kuhn, T.S. (1962; 2nd edn 1970) *The Structure of Scientific Revolutions*, Chicago: University of Chicago Press.

Laibson, D. (1997) 'Golden Eggs and Hyperbolic Discounting', *Quarterly Journal of Economics*, 112: 443–77.

Lakatos, I. (1970) 'Falsification and the Methodology of Scientific Research Programmes', in I. Lakatos and A. Musgrave (eds) *Criticism and the Growth of Knowledge*, pp. 91–196.

Lakatos, I. and Musgrave, A. (eds) (1970) *Criticism and the Growth of Knowledge*. Cambridge: Cambridge University Press.

Latour, B. (1987) *Science in Action*, Cambridge, Mass.: Harvard University Press.

Latour, B. and Woolgar, S. (1979; 2nd edn 1986) *Laboratory Life: The Construction of Scientific Facts*, Princeton: Princeton University Press.

Lawson, T. (1997) *Economics and Reality*, London: Routledge.

Leamer, E. (1983) 'Let's Take the Con Out of Econometrics', *American Economic Review*, 73: 31–64.

Leonard, R.J. (1994) 'Laboratory Strife: Higgling as Experimental Science in Economics and Social Psychology', in N.B. De Marchi and M.S. Morgan (eds) *Higgling*, History of Political Economy Supplement, Vol. 26. Durham: Duke University Press, pp. 343–69.

Levine, D.K. (1998) 'Modeling Altruism and Spitefulness in Experiments', *Review of Economic Dynamics*, 1: 593–622.

Lichtenstein, S. and Slovic, P. (1971) 'Reversals of Preference Between Bids and Choices in Gambling Decisions', *Journal of Experimental Psychology*, 89: 46–55.

——(1973) 'Response-Induced Reversals of Preference in Gambling: An Extended Replication in Las Vegas', *Journal of Experimental Psychology*, 101: 16–20.

Lipsey, R. and Chrystal, A. (1995 8th ed.) *An Introduction to Positive Economics*, Oxford: Oxford University Press.

Loewenstein, G. (1999) 'Experimental Economics from the Vantage-Point of Behavioural Economics', *The Economic Journal*, 109: F25–34.

Longino, H.E. (1990) *Science as Social Knowledge: Values and Objectivity in Scientific Inquiry*, Princeton, N.J.: Princeton University Press.

——(1991) 'Multiplying Subjects and the Diffusion of Power', *The Journal of Philosophy*, 8: 666–74.

——(1994) 'The Fate of Knowledge in Social Theories of Science', in F.F. Schmitt (ed.), *Socializing Epistemology: The Social Dimensions of Knowledge*, Lanham, MD: Roman and Littlefield, pp. 135–57.

——(2002) *The Fate of Knowledge*, Princeton: Princeton University Press.

Loomes, G. (1991) 'Experimental Methods in Economics', in D. Greenaway, M. Bleaney and I. Stewart (eds), *Companion to Contemporary Economic Thought*, London: Routledge, pp. 593–613.

——(1998) 'Probabilities vs Money: A Test of Some Fundamental Assumptions about Rational Decision Making', *The Economic Journal*, 108: 477–89.

——(1999a) 'Some Lessons from Past Experiments and Some Challenges for the Future', *The Economic Journal*, 109: F35–45.

——(1999b) 'Experimental Economics: Introduction', *The Economic Journal*, 109: F1–4.

Loomes, G. and Sugden, R. (1982) 'Regret Theory: An Alternative Theory of Rational Choice under Uncertainty', *The Economic Journal*, 92: 805–24.

——(1983) 'A Rationale for Preference Reversal', *The American Economic Review*, 73: 428–32.

Loomes, G., Starmer, C. and Sugden, R. (1989) 'Preference Reversal: Information-Processing Effect or Rational Non-Transitive Choice?', *The Economic Journal*, 99: 140–51.

——(1991) 'Observing Violations of Transitivity by Experimental Methods', *Econometrica*, 59: 425–39.

Mäki, U. (1996) 'Scientific Realism and Some Peculiarities of Economics', *Boston Studies in the Philosophy of Science*, 169: 425–45.

——(1998) 'Aspects of Realism about Economics', *THEORIA*, 13: 301–19.

——(2001) 'Models', in N.J. Smelser P.B. Baltes (eds) *International Encyclopedia of the Social and Behavioral Sciences*, Volume 15, Elsevier, pp. 9931–37.

——(2002a) 'Some Non-reasons for Non-realism about Economics', in U. Mäki (ed.) *Fact and Fiction in Economics. Realism, Models and Social Construction*, Cambridge: Cambridge University Press, pp. 90–104.

——(ed.) (2002b) *Fact and Fiction in Economics. Realism, Models and Social Construction.* Cambridge: Cambridge University Press.

——(2005) 'Models are Experiments, Experiments are Models', *Journal of Economic Methodology*, 12: 303–15.

Mäki, U., Gustafsson, B. and Knudsen, C. (eds) (1993) *Rationality, Institutions and Economic Methodology*, London: Routledge.

Machina, M.J. (1982) '"Expected Utility" Analysis Without the Independence Axiom', *Econometrica*, 50: 277–323.

McAfee, R.P. and McMillan, J. (1996) 'Analysing the Airwaves Auction', *Journal of Economic Perspectives*, 10: 159–75.

McCabe, K., Rassenti, S.J. and Smith, V.L. (1989) 'Designing "Smart" Computer-Assisted Markets: An Experimental Auction for Gas Networks', *European Journal of Political Economy*, 5: 259–83.

McDaniel, T. and Starmer, C. (1998) 'Experimental Economics and Deception: A Comment', *Journal of Economic Psychology*, 19: 403–9.

MacKenzie, D. (1981) 'Interests, Positivism and History', *Social Studies of Science*, 11: 498–504.

McMillan, J. (1994) 'Selling Spectrum Rights', *Journal of Economic Perspectives*, 8: 145–62.

McMillan, J., Rothschild, M. and Wilson, R. (1997) 'Introduction', *Journal of Economics and Management Strategy*, 6: 425–30.

Magnani, L. and Nersessian, N.J. (eds) (2002) *Model-Based Reasoning: Science, Technology, Values*, Dordrecht: Kluwer.

Mayer, T. (1980) 'Economics as Hard Science: Realistic Goal or Wishful Thinking', *Economic Inquiry*, 18:165–77.

Mayo, D.G. (1996) *Error and the Growth of Experimental Knowledge*, Chicago: University of Chicago Press.

Milgrom, P. (2000) 'Putting Auction Theory to Work: The Simultaneous Ascending Auction', *Journal of Political Economy*, 108: 245–72.

Mill, J.S. (1844; 2nd edn 1874) 'On the Definition and Method of Political Economy; and the Method of Investigation Proper to It', in *Essays on Some Unsettled Questions of Political Economy*, London: Longmans, Green, Reader & Dyer.

Miller, R.M., Plott, C.R. and Smith, V.L. (1977) 'Intertemporal Competitive Equilibrium: An Empirical Study of Speculation', *Quarterly Journal of Economics*, 91: 599–624.

Mirowski, P. (2002) *Machine Dreams: Economics Becomes a Cyborg Science*, Cambridge: Cambridge University Press.

Morgan, M. (2002) 'Model Experiments and Models in Experiments', in L. Magnani and N.J. Nersessian (eds) *Model-Based Reasoning: Science, Technology, Values*, Dordrecht: Kluwer, pp. 41–58.

——(2003) 'Experiments without Material Intervention: Model Experiments, Virtual Experiments and Virtually Experiments', in H. Radder (ed.) *The Philosophy of Scientific Experimentation*, Pittsburgh: University of Pittsburgh Press, pp. 216–35.

——(2005) 'Experiments versus Models: New Phenomena, Inference and Surprise', *Journal of Economic Methodology*, 12: 317–29.

Morrison, M.C. and Morgan, M.S. (1999) 'Models as Mediating Instruments', in M.S. Morgan and M.C. Morrison (eds), *Models as Mediators*, Cambridge: Cambridge University Press, pp 10–37.

Mulkay, M. and Gilbert, G.N. (1986) 'Replication and Mere Replication', *Philosophy of the Social Sciences*, 16: 21–37.

Nersessian, N.J. (ed.) (1987) *The Process of Science*, Dordrecht: Martinus Nijhoff Publishers.

Nickles, T. (1989) 'Justification and Experiment', in D.C. Gooding, T. Pinch and S. Schaffer (eds) *The Uses of Experiment*, Cambridge: Cambridge University Press, pp. 299–333.

Nik-Khah, E. (2008) 'A Tale of Two Auctions', *Journal of Institutional Economics*, 4: 73–97.

Ochs, J. and Roth, A.E. (1989) 'An Experimental Study of Sequential Bargaining', *The American Economic Review*, 79: 355–84.

Palfrey, T. and Porter, R. (1991) 'Guidelines for Submission of Manuscripts on Experimental Economics', *Econometrica*, 59: 1197–98.

Pickering, A. (1981) 'The Hunting of the Quark', *Isis*, 72: 216–36.

——(1984) *Constructing Quarks*, Chicago: University of Chicago Press.

——(1987) 'Against Correspondence: A Constructivist View of Experiment and the Real', in A. Fine and P. Machamer (ed.), *PSA 1986*, Pittsburgh: Philosophy of Science Association, 2: 196–206.

——(1989) 'Living in the Material World: On Realism and Experimental Practice', in D.C. Gooding, T. Pinch and S. Schaffer (eds) *The Uses of Experiment*, Cambridge: Cambridge University Press, pp. 275–97.

——(1990a) 'Reason Enough? More on Parity-Violation Experiments and Electroweak Gauge Theory', in A.I. Fine and P.K. Machamer (eds) *Proceedings of the Biennial Meeting of the Philosophy of Science Association*, East Lansing, MI: Philosophy of Science Association, pp. 459–69.

——(1990b) 'Knowledge, Practice and Mere Construction', *Social Studies of Science*, 20: 682–729.

——(1992a) *Science as Practice and Culture*, Chicago: University of Chicago Press.

——(1992b) 'From Science as Knowledge to Science as Practice', in A. Pickering (ed.), *Science as Practice and Culture*, Chicago: University of Chicago Press, pp. 1–26.

——(1994a) 'The Mangle of Practice: Agency and Emergence in the Sociology of Science', *American Journal of Sociology*, 99: 559–89.

——(1994b) 'After Representation: Science Studies in the Performative Idiom', in A.I. Fine and P.K. Machamer (eds) *Proceedings of the Biennial Meeting of the Philosophy of Science Association*, East Lansing, MI: Philosophy of Science Association, pp. 413–19.

——(1995a) *The Mangle of Practice: Time, Agency, and Science.* Chicago: University of Chicago Press.

——(1995b) 'Context and Constraints', In J. Z. Buchwald (ed.) *Scientific Practice: Theories and Stories of Physics.* Chicago: Chicago University Press, pp. 13–41.

——(1995c) 'Beyond Constraint: The Temporality of Practice and the Historicity of Knowledge', in J. Z. Buchwald (ed.) *Scientific Practice: Theories and Stories of Physics.* Chicago: Chicago University Press, pp. 42–55.

Pinch, T. (1986) *Confronting Nature*, Dordrecht: Reidel.

Plott, C.R. (1979) 'The Application of Laboratory Experimental Methods to Public Choice', in C.S. Russell (ed.) *Collective Decision Making: Applications from Public Choice Theory*, Baltimore MD: John Hopkins University Press, pp. 137–60.

——(1982) 'Industrial Organization Theory and Experimental Economics', *Journal of Economic Literature*, 20: 1485–1527.

——(1987) 'Dimensions of Parallelism: Some Policy Applications of Experimental Methods', in A. E. Roth (ed.) *Laboratory Experimentation in Economics: Six Points of View*, Cambridge: Cambridge University Press, pp. 193–219.

——(1991) 'Will Economics Become an Experimental Science?', *Southern Economic Journal*, 57: 901–19.

——(1995) 'Rational Individual Behaviour in Markets and Social Choice Processes: the Discovered Preference Hypothesis', in K. J. Arrow, E. Colombatto, M. Perlman, and C. Schmidt (eds) *The Rational Foundations of Economic Behaviour*, IEA Conference, London: Macmillan Press, pp. 225–50.

——(1997) 'Laboratory Experimental Testbeds: Application to the PCS Auction', *Journal of Economics and Management Strategy*, 6: 605–38.

Plott, C.R. and Levine, M.E. (1978) 'A Model Agenda Influence on Committee Decisions', *The American Economic Review*, 88: 146–60.

Plott, C.R., and Smith, V.L. (1978) 'An Experimental Examination of Two Exchange Institutions', *Review of Economic Studies.* 45: 133–53

Polanyi, M. (1958) *Personal Knowledge*, Chicago: Chicago University Press.

Pommerehne, W.W., Schneider, F. and Zweifel, P. (1982) 'Economic Theory of Choice and the Preference Reversal Phenomenon: A Reexamination', *The American Economic Review*, 72: 569–74.

Popper, R.K. (1959) *The Logic of Scientific Discovery*, New York: Basic Books (translation of Popper 1934).

——(1965; 2nd edn 1963) *Conjectures and Refutations*, New York: Harper and Row.

——(1979; 2nd edn 1972) *Objective Knowledge: An Evolutionary Approach*, Oxford: Clarendon Press.

——(1994) *The Myth of the Framework: In Defense of Science and Rationality*, London: Routledge.

Prasnikar, V. and Roth, A.E. (1992) 'Considerations of Fairness and Strategy: Experimental Data from Sequential Games', *The Quarterly Journal of Economics*, 107: 865–88.

Quiggin, J. (1982) 'A Theory of Anticipated Utility', *Journal of Economic Behavior and Organization*, 3: 324–43.

Rabin, M. (1993) 'Incorporating Fairness into Game Theory and Economics', *The American Economic Review*, 83: 1281–1302.

——(1998) 'Psychology and Economics', *Journal of Economic Literature*, 36: 11–46.

Radder, H. (1988) *The Materialization of Science*, Assen: Van Gorcum.

——(1995) 'Experimenting in the Natural Sciences: A Philosophical Approach', in Jed Z. Buchwald (ed.) *Scientific Practice: Theories and Stories of Physics*, Chicago: Chicago University Press, pp. 56–86.

——(1996) *In and About the World – Philosophical Studies of Science and Technology*, Albany, New York: State University of New York Press.

——(1998) 'Issues for a Well-Developed Philosophy of Scientific Experimentation', in M. Heidelberger and F. Steinle (eds) *Experimental Essays: Versuche zum Experiment*, Baden-Baden: Nomos Verlagsgesellshaft, pp. 392–404.

——(ed.) (2003a) *The Philosophy of Scientific Experimentation*, Pittsburgh: University of Pittsburgh Press.

——(2003b) 'Toward a More Developed Philosophy of Scientific Experimentation', in H. Radder (ed.) *The Philosophy of Scientific Experimentation*, Pittsburgh: University of Pittsburgh Press, pp. 1–18.

——(2003c) 'Technology and Theory in Experiment', in H. Radder (ed.) *The Philosophy of Scientific Experimentation*, Pittsburgh: University of Pittsburgh Press, pp. 152–73.

Rassenti, S.J., Smith, V.L.and Bulfin, R.L. (1982) 'A Combinatorial Auction Mechanism for Airport Time Slot Allocation' *Bell Journal of Economics*, 13: 402–17.

Reilly, R.J. (1982) 'Preference Reversal: Further Evidence and Some Suggested Modifications in Experimental Design', *The American Economic Review*, 72: 576–84.

Reiter, S. (1977) 'Information and Performance in the (New) Welfare Economics', *American Economic Review Proceedings*, 67: 226–34.

Rizvi, S.A.T. (2005) 'Experimentation, General Equilibrium and Games', in P. Fontaine, and R. Leonard (eds) *The Experiment in the History of Economics*, London: Routledge, pp. 50–70.

Roth, A.E. (ed.) (1987) *Laboratory Experimentation in Economics: Six Points of View*, Cambridge: Cambridge University Press.

——(1988) 'Laboratory Experimentation in Economics: A Methodological Overview', *Economic Journal*, 98: 974–1031.

——(1995a) 'Introduction to Experimental Economics', in J.H. Kagel and A.E. Roth (eds) *The Handbook of Experimental Economics*, Princeton: Princeton University Press, pp. 3–109.

——(1995b) 'Bargaining Experiments', in J.H. Kagel and A.E. Roth (eds) *The Handbook of Experimental Economics*, Princeton: Princeton University Press, pp. 253–348.

Roth, A.E. and Erev, I. (1995) 'Learning in Extensive-Form Games: Experimental Data and Simple Dynamic Models in the Intermediate Term', *Games and Economic Behavior*, 8: 164–212.

Roth, A.E., Prasnikar, V. Okuno-Fujiwara, M. and Zamir, S. (1991) 'Bargaining and Market Behavior in Jerusalem, Ljubljana, Pittsburgh, and Tokyo: An Experimental Study', *The American Economic Review*, 81: 1068–95.

Samuelson, P.A. and Nordhaus, W.D. (1985) *Principles of Economics*, McGraw-Hill, Irwin. 12th ed.

Sauermann, H. and Selten, R. (1960) 'An Experiment in Oligopoly', in L. von Bertanlanffy and A. Rappoport (eds) *General Systems Yearbook of the Society for General Systems Research*, Ann Arbor: Society for General Systems Research.

Savage, L.J. (1954) *The Foundations of Statistics*, New York: Wiley.

Schaffer, S. (1989) 'Glass Works: Newton's prisms and the uses of experiment', in D. Gooding, T. Pinch, and S. Schaffer (eds) *The Uses of Experiment: Studies in the Natural Sciences*, Cambridge: Cambridge University Press, pp. 67–104.

Schelling, T.C. (1957) 'Bargaining, Communication, and Limited War', *Journal of Conflict Resolution*, 1: 19–36.

Schkade, D.A. and Johnson, E.J. (1989) 'Cognitive Processes in Preference Reversals', *Organizational Behavior and Human Decision Processes*, 44: 203–31.

Schmitt, F. (1994) 'Socializing Epistemology: An Introduction through Two Sample Issues', in F. Schmitt (ed.) *Socializing Epistemology: The Social Dimensions of Knowledge*, Lanham, MD: Roman and Littlefield, pp. 1–27.

Schmitt, F.F. (ed.) (1994) *Socializing Epistemology: The Social Dimensions of Knowledge*, Lanham, MD: Roman and Littlefield.

Schotter, A., Weiss, A. and Zapater, I. (1996) 'Fairness and Survival in Ultimatum and Dictatorship Games', *Journal of Economic Behavior and Organization*, 31: 37–56.

Schotter, A., Weigelt, K. and Wilson, C. (1994) 'A Laboratory Investigation of Multiperson Rationality and Presentation Effects', *Games and Economic Behavior*, 6: 445–68.

Schram, A. (2005) 'Artificiality: The Tension Between Internal and External Validity in Economics Experiments', *Journal of Economic Methodology*, 12: 225–37.

Segal, U. (1988) 'Does the Preference Reversal Phenomenon Necessarily Contradict the Independence Axiom?', *The American Economic Review*, 78: 233–36.

Siakantaris, N. (2000) 'Experimental Economics under the Microscope', *Cambridge Journal of Economics*, 24: 267–81.

Siegel, S. (1961) 'Decision Making and Learning Under Varying Conditions of Reinforcement', *Annals of the New York Academy of Science*, 89.

Siegel, S. and Fouraker, L. (1960) *Bargaining and Group Decision Making*. New York.

Slonim, R. and Roth, A.E. (1998) 'Financial Incentives and Learning in Ultimatum and Market Games: An Experiment in the Slovak Republic', *Econometrica*, 66: 569–96.

Slovic, P. (1975) 'Choice Between Equally Valued Alternatives', *Journal of Experimental Psychology: Human Perception and Performance*, 1: 280–87.

——(1995) 'The Construction of Preferences', *American Psychologist*, 50: 364–71.

Slovic, P. and Lichtenstein, S. (1968) 'The Relative Importance of Probabilities and Payoffs in Risk Taking', *Journal of Experimental Psychology*, 78: 1–18.

——(1983) 'Preference Reversals: A Broader Perspective', *The American Economic Review*, 73: 596–605.

Smith, V.L. (1962) 'An Experimental Study of Competitive Market Behaviour', *The Journal of Political Economy*, 70: 322–23.

——(1964) 'Effect of Market Organization on Competitive Equilibrium', *Quarterly Journal of Economics*, 78: 181–201.

——(1965) 'Experimental Auction Markets and the Walrasian Hypothesis' *Journal of Political Economy*, 73: 387–93.

——(1967) 'Experimental Studies of Discrimination versus Competition in Sealed-Bid Auction Markets', *Journal of Business*, 40: 56–84.

——(1976a) 'Experimental Economics: Induced Value Theory', *American Economic Review*. 66: 274–79.

——(1976b) 'Bidding and Auctioning Institution: Experimental Results', in Y. Amihud (ed.), *Bidding and Auctioning for Procurement and Allocation*, New York: New York University Press, pp. 43–64.

——(1979a) 'An Experimental Comparison of Three Public Good Decision Mechanism', *Scandinavian Journal of Economics*, 81: 198–215.

——(1979b) 'Incentive Compatible Experimental Processes for the Provision of Public Goods', in V. L. Smith (ed.) *Research in Experimental Economics*, vol.1. Greenwich, Conn.: JAI Press, pp. 59–168.

——(1980a) 'Experiments with a Decentralized Mechanism for Public Goods Decision', *American Economic Review*, 70: 584–99.

——(1980b) 'Relevance of Laboratory Experiments to Testing Resource Allocation Theory', in J. Kmenta and J.B. Ramsey (eds) *Evaluation of Econometric Models*, New York: Academic Press.

——(1981a) 'An Empirical Study of Decentralized Institutions of Monopoly Restraint', in J. Quirk and G. Horwich (eds) *Essays in Contemporary Fields of Economics in Honor of E. T. Weiler (1914–1979)*, West Lafayette: Purdue University Press, pp. 83–106.

——(1981b) 'Theory, Experiment and Antitrust Policy', in S. Salop (ed.) *Strategy, Predation, and Antitrust Analysis*, Washington, D.C.: Federal Trade Commission, Bureau of Economics, pp. 579–603.

——(1982) 'Microeconomic Systems as an Experimental Science', *American Economic Review*. 72: 923–55.

——(ed.) (1985) *Research in Experimental Economics*, Vol. 3, Greenwich, CT: JAI Press.

——(1987) 'Experimental Methods in Economics', in J. Eatwell, M. Milgate and P. Newman (eds) *The New Palgrave: A Dictionary of Economic Theory and Doctrine*, Macmillan Press, Inc., pp. 241–48.

——(1989) 'Theory, Experiment and Economics', *Journal of Economic Perspectives*, 3: 151–69.

——(1990) *Experimental Economics. Schools of Thought in Economics*, Vol. 7 Aldershot, England: Edward Elgar; and Brookfield, V.: Gower Publishing.

——(1991) 'Experimental Economics at Purdue', in V. L. Smith (ed.) *Papers in Experimental Economics*, Cambridge: Cambridge University Press.

——(1992) 'Game Theory and Experimental Economics: Beginnings and Early Influences', in E. R. Weintraub (ed.) *Toward a History of Game Theory*, Annual Supplement to vol. 24, History of Political Economy, Durham, N.C.: Duke University Press, pp. 241–82.

——(1994) 'Economics in the Laboratory', *Journal of Economic Perspective*, 8: 113–31.

——(2002) 'Method in Experiment: Rhetoric and Reality', *Experimental Economics*, 5: 91–110.

——(2003) 'Autobiography' in Tore Frängsmyr *(ed.) The Nobel Prizes 2002*, Stockholm: Nobel Foundation, http://nobelprize.org/nobel_prizes/economics/laureates/2002/smith-autobio.html

Smith, V.L. and Williams, A.W. (1983) 'An Experimental Comparison of Alternative Rules for Competitive Market Exchange', in R. Englebrecht-Williams et al. (eds) *Auctions, Bidding and Controlling: Uses and Theory*, New York University Press.

Smith, V.L., McCabe, K. and Rassenti, S. (1991) 'Lakatos and Experimental Economics', in N. de Marchi and M. Blaug (eds), *Appraising Economic Theories*, Edward Elgar.

Smith, V.L., Suchanek, G.L. and Williams, A.W. (1988) 'Bubbles, Crashes, and Endogenous Expectations in Experimental Spot Asset Markets', *Econometrica*, 56: 1119–52.

Smith, V.L., Williams, A.W., Bratton, W.K. and Vannoni, M.G. (1982) 'Double Auctions vs Sealed Bid-offer Auction', *American Economic Review*, 72: 58–77.

Solomon, M. (1992) 'Scientific Rationality and Human Reasoning', *Philosophy of Science*, 59: 439–54.

——(1994a) 'Social Empiricism', *Noûs*, 28: 325–43.

——(1994b) 'A More Social Epistemology', in F.F. Schmitt (ed.) *Socializing Epistemology: The Social Dimensions of Knowledge*, Lanham, Md: Rowman & Littlefield, pp. 217–33.

——(1995) 'Legend Naturalism and Scientific Progress', *Studies in History and Philosophy of Science*, 26: 205–18.

——(2001) *Social Empiricism*, Cambridge, Mass.: MIT Press.

Starmer, C. (1999a) 'Experiments in Economics: Should we Trust the Dismal Scientists in White Coats?', *Journal of Economic Methodology*, 6: 1–30.

——(1999b) 'Experimental Economics: Hard Science or Wasteful Tinkering?' *The Economic Journal*, 109: F5–15.

——(2000) 'Developments in Non-Expected Utility Theory: The Hunt for a Descriptive Theory of Choice under Risk', *Journal of Economic Literature*, 38: 332–82.

Starmer, C. and Sugden, R. (1991) 'Does the Random-lottery Incentive System Elicit True Preference? An Experimental Investigation', *The American Economic Review*, 81: 971–78.

——(1998) 'Testing Alternative Explanations of Cyclical Choices', *Economica*, 65: 347–61.

Sugden, R. (2002) 'Credible Worlds. The Status of Theoretical Models in Economics', in U. Mäki (ed.) *Fact and Fiction in Economics: Models, Realism, and Social Construction*, Cambridge: Cambridge University Press, pp. 107–36.

——(2005) 'Experiments as Exhibits and Experiments as Tests', *Journal of Economic Methodology*, 12: 291–302.

Sunder, S. (1995) 'Experimental Asset Markets: A Survey', in J.H. Kagel and A.E. Roth (eds) *The Handbook of Experimental Economics*, Princeton, NJ: Princeton University Press, pp. 445–500

Tammi, T. (1999) 'Incentives and Preference Reversals: Escape Moves and Community Decisions in Experimental Economics', *Journal of Economic Methodology*, 6: 351–80.

——(2003) 'On Experimental Discourse in Economics', *Philosophy of the Social Sciences*, 29: 62–88.

Thaler, R.H. (1988a) 'The Winner's Curse', *Journal of Economic Perspectives*, 2: 191–202.

——(1988b) 'The Ultimatum Game', *Journal of Economic Perspectives*, 2: 195–206.

——(1992) *The Winner's Curse: Paradoxes and Anomalies of Economic Life*. Princeton: Princeton University Press.

Thaler, R.H. and Sunstein, C.R. (2003) 'Libertarian Paternalism', *American Economic Review*, 93: 175–79.

——(2008) *Nudge: Improving Decisions About Health, Wealth, and Happiness*, New Haven & London, Yale University Press.

Thrall, R.M., Coombs, C.H. and Davis, R.L. (eds) (1954) *Decision Processes*, New York: Wiley.

Tversky, A. and Thaler, R.H. (1990) 'Anomalies: Preference Reversals', *Journal of Economic Perspectives*, 4: 201–11.

Tversky, A., Slovic, P. and Kahneman, D. (1990) 'The Causes of Preference Reversal', *The American Economic Review*, 80: 204–17.

Tversky, A., Slovic, P. and Sattah, S. (1988) 'Contingent Weighting in Judgment and Choice', *Psychological Review*, 95: 371–84.

von Neumann, J. and Morgenstern, O. (1944) *Theory of Games and Economic Behavior*, Princeton: Princeton University Press.

Whewell, W. (1840, 1967) *The Philosophy of Inductive Sciences, Founded Upon their History*, London.

Wilde, L.L. (1981) 'On the use of laboratory Experiments in Economics', in J.C. Pitt (ed.), *The Philosophy of Economics*, Dordrecht, Reidel, pp. 137–48.

Woodward, J. (2009) 'Experimental Investigations of Social Preferences', in H. Kincaid and D. Ross (eds), The Oxford Handbook of the Philosophy of Economics, New York: Oxford University Press, pp 189–222.

Witt, U. (ed.) (1992) *Explaining Process and Change: Approaches to Evolutionary Economics*, Ann Arbor: University of Michigan Press.

Yaari, M. E. (1987) 'The Dual Theory of Choice Under Risk', *Econometrica*, 55: 95–115.

Index

For Product Safety Concerns and Information please contact our EU representative GPSR@taylorandfrancis.com
Taylor & Francis Verlag GmbH, Kaufingerstraße 24, 80331 München, Germany

www.ingramcontent.com/pod-product-compliance
Lightning Source LLC
LaVergne TN
LVHW011129300926
849160LV00008B/572

* 9 7 8 1 1 3 8 8 0 5 0 9 5 *